DISCRETIONS

What thou lovest well remains,
                              the rest is dross
What thou lov'st well shall not be reft from thee
What thou lov'st well is thy true heritage . . .

                    Ezra Pound, Canto LXXXI

Ezra Pound, Father and Teacher:

DISCRETIONS ✤

Mary de Rachewiltz

A NEW DIRECTIONS BOOK

Manufactured in the United States of America
Originally published clothbound, as *Discretions,* in 1971 by Atlantic-
Little, Brown Books
First published as New Directions Paperbook 405
(ISBN: 0-8112-0589-4) in 1975
Published simultaneously in Canada by McClelland & Stewart, Ltd.

New Directions Books are published for James Laughlin
by New Directions Publishing Corporation,
333 Sixth Avenue, New York 10014

Thanks to Leonard

Illustrations

Illustrations follow page 152

Note to the Reader

Quotations from *The Cantos of Ezra Pound* appear in **boldface** type. An appendix of citations for all sources quoted follows the text.

P. S. / 1975

This book was drawn from memory, for memory, and I shall make no changes. But since I have been quoted out of context by people whose opinion differs from mine on the matter of Ezra Pound's broadcasts, I want to make it clear that my sentence, "He was losing ground," refers exclusively to his excessive use of vituperative terms.

'Acquit of evil intention...'

M de R

DISCRETIONS

1.   "If that's how you see it, or saw it, O.K. that's that," was Homer's comment to his son's *Revue de Deux Mondes*.

For years I have resisted a voice: "Write it down, write it down!" — Knowing that I shall probably get no comment from the author of *Indiscretions* takes the edge off my story, blunts the keenness to tell. Too late now.

"Too late," says the voice. And yet, having crossed the Equator and discovered in the process that the much-exalted Kilimanjaro — whether looked down upon from the heights of a plane or glimpsed in the early morning from the scorching plains — cannot compete in mystery and stateliness with

Plan de Corones, towering in my mind, I seem to have gained a perspective peculiarly fit for looking back on things at their beginning.

The bias and the contradiction inherent in the foregoing sentence should indicate that several realities are playing in counterpoint. Some minds take pleasure in counterpoint.

Pleasure in counterpoint: Plan de Corones and the Beitlerkofl were the Hercules Columns of my childhood. Their shape has been inside me for over forty years. I have climbed them, I have walked about, but still I cannot say with precision what stands behind them, their configuration seen from the south. Seen from the north: in a loop, side by side, two giants.

Plan de Corones, green, russet, white, and spotted in spring, squats like a telluric bust against the bronze, dolichocephalic, bald, doublefaced, cleft-at-the-top Beitlerkofl.

In the pan at their feet rests serenely an egg-shaped valley. Perfect, pregnant and aloof as Brancusi's ovoid. And Gais stands in the center: the yolk sac for *The Beginning of The World*. The light there almost solid. A root and a beginning after the deluge.

According to oral tradition, in times immemorial, there had been a great flood and all perished save an old woman who lived with a goat. On the day it started to rain, the goat, until then a well-disciplined, sensible animal returning each evening of her own free will to the stable, kept on grazing upwards.

Agatha was the name of the old woman. She worried because of the black clouds threatening. She called after the goat: *Goas Goas*. The goat answered *bhê bhê* and kept moving upwards, as much as to say, "Come and get me." Agatha went after her. Three days and three nights in the pouring rain. A calling and beckoning, a bickering back and forth until Agatha spoke like the goat, *bhê bhê,* and the goat said: *Goas Goas.*

All the while the river Aar rose: higher than the rooftops in the valley, higher than the steeple, higher than the houses on the mountainside.

When the goat reached the grass-green indent on the mountain crest, the rain stopped and a rainbow appeared. Heaven and earth had made peace. When Agatha, panting and still calling *bhê bhê,* caught up with the goat, she was struck blind at the sight of the portent: the animal had given birth to kids that looked like children, very hairy, but no tails, yelling like human beings. The goat then resumed the voice of goats and Agatha regained her speech, but never her sight, which was just as well, for she would not have liked those two creatures if she had seen what they were up to. One was a male and the other a female.

The goat allowed them to suck and Agatha instructed them in all a spinster knows. They made a home for themselves under a protruding rock, learned how to distinguish edible herbs by their odor, and fed mainly on sweet fern roots and sour clover.

In those days women wore knickers to their ankles and three layers of petticoats and a wide apron over all. Agatha had swaddled the kids in her apron; later she took off her first petticoat, tore it in the middle and laced it in front. The children were by now standing upright. Years passed and she had to take off her second petticoat; this one had a bodice attached to it, so she tore it off around the waist and stuck the boy's legs into the sleeves, which reached the knees and were tight. The garment was held up with her black velvet headband. Her hair grew thin and disheveled.

Then one day the goat died, for goats die sooner than women. Agatha told the boy how to take off the hide and dry it and how to quarter the meat. She taught the girl how to roast it. The meat lasted for a while, but Agatha grew weaker and weaker and said: "Before I forget everything, remember that my house stood in a meadow called Sâm, near the river, and the church stood on the other side of the river. You will have to rebuild a bridge to get to it, and if all the animals have perished as well as the people, remember that right under the Beitlerkofl, at the feet of the Kronplatz, they hold a market on Saint Michael's Day and there you will find everything you need. Keep the hide for barter and gather herbs and mushrooms, dry them and remember what they are good for." And so speaking, she pulled them near her, for they were after all the children of her beloved goat, and she found that they had once more grown out of their clothes and were big and strong. She took off her last petticoat and it barely covered the girl. She hesitated and then said: "Now turn your back, and as soon as I throw you my bloomers run down the mountain. Don't look back." And so they did, but after a while the boy caught a hare and thought: Something to keep my mother company. He turned back and found the blind old woman sitting naked in the grass. He knew he must not look at her.

Stealthily he threw the wriggling hare into her lap and ran. Either because of the scare from the furry creature in her lap, or because she realized that the goat-son had seen her naked, Agatha was petrified — turned into a rock. One can still see the semipellucid milk-white hump to one side of the crescent. It is an important landmark in the boundaries of the woods, and known as the Agathastoan.

Thus, some of the ways of the people in Gais can be explained by their origin. The greatest sin and shame is nakedness. Children have to be swaddled. Little boys and girls wear frocks until they grow out of them. During the day, from early mass to evening rosary, morals conform to the standards of pious old spinsters. But in the blindness of night restraint is put aside. If judged by the number of illegitimate children in Gais, the Totem's animal instincts are stronger than the heritage of Agatha's spinsterhood. Sweethearts must be let in through the window. And a girl to whom no one goes *fensterln* — courting at the window — isn't worth her salt. But great discretion is required, else the girl turns into a *Kitz* and the man into a *Bock* — nymph and satyr — today called gay-young-she and tough-old-he-goat.

Hares are considered evil, tricky animals. Everyone, including the priest, has faith in the power of herbs.

"Fools, how else did they expect me to do it. Five people watching your first suck, as though I were not giving it to you straight. You can't stop the flow when you have it in you. And all the fuss for money because you come from *Pessere Lait* — upper class. Weighing you before and after the feeding. All in white aprons and gloves. Three doctors and that hag of a midwife around my bed. But Er — he — my own husband — had to leave the room. Only the Herr was kind and always asked me if there was anything I needed. And smiled. *A Pildung!* — good manners." A gentleman with an education who looked tenderly on the young woman all dimples. And he recognized in those light gray eyes the seminal intelligence, the love that is energy and makes things grow. And he understood the vague, deep-hidden grudge that now and then came to the surface.

What power had stayed the hand that with a simple Caesarean could have delivered to this girl her own boy alive? No one had bothered. She was only a healthy, poor peasant, with too much spirit for such a small body. Her baby was too big. It choked in her womb. Scientifically it might be explained otherwise. A blue baby. The overflow of her milk, energy and compassion was diverted towards a small creature all skin and bones. These city-ladies never think of the creature inside them, want to keep *schlonk wi a Schlonge* — thin. Like a starving nestling, she says, did I stretch my long neck and open my beak wide. We had need of each other.

Then Joggl, her husband, came. A humane man. He wept and buried his firstborn after having given him his own name: Jakob — Joggile. Unbaptized. And he was going to take his wife home immediately. It was July; corn and hay need gathering while the sun shines.

Couldn't he stay a few days while his wife's milk was being tested? — He certainly could not. — His expenses would be paid. — No, he had two cows to milk and feed, can't keep animals waiting, and the mare is temperamental, she takes water only from him or from Hanne, his wife.

He was prevailed upon by his wife — for only she had power of persuasion over him — to leave her behind. "The Lady would like me to stay a month, but she is crazy. In a few days they'll see the baby gains weight. If they want it to live they will have to let me take it home with me."

"*In insra Hitt!* — that shack." "I told them to go and look at the house first, but they say the house does not matter. They will come with me, bring me home in a car. The doctor says they are rich people, people who can pay."

A determined little woman, always taking care of other people's children. She says it comes from having lost her own parents at the age of fourteen. There were seven brothers, one aged sixteen and all the others younger. A plucky brood, they survived and saved the farm. The oldest brother, the heir, later was forced to sell it, but at a small profit, so that each got a share for ten years' unpaid labor.

Klöcka Hanne had married Sâma Joggl for love. There was no one to stop her. From seventeen cows down to two. Into a house all a shambles, with a leaky roof and a hungry gang of relatives. In less than two years she had swept the house clean of in-laws, mice and grime. The Sâma family became respectable.

And over the past forty years the Sâma have reared seventeen children: Mamme and Tatte to all. But I was the only one Mamme breastfed, except Hansile for a few weeks after her second-born died. With the exception of the last, whose brain is permanently damaged and who will remain a child as long as he lives, they have now all gone to live their own mistakes, carried away by their bad blood — *schlechts Bluit*. Nine of them were abandoned by peddlers, vagabonds, beggars and whores. The rest came from sick or bewidowed relatives.

My milk-brother is now a riotous bum who earns a dubious living as butcher-boy. His grandmother is to blame for it, Mamme says, since she took him away from her when he started going to school, hoping he would be useful and keep her in old age. With the first month's pay — the Fascist regime had introduced subsidies for the illegitimate (to engender corruption, old people said) — the mother had vanished without having revealed the father's name. As always in such cases, an Italian carabiniere was blamed. A few years later, the police informed the "place of origin" that Hansile's mother had been found dead in a basement at the outskirts of Rome. A strangled prostitute — *mondana strangolata*. She made headlines. Villon's world has always been familiar: "*Les frères humains . . .*"

Margherita — we called her Margit — was the oldest of us

all. Before Mamme's marriage, Margit had been parked with her by a *Kornarin,* just for a few hours, so that she could get a new supply of willow branches to make baskets. Good nature ruled out suspicion. The *Kornarin* never came back. Mamme's brothers were angry and told her to inform the police. But by then the police were Italian, and she had little faith in them. And Margit was a dear little girl, truly wasted on such a *Luido* — slut — of a mother who would have brought her up to beg on the roads. *Korner* are vagabonds; all their belongings are in their *Korn* — cart. Often they don't even have a cart. They camp and cut willows along the rivers in summer. They make baskets and sell them and spend the money on wine. So into marriage along with her scanty dowry, Mamme had brought Margit, and her husband, Tatte, did not mind.

⁂

It is dawn at Jerusalem while midnight hovers over the Pillars of Hercules.

And the discovery of America must have dawned upon Gais, when out of a black car stepped Outis and a trim-coiffed goddess. All the peasants had paused in their second hay-making and those on the road had pressed their carts and horses against the hedges to let the black monster stirring up clouds of dust pass.

Si om la olla pleit hergschaugh. Flabbergast. *Grüss Gott.* Tatte took his hat off and skeptically shook hands with the tall blond Herr who had helped his bustling little wife, bearing a soft white bundle, out of the car. Good. *"Gut, gut,"* the Herr commented on the low, wood-paneled room, the black vaulted kitchen, the stable leading off from the entrance. The air was good. Clean smell of hay and manure. Sound of swift river under swishing elm boughs. And when Margit was brought in, his face lit up. "I said I could not guarantee that you would grow into such a beautiful and healthy child, but I would do all I can. And thought: then it is not a question of a few months, they must mean to leave her here for a few years." It is always Mamme speaking. "And he put a five-hundred-lire note on the table. Two months payment in advance, the hundred lire extra was a gift. *Trinkgeld.* I looked astounded, and he said, 'Is it not enough? I thought the doctor had explained, he said it would be all right.'" And again he shook hands warmly with Mamme and Tatte and laughed at Margherita and said: *Gross, stark;* his girl, too, would grow big and strong. They would come again at the end of two months, and left in the big black car. Strangers with strange names. *Gspassiga Lait.* Speaking in a strange tongue. *Mir om la pleit hergschaugh* — flabbergast — at the five-hundred-lire note. Such a big note they had never before seen. Italian money was still somewhat of a novelty, although the silver Kronen and the Groschen — *l'aigle à deux têtes* — had been exchanged for flimsy Italian lire ever since the Treaty of St. Germain, when the South Tyrol had been allotted to Italy.

"You'll never see them again." Tatte's diffidence towards Lords and Ladies was as unshakable as Mamme's trust in Divine Providence. "Even so, look at that money; it's a gift from heaven." And a child in place of their own. The strangers nestled in her mind. What if after two months they came back to take this gift-from-heaven away? It must grow big and strong, must have color in its cheeks. Her milk and the good air would do it. *Immer in die gute Luft.*

For her own baby she had prepared the big wicker baby carriage, well upholstered, deep and safe, but unwieldy on the roads — it had never left the room when in use for herself and her seven brothers. She found an ancient perambulator and repainted it a shiny brown. A remarkable vehicle, fit for any road, a combination of rickshaw and sedan, in solid wood, with two big spiked wheels and a detachable roof.

Like Cocteau: *"Sont-ils nègres ou comme tout le monde?"* the Herr Lehrer asked — "They say you have an American baby, is it black, or white like us?" Even the churchwarden, the most impassible and unapproachable man in the village, was curious and stopped Mamme in her perambulating. I suspect at that moment she wished I had been black, for it would have given her great satisfaction to startle him. Until 1919 he had been the village teacher. One teacher, one book, one slate and no nonsense. Reading, writing, arithmetic for counting, and the catechism as a guide for the soul. After the war the Church preserved the dignified isolation of the old teacher by electing him churchwarden and organist. This is the only time he has been known to stop a woman in the street and show curiosity. The event was followed by a more important one: one of the Bacher brothers, Michael, left for America. Up to 1925 no one from the valley had been known to have undertaken a voyage by sea.

At the end of the summer, without warning, the strangers returned. A busy harvest time, with the cold pressing down from the mountains. And they hit baking day, the most hectic of all days. Bread is baked every two or three months on farms in the Pustertal. Houses have bread rooms, with long wooden racks to keep the loaves dry and ventilated. Our black vaulted kitchen, with its two chicken coops serving as tables to eat on and the cement swill trough, was dominated by an enormous bread oven, the heating of which took a good seven hours. Tatte started to pile up logs in the middle of the night. In the early morning when Mamme lifted the lid off the wooden yeasting tub, the whole house heaved with the smell of fermented dough. The making of bread is difficult; it requires practice and training. Mamme's hands tossed the loaves like butterflies, light, swift, expert; and Tatte with a long wooden oar shoved them into the oven. It was a great day for children who could pitch in and make themselves useful. But the smaller ones were pushed aside and babies neglected.

So they found me unkempt and wet in the wicker carriage. The lady frowned. Mamme blushed. "Until that day I had you spotless!" Tatte shrugged: *Man muss essen a.* And the Herr understood: *Gut, gut.*

> Earth is the nurse of all men . . .
> Bread is the base of subsistence . . .
> 'Wheat is by sweat of the people . . .'
>   . . . .
> Dress 'em in folderols
>   and feed 'em with dainties,
> In the end they will sell out the homestead.

Do Mensch hot an Voschtont — a wise man.

The strangers left and it was agreed that next day I would be brought to them at their hotel in town. Mamme had seldom been in Bruneck. The idea that she would have to cross the threshold of the awe-inspiring Hotel Post worried her greatly. With what care she dressed up! It is a good hour's walk from Gais to Bruneck. She must have hurried and talked and sung to me all the way, as she pushed the pram, talked and sung out her excitement, her fears, her pride, her hopes. My earliest memories are of Mamme singing and talking and confiding in me as though I were a little Lord Jesus.

How did she get the pram up Herr Photograph Kofler's dark and narrow stairs? Or was he summoned with his equipment to the hotel? Details are not available, but a picture testifies that I was a healthy, happy baby. The Frau was appeased and satisfied and Mamme was allowed to take her gift-from-heaven back home in the late afternoon. Again a big bill tucked away in her bosom and a great weight off her chest.

The strangers were leaving next day for unknown places. . . .

How is it far, if you think of it?

Paris is how far? Ages in understanding. Venice, Rapallo, Rome? A bit nearer.

And she shall have music wherever she goes . . . In the style of the twenties. Their style: *"M. et Mme. vous invitent . . ."*

things have ends and beginnings

And feigning? Ah, it will take generations to put an end to things started in feigning — to the despair of it.

Our dynasty came in because of a great sensibility.

Ours? For the sake of Art? . . . we seek to fulfill . . . Over the chaos hovers one certainty: I, the child, was wanted. The rest is music and poetry.

The young violinist stands beside the poet's chair playing arie from *Le Nozze*. No, not a painted paradise. They go to heaven with their shoes on, to a heaven where even angels experience a change of state and are sad, at times.

And from now on whenever the scrupulous biographer will report a concert in Budapest, a performance in Vienna, a trip to Frankfurt, Wörgl, Salzburg, it may be assumed that the journey was interrupted, for a few hours or for a few days, in Bruneck.

On a balcony of the Hotel Post, the Herr and the Frau, enthroned on wicker chairs. I pastured a flock of thin caoutchouc flat-bellied geese precariously floating in a bowl of water at their feet. And I wanted to stroke the shoes dangling in front of my eyes, so smooth and shiny. "*Net!*" Mamme warned watching over me from the doorway. *Net.* I must not touch the Lord and the Lady's shoes and I must call them Tattile and Mamile.

Mamile pulled a huge raffia hat over my ears; it hid me from their eyes and felt as prickly as the stacks of cornsheaves Mamme made me crawl under in the fields to hide from the sun.

Otherwise: *celuy temps passa comme les petits enfans du pays c'est assavoir: a boire, manger, et dormir* . . . Hey ho! When the snow came the perambulator was replaced by a sledge, which I remember bright green, covered by a fleecy white bearskin.

And I grew up like one of them and was "'s Sâma Moidile." Imbued with love for sheep, cows and horses. Always hungry for *Knödl* and *Speck,* for stories and songs. *En plein air — die gute Luft.* Art? In the shade of two greenish, faded stereotyped prints that impressed upon me the dangers and possibilities of transgression and adventure. Two popular themes in the Tyrol. One can still find the prints in many old inns. The poacher, hero of folksongs. It took me years of growing up to patch the story together. A man with a green cap and a gun slung lawfully, nonchalantly, over one shoulder, waits. For the stubborn, bewhiskered, tall hunter, staring defiantly ahead, hands clutched low behind his back, defending his ideas barefooted in studded low shoes, bare knees and wool leggings. His kneeling wife clutches his knees. To one side a barefooted, long-skirted girl holds a little boy. A *fait accompli* or a warning? The picture lends itself to speculation. Its companion is more specific: a North Pole bear hunt. A huge white bear biting into the bleeding throat of a falling man. A bustling group of inefficient men with hatchets and guns held awkwardly. Did the man get killed? Did they kill the bear? His white fleece was my earliest pride and comfort. Into the snow I went bear-hunting, pulling and strangling the fleece, for fear of losing it each time I had to kill it anew. And where did it come from, anyway? A smart shop in Paris?

"Would I had seen a white bear"? Miss Stein.

My curiosity was insatiable and Mamme's natural gift for making up stories during the day was supplemented in the evening by the talk of men. Tatte simply had to go out, to rest and smoke his pipe in company. Mamme's protests were to no avail. She too liked company, would have liked visitors. But when they came, she dominated the conversation and Tatte twitched nervously, spitting more often than was necessary. He was interested in politics, wanted the latest news. Mamme was interested in miracles and old legends. Tatte's sister, by all referred to as Töite because she was godmother to twenty-two nieces and nephews, in due course, including Margit and myself, was married to a tobacco-chewer and heavy drinker, a one-cow farmer, Leo. He subscribed to the weekly paper and she earned the money for it by her skill at turning old rags into slippers. She kept late hours and had to have a well-heated room for her fingers to remain supple and for the flour-and-water glue not to get hard. Moreover, she had to give all her attention to the sewing and keep tight lips. The house stood by the roadside in the middle of the neighborhood, an ideal meeting place and a natural magnet for the *Faira*:

Fairn: Seneca's *Otium*. *Faira* are people of leisure.

> Sun up; work
> sundown; to rest

As soon as I would see Tatte pocket his tobacco pouch — after he had, in Mamme's opinion, "simply rattled off" the evening rosary — I would stand up on the bench and jump onto his bent back. And he would protest, but never pry loose my arms tight around his neck.

Mamme's objection was tempered by the notion that if he had me with him he would come home sooner. I was usually carried back fast asleep. But for a few hours, I remained wide-awake, taking in every word and gesture; and the next day I would practice mannerisms in front of the looking glass, spitting at a great distance, blowing my nose with my thumb:

> *Do Paur isch so keck*
> *unt wirft in Rotz weck . . .*
> *Do Hear isch a Fock*
> *unt schtecktn in Sock*

Fairn is a winter luxury, when . . . a world is covered with jade and the peasants assembled around the stove. I watched them from behind the table, next to Töite, cutting miniature slippers out of snippets thrown under the table or shoved over to me. The stoves in the Tyrol are vaulted, in white plaster, surrounded by benches. Four uprights hold up a broad bench over the stove, the crossbars around the middle of the stove serve to lean against and to hang up socks and diapers. Leo always lay on the plank over the stove and at regular intervals,

[17]

from that height would let fly over the heads of the men seated on the bench below, a dark clot, . . . hittin' the gob at 25 feet

Every time, ping . . . in the middle of the square wooden box by the door into which the others emptied their pipes and spat from a short distance with lesser skill.

With the exception of Wonga, the men had all fought against Italy in the 1914–1918 war. Persistently, vaguely, they still longed for a Kaiser. Daily news and gossip invariably merged into reminiscing about the war. The stories were mostly of cunning, often gruesome. Leo had served in the ambulance corps. Built like — and with the strength of — a bear, he could lift any deadweight, but he had no skill at pulling triggers. He was full of tales about severed limbs and robbing corpses and probably worse. He claimed that from all the looting he had kept only the ring he wore on his little finger as a souvenir. He had picked up a blanket and a very white hand fell to the ground. It must have been an officer's. Spitting on the dead finger, he managed to get off the ring and then threw the hand into a ditch. That lonesome hand troubled me much.

Tatte had been a hero. Invariably duped. He spoke of the war as though it had all been a great joke. The telephone line had been interrupted. He was asked to carry a message under heavy enemy fire. A bullet shattered his left hand, but he kept running. He met another soldier and told him his errand in a sort of fever. The other soldier ran faster. When, fainting, Tatte reached the officer and expected to be at least praised for his bravery, he was shouted at: *Raus* — clear out. The message had already been delivered. Instead of a bonus he was kicked into hospital. It's all a big swindle. Luckily, at the battle of Caporetto he was wounded again, and too seriously to be fit for the front thereafter.

A writer on "Caporetto" attributes the loss of the battle to Italy's lack of bourgeoisie from which officers can be made. In my young mind that German victory was due to the Kaiser-jäger Jakob Marcher and young peasants like him, fighting like devils, throwing hand grenades and insults at the fleeing *Walschn.*

Caporetto, Monte Grappa, Rovereto, Pasubio. The refrain of such glorious names and all the military ranks from *Feldmarschall* to *Schorsch* and *Pfeiflschtirggla,* whatever that may have been, were etched deep into my mind. Strangely mingled with the word *catacomb* in Prenn's story of his visit to Rome.

Prenn Hans was a gifted raconteur. Famous for his credulity, for his luck with honey and bees and for his imaginative way of swearing. He was a small farmer who did the plowing with his cows. His wife had to lead them, and if anything went wrong, which it often did, he would kneel down in the middle of the furrow and, at the top of his voice, intone a litany of invectives: By the seven holy martyrs, Lucifer, I beseech thee, ascend from burning hellfire and bugger the Schnegge-cow and bugger the Mause-cow and bugger that cow of my wife who is the greatest, etc.

The Italians in their effort to conquer the Tyroleans also tried persuasion. The men who signed up for evening courses in Italian were offered a trip to Rome. Prenn had an open mind. He learned about half a dozen words of Italian and set off, with a few others, for the great voyage to the Pope. Was I spellbound by his narrative, or was he so long-winded? The fact is that I would invariably reach full awareness only at the words "They said they would now show me the catacombs." More likely, I was awakened by roars of laughter, since the story had been told many times and everyone knew what was coming. "We climbed upstairs. I said I had read they were underground. The shutters were closed and there was a strange smell. A woman sat on my knees, the dress cut so low I could see down to her navel. Boys, did I run and curse when I caught on. Those devils leading me to perdition in the Holy City."

The next thing I would be aware of was Mamme leaning over the bed whispering: Repeat! *Heiliges Schutzengile mein . . . mach mich immer kaisch und rain. Amen.* The evening prayer to my guardian angel, asking for chastity.

Needless to say, the only language heard, known and mastered was Tyrolese. *Puschtrerisch,* more precisely. Thus when grandfather Homer, alias "Euripides, . . . the naïvest man who ever possessed sound sense," was brought to Gais, we could not communicate. He had been informed of my existence and his advice was being sought. Should the nature-child be brought into civilization? His verdict: "It would kill her. The plant is too tender to be uprooted." He added that one could try acclimatization — slowly, short visits — but at no cost must I be separated from Mamme yet. We all loved him for his wisdom.

Grandfather's visit conferred a sense of stability. The Herr and the Frau were difficult to figure out, but a *Grossvater* you do not conjure up out of nowhere. It means there is a background. His first visit left a landmark. He gave me a beautiful doll, and I called it Rosile, for she had pink porcelain cheeks. The black eyes that snapped open and shut became an exotic ideal. Everyone I knew had green, gray or blue eyes. The picture of three generations was taken by Photographer Mariner in Bruneck.

Through his son's translations into German and much sign language, Grandfather told Tatte about his own experiences in farming. Wisconsin, yes, there too it is very cold. Comparisons were made between Wisconsin and the Pustertal. Homer and Tatte clearly liked each other and the story of the clipped longhorns entered into Tatte's *Fairn* repertoire: *"Do Gischns Groussvotto hot mo dozeilt . . ."* Yes, my grandfather had told him.

Tatte would have liked to try it too, for the fun of it. But it is all very well for a lord to experiment with a hundred cows and clip their horns because of the theory that they will produce more milk and take up less space. Na na, if two cows are all you have, you had better stick to common sense.

Mamme and Tatte tossed questions, intrigued, intriguing: "The house in Venice belongs to the Frau, if I got it right, she said her father bought it for her. The outside is nothing much; I don't know why she does not get it painted. But inside she has it beautiful on three floors — though such open fires as we wouldn't have any more . . ."

I was placed on a high dark-blue armchair, on a pile of cushions over which was spread a leopard skin. Facing me, over a monumental dark table, on a high dark-blue armchair, sat Mamile, majestic and beautiful like a queen towards me; soft and willowy, smiling like a fairy towards Tattile.

Tattile occupied a dark-blue broad bench against the wall. The wall was bright yellow with painted ocher columns and a bright glass star hung over us. This was the dining room on the ground floor. I liked Mamile's room upstairs the best; it had no open fire and the most beautiful dress hung on the door. The door was a looking glass, facing the king-size, pearl-gray velvet couch. On the long, low bookcase stood two pairs of strange shoes, one of straw and one of black wood. Later I learnt that these were Japanese shoes and the dress a kimono, and the jewel-studded silver bird on the same shelf a gift from d'Annunzio. To me all these things were objects of great veneration, like the brocade mantle, the tiara and the rings covering the bones and the skull of a saint in our village church.

The wall along the stairs leading to the top room was taken up completely by a gray opaque canvas into which I read nothingness; chaos, the universe or the torso of a giant, crucified. Tami Koume's Super-artificial-growing-creation, whispering: "We are now standing at the critical moment of humanity. We must be saved by something." And he was killed in the Tokyo earthquake and his big canvas in Venice torn to pieces during the war. And on the studio bookcase the great Ovid bound in wooden boards and the marble bas-relief of Isotta da Rimini set in the wall by the desk

> and the gilded cassoni neither then nor up to the present
> the hidden nest, Tami's dream, the great Ovid
> bound in thick boards, the bas relief of Ixotta
> and the care in contriving

To this house of elegance, tense symbols, charged with learning, wisdom and harmony, I was first brought I think at the age of four, following Homer's advice of gradual weaning from the soil.

My impressions may have been blurred by Mamme's forceful account of her great adventure. Via Calalzo, change trains . . . sounded as though the trip from Gais to Venice had taken three nights and three days, instead of ten hours. And how those signori in the first class compartment laughed — yes, first class on the first trip, second class the second — and they laughed because I tied a curtain strap around their necks and said: Кин-*Kui*. A family trait, it seems, comparing humans to animals. Gargantua reports that he called his grandmother a steer, and allegedly the first thing I ever called my mother was *Fock,* which, it would seem, she luckily did not understand, and which serves to illustrate my position and the abyss between Mamme and Mamile. I had only seen women with skirts to their ankles, and heavy winter-woollen, summer-cotton stockings tied under grubby knees with a string. No doubt Mamme had impressed upon me the sinfulness of immodesty. So I pointed at the lady's legs and said: *A sella Fock*. And she wanted to know what I had said, and Mamme with Tyrolean tact toned it down to a concern about her wearing no stockings: *Nix Strumpf*. The lady took my hand and stroked it against her leg to show me that she was wearing stockings. I was not convinced; but my conclusion apparently amused them: Oh well, if you will wear them of glass!

The first trip took place in the fall. And the first tantrum over a pair of gloves. I did not think it was cold enough to wear gloves; neither Mamme nor I could see the point of wearing gloves when there was no need for them. My hand went limp and the glove would not go on. The Frau became very impatient and proved to us that the gloves were big enough because she was able to stick her little finger in, and my usual comment was: Oh well, the kind of food you eat of course makes you thin. I hated vegetables; spinach was simply a variety of grass that at home one fed to the pigs. I also objected to the water. Instead of being impressed with the grandeur of restaurants I asked for fizz because the water smelled foul. I had my standards too. In Gais one was very fussy about water, always had to go to the main fountain for a pitcher of spring water before meals. But it seemed to be part of my education to drink foul water and wear gloves. Mamme cried secretly at the tortures I had to endure. *Sella Sektn*. She sought comfort in the Chiesa della Salute reciting one rosary after another while we were supposed to be walking on the Zattere. And the Herr rewarded her with little presents, souvenirs of Venice. In his best German he consoled her of *Heimweh* —

she was homesick — and he never had any whims and looked at me approvingly and hugged me and stooped to put his arm around her shoulder when he caught her frowning. *Gut, alles gut.*

Sometimes there were small parties downstairs. Adrian Stokes, at the time exploring the stones of Venice, was brought upstairs. Mamme had a notion that when we were sent upstairs instead of being asked to participate, it was because the Frau was ashamed of us; we did not know how to behave, how to be *hearrish.* But because I had kept so very quiet, we were given the dessert left over from the dinner. And forever after, I have associated Adrian Stokes with crème caramel, because at the top of the stairs first appeared the plate with the sweet, carried high by the Frau, very gay that evening. Of Adrian, I remember only the name. Don Arturo, another name with a story: a very rich South American, who lived in Paris and had his clothes tailored in London and flown to him, tailor and all. Mamme was very impressed by him, or rather, by the gorgeous boxes of sweets he brought the Frau. In Venice she wept, but back in Gais she talked like a Marco Polo returning from Cathay: the marvels of the churches and the marketplace. Rialto, the musicians in the Markusplatz: white jackets, gold buttons, blue jackets, silver spangles, and why did not the Frau play in the Piazza? — *"si kons wol a"* — she dismissed the problem, and the frown it had provoked, and described in detail the dream of Saint Ursula, and the mosaics, and her fright lest we fall into the water, the immeasurable depth and vastness of the sea. She imitated the cries of the gondoliers, of the milkman and the fishmongers. But the food, oh the Italian food was terrible: and proof was a packet of green olives which the Frau had given her with sandwiches to eat on the train. You found olives everywhere in Venice and everyone eats them, but back in Gais everyone who was given them to taste spat them out.

What I remember most clearly is leaning out of a gondola, splashing with my hands. The pleasant sensation of floating on quiet waters.

Whereas at home the river was a great menace. It came racing down from the glaciers and one would go near it only to dispose of a sheep's entrails or a dead cat. The current swished them out of sight in an instant. There were a few bends where the water slowed down and on the south side of the bridge one bank sloped into a sand-stretch where one could take cows and horses to water. But under no circumstances were children allowed to play there. It was more than fear: a deep-rooted, unexpressed superstition about the deadliness of the current.

As soon as I went to school I experienced the danger, or the attraction. On the bank opposite the strip of sand, the grass was high and backed by alders. Almost under the bridge, fastened to a protruding rock, was a wooden fish trap. A solid square box with holes in it. I was going to afternoon class with Prenn Agnes, one of our neighbor's fourteen daughters. She was a model of piety and righteousness who, nevertheless, when her twin sister, Lene, stayed too long at our house, came to fetch her with a stick hidden behind her back, and tied to the stick were nettles. Lene was a somewhat unpredictable moron, incapable of speech; she could, however, hoot like a truck, and was encouraged to do so by the older boys. Generally she was affectionate and joyful. In the course of history she met a "painless death."

A gypsy girl was sitting on the wooden box, and naturally, I stopped and leaned over the parapet. Agnes reminded me that I had better hurry or we would be late. This seemed to me utterly unimportant compared to the novelty of the girl on the box. The gypsy beckoned: "I bet you wouldn't dare come down and sit here." I hesitated. "It's like being on a boat. You are a coward." What! Hadn't I been on a boat, a real boat on a real sea, in a city built on a huge fish trap? The challenge had to be met, although I knew I must not associate with gypsies, let alone sit on the fish trap — not that it had ever entered anyone's head to forbid something so improbable! I crossed the bridge and turned towards the river. Agnes ran off, throwing over her shoulder: *"Passau!* I'll tell." Blissfully I slid down the high grass and leaped from the rock onto the box, clutching at the hand the gypsy held out to me. And there we sat, after an initial *fain,* on the swinging box for a while, until I suddenly realized that I did not like the mocking smile of the girl. She was much older than I; we had nothing to say to each other. Silence and the swish of water. The fish inside the box, if indeed there were any, were quiet. Or perhaps dead? Dead! — as surely I would be in a minute. It was a very quiet afternoon. The girl stopped smiling, she leered at me, or so it seemed. I noticed her unkempt hair. She was filthy and smelly.

How I managed to extract myself I do not remember. In later years I was frightened in retrospect and had nightmares, but at the time I must have forgotten quickly because the following winter in exactly the same spot I nearly crashed through thin ice. That was because of my passion for skating. Skating on the river was also forbidden, but the boys did it, close by the bank, and so did I. No one had skates, merely solid nailed boots. When the boots were made for me, I insisted on having big nails protruding and bending over the sole, not the round feminine kind, so that on ice I could more easily swing around in circles instead of going in a straight line. The cobbler rocked with laughter at my request, and Mamme said to him in mock anger: "Shut up, you ass."

Shoes, like most things, were made at home. Once a year the living room was taken over by the cobbler. It was one of the highlights of the winter season, much better than when the dressmaker came. I liked the smell of leather and glue, the sight of all those tools neatly laid out on the bench, the soaking leather in the bucket, the big smooth stone to flatten and mold the leather with, the various little piles of nails, separated according to their gender. And then the waxing of the thread and the quick hammering, and all one had to do was to look on and every now and again put one's foot gently into the cobbler's hand to have it sized. Whereas with the dressmaker one had to undress and be measured clumsily all over. And worse than that, one had to help rip up bundles of old clothes and sew on buttons, and the smell was musty and choking.

During the first winter I went to school, not only the cobbler and the dressmaker came *af Stearn,* to work and live with us, but also the saddler, because Fuchs, the mare, needed a new harness. The finished harness remained on display for many days, propped up in a corner of the room, and I kept polishing the brass ornaments and rings. The saddler was Mamme's youngest brother and was in no hurry to leave the house.

It was decided he should make a couch for the living room so that when the Herr and the Frau came they would not look so uncomfortable on our hard benches. But the couch never looked at home. The wood-paneled room was proportioned for the stove, the benches and the gothic table in the corner. Some leather and some material were left over, enough to make satchels for Margit and myself. The satchels turned out very square and hard and awkward to strap on our backs. But useful: one day I was so swift with my new boots on the ice, and felt it give way under me, and the water foaming, I flung myself on my back and was saved.

The satchel also shielded me from the stones that flew between the two factions of the village. *Hiogopruggla* and *Endopruggla*. We *Hiogopruggla* — of this side of the bridge — had to venture into foreign territory — the other side of the bridge — when going to school and to church. Gais was ill famed for its stone-flinging children. Most boys had slings. The ultimate purpose was to defend the Kirchtamichl — our Bacchus or John Barleycorn — on thanksgiving. The boys practiced for the great day when they would be old enough to take part in the battle.

The Kirchtamichl — Mihil: the strong one, the big one, a god once upon a time — is born in great secrecy. The unmarried girls lock themselves up in a room to dress the life-size straw figure in the traditional Tyrolean costume: white shirt, leather breeches with green suspenders, white stockings, low black boots, a stiff brown jacket and a wide-brimmed hat over the mask of a laughing young man. To keep him nourished, they tie a *Kirchtakropfn* — a kind of sour, highly yeasted, oblong doughnut — to his hat.

With equal secrecy, the young men fell the tallest tree, dig a deep hole in front of the inn or in a nearby meadow. Then they fetch the Michl and stick a red-and-white feather or the tail of a heathcock on his hat, to signify that they are ready for the fight. To one hand they tie a bottle of wine, to the other a gourd, and a loaf of bread is tucked under the jacket. With heavy drinking and shouts of *"Juhui!"* the Michl is sat astride a wine barrel and fastened to the top of the pole. Then *"Ruck! Ruck!"* — the pole is hoisted and steadied while an accordion drowns the threatening cries of the enemy, the sound of clashing sticks and the howling of the wounded. At the break of dawn, on the top of a mountain an ancient mortar fires three salvos. The fight is over, either won or lost. The village wakes up and the church bells toll: the great day of eating and drinking to which all the relatives are invited has begun. One speculates as to whether the red spots on the stones and sticks left on the battleground under the standing or missing Michl are wine or blood.

The young men from the neighboring villages try to steal the Kirchtamichl, or to tear him to pieces or to prevent him from being hoisted.

If our people did not succeed in setting up the Kirchtamichl, the disgrace was felt by the entire village, spirits sagged and appetites waned: the *Kropfn* tasted dry, the *Sulze* was bitter. Nor could one look forward to the invitation from relatives in the next village on their Kirchtag, for one might encounter the Gais Kirchtamichl, disfigured and tied like a prisoner to their pole. Oh, but if our side managed to ward off the onslaughts of the enemy and, on glorious occasions, even succeed in capturing *their* Michl, then eating and drinking became a feast.

Being a girl, I was cured early of the habit of stone-throwing. A new signpost had been erected at the local railway crossing, with little round red glasses like the reflectors on the back of bicycles, and we immediately used it as a target. I was caught by the roadsweeper. He was an employee of the Italian government, thus someone not to be trusted, and Tatte did not like it at all when he came to our house: "If I catch your *Frotz* again, *you* will be fined, and if you don't pay you'll be put in jail." It was the only time Tatte boxed my ears. I realized he had to, the roadsweep was expecting it and Tatte could not lose face: he had to show he was a stern father. I kept my resolve never to throw stones again.

2. The urge to write my own story took hold of me at an early age. I must have been eight when I started very formally: "My name is Maria Rudge. I was born on the 9th of July 1925 in Bressanone. Nine days I had to live under a glass bell because I was not ripe. Then I came to Gais and I lived with my mother and my father who has a crippled hand and many bullets in his legs and in his back which hurt when the weather changes. He won a medal in the war and we keep it in our glass cabinet. My older sister Margherita loves cats, she has brown hair and green eyes. I have blond hair and blue eyes. My friends are called Andreas Hofer and Adolf

Schuster, and I also have a little white dog called Turggile and a black lamb which lives with me because it has a wicked mother who does not allow it to suck because she likes the two white lambs better and three lambs is too much, so I feed it with a bottle and sometimes give it an egg and a little sugar in the milk. It is a nice fat lamb with very curly fleece."

That is as far as my first autobiography went, written in almost incomprehensible Italian since I did not know how to spell our dialect. My writing was prompted, as is most writing in the Tyrol, by Raimmichl's *Volkskalender*. Mamme had a great passion for reading out loud. She was very proud of the two enormous gothic tomes that sat among the milk bowls stacked for the skimming on the shelf in the *Stube* — *The Life of Christ* and *The Lives of the Saints* were the only two books in the house and she knew them almost by heart. For entertainment she read to us the feature stories in Raimmichl's calendar. That year, the main feature was the diary of a husbandman recorded on the blank columns of the calendars over a span of forty years. A peasant's life, simple and straightforward. Today I seem to remember only the ending because, as it often happened with the "Life of Christ," we were all moved to tears, aware only of that unforgettable tremor in Mamme's voice which indicated that she was no longer reading what was on the page, but was weaving a mysterious tale of her own. The farmer's last entry was made on the evening his wife was buried. And now he would sit back, waiting to join her, be it in Purgatory or in Paradise. He was ready and would abide his time patiently sustained by an occasional glass of wine! (". . . piety & uxoriousness, combining to make him long for death in order that he may meet her in heaven," to use the words of W. B. Yeats).

I decided then and there that I, too, must start writing my diary, while Mamme, stepping out of her spell — an ordinary

[31]

small farmer's wife, no longer the glorious universal foster mother — nagged Tatte good-humoredly and with good reason. His entries in the yearly calendar were anything but edifying. Granted, his left hand was crippled, and therefore one could not expect much in the way of writing, but the language, she said, the language was appalling:

> *Shegge giritn*
> *Focke gfacklt, 7 Facklan, 3 hin*
> *Tull giklemp*
> *Schof gschorn, 20 kilo Wolle*
> *Mause gikelbort, 16 litto Milch*

to remind him that on such and such a day

> spotted cow in heat
> sow littered 7, 3 dead
> rams castrated
> sheep shorn, 20 kg. wool
> the gray cow calved, 16 liters of milk.

This was his life. His feelings he would not put into writing but act upon.

I do not know where I had picked up the fancy notion that at Easter one had to make a nest for a rabbit to lay eggs in. Mamme dismissed it as sheer nonsense. Easter meant our Lord's fear and agony on Maundy Thursday, his death at the hands of the wicked Jews on Good Friday, the Descent into hell on Easter Saturday to deliver the souls of believers and His glorious Resurrection on Sunday. In memory of this, the custom was to scrub the house from top to bottom, to bake a cake, to dye eggs by boiling them wrapped up in onion peel, crocuses and rags, to look in the sunniest corner of the kitchen garden for the kren root, and to prepare the food basket for the blessing in church. First Margit would be told to go and look for the kren, and she would come back and say there was none, that the snow was still too high. Then I would be sent to look for it and come back and say there was too much soot on the ground — the soot from the chimneys was always strewn over the snow in the garden as the best fertilizer. Then, to keep Mamme's temper down, Tatte would go and poke around for a while and come back with a root as long as a pig's tail. A big kren root was a good omen: healthy soil.

It was Margit's job to carry the basket filled with the painted eggs, the cake, the chunk of smoked bacon and the kren root to be blessed in church on Easter Sunday. The sight and smell of these bounties proudly displayed before the altar, in laundry baskets by big farmers, knitting baskets by small farmers like us, kerchiefs by the poor people who grew no wheat and killed no pig, seemed to make High Mass last forever. In the course of years the Easter rites became more meaningful in their details. But of that year only the rabbit nest stands out. I had made it behind the house under the east side wall of the dungheap, lined with heather and crocuses. My expectations were great, though rabbits, as such, I did not trust. I knew their tricky traits well. Margit had great trouble tending her rabbit hutch, and I will tell later of how my own attempt to raise rabbits failed.

What I saw then was Tatte's jacket flap round the corner of the house. On my first inspection early in the morning I had found only frost. This meant that Tatte after Mass had been to the shop. Farmers, however small, thought it below their dignity to enter the village shop. That was a place for women and children. They had need of nothing. For trading and selling, there were the markets in the right season at the appropriate places and intervals. I suppose he used tobacco as the only face-saving pretext, and then with a snicker he must

[33]

have tossed off: "And give me three of those yellow things" —
if he had to buy them, he would not admit knowing the name
of something so foreign and extravagant.

In the nest I found three oranges. Unforgettable, like the
laughter dancing in Tatte's eyes at my real delight and feigned
surprise.

Spring comes late in the Pustertal. As everywhere, children
throw off their shoes when the ground is no longer frozen and
draw the temple for hopscotch and the ring with the dip in the
middle for marbles. I could never keep marbles from one year
to another, while Margit always had a bagful. Clay marbles
and plenty of the colored glass ones too. I suppose she knew
she was poor and had to save, whereas I felt rich; not because
of those trips to Venice, the visits from my *Pessan Lait,* or
those registered letters that smelled deliciously of sealing wax
and contained the money for my keep, which, even after having been reduced from the initial munificence of two hundred
lire per month to a hundred and fifty, and no extras, was still
a handsome gift of the gods. To me those letters were on the
whole vaguely disturbing, for whenever I behaved like the rest
of the village urchins, which was usual, I would hear: *sham
de* — fie! — your people don't pay for you to grow up like a
Strousnraba!

I felt rich because I could always count on Tatte. He
smoked a lot and I had to run to the shop to buy his 1.40 lira
tobacco. He usually gave me 1.50, so that there was 10
centesimi change: the equivalent of three *Stollwerk* toffees;
two *Napolitana* wafers; two glass or five clay marbles; or a
Pearnsdreck — a stick of licorice. I first had to bring back the
change with the tobacco, and then cajole it back, while
Mamme protested: there he was ruining his own health by
smoking that filthy tobacco — not to mention that he spent his

entire invalid pension on smoking, and she had to think of everything and bring up other people's children to earn a little money; that the house, when she married, was ramshackle and now it had a new roof; and Margit would join in and say that the *Letze* (I was referred to as the minor; she was the *Groese,* the major) was allowed to go to the shop while she had to work — ruining my stomach, ruining my teeth, giving me a bad complexion and no appetite and so on. But I was Tatte's pet, and he asserted his authority by giving me the ten centesimi and I reasserted my independence by running to the shop.

I followed him around the fields and always joined him in the stable to help with the cows. If he was in an exceptionally good mood he would even allow me to milk them, though he said it meant losing at least one-third of the milk; cows don't like a different hand and mine were still too small anyway. Most of all I loved to wheel the dung cart from the stable to the dungheap. I could show off my skill at keeping the wheelbarrow balanced. Dung is the main wealth on a farm and one must never spill or waste a straw. Tatte was very particular about that. I knew nothing of the sacredness of the *sterquilinium* in those days, but it was undoubtedly a respected place with a code of its own. City people had to be told that a dungheap is not a rubbish heap and had to be kept clean. A compost heap is something different again; Tatte thought it was merely an excuse for wasting and he never kept one.

On the main dungheap only the cleaned-out bedding of the cows and horse went. The bedding of sheep and pigs went on a different pile. It smelt differently and had other properties, good only for the lesser fields. Tatte alone remembered the exact rotation. A well-kept dungheap smells good, especially if the bedding is of leaves and not of sawdust or shavings. And again: forest bedding smells best; it is mostly moss, ferns, fir-tips and birch leaves. Alder-leaf bedding was, at that time, the easiest to come by, for there was a great stretch of communal grazing ground, mainly along the river from Gais to Uttenheim, overgrown with alders. After harvest, a full week was set aside for the raking of leaves. Everyone was allowed to rake as much as he needed, and all the family went along. Children too small to rake had to look for snail shells. Shells are excellent chicken feed; it was a real feast for the hen when one returned with an apronful. I always made sure that the shell was empty, with the ditty: *Schneggile, Schneggile,* show me your horns. . . . One had to say it at least three times; if no horns peeped round the curve of the shell it meant the snail was not at home or dead, or a cussed one deserving to be fed to chickens.

Alder leaves have to smolder before they can be used for bedding; thus the stack was used as a hearth and one carried lunch along and it kept warm, burrowed in a tightly covered pail.

All that is gone now. In its place there is a new school, a post office, a hotel and a cement factory near the river.

Sold the school-house at Gais,
cut down the woods whose leaves served for bedding cattle
so there was a lack of manure . . .

And one waited for the snow to settle, for the roads to be good. The horseshoes were sharpened. The big sledge stood by the dungheap to be loaded. A perfect, huge, brown egg and on top of it the horse blanket and on top of it me. On Thursday there was no school, on Thursday we took dung to the fields and Fuchs wore his jingle bells because sledges are so swift and so silent. On the way home Tatte tipped the empty crate and in the big oval shell we sat, I huddled up against him; he smoked placid and silent all the way.

The pleasure lasted long into my school years.

Mamme was rushed to the Bruneck hospital early one morning, a straw mattress and an eiderdown hastily thrown into the four-wheeler. It was one of the few times I saw Tatte whip the horse; and to no avail. Another stillbirth. But the loss of a soul was more unbearable than the loss of a life. To comfort Mamme, a nun gave it emergency baptism before removing the little corpse to a box of sawdust in the hospital morgue.

Tatte came home with red eyes and with a tiny coffin under his arm. In the afternoon Töite, Margit and I went to see Mamme and to prepare the baby for burial, taking the coffin with us. Such a weary dragging of feet; we recited rosaries all the way. Margit and I took turns at carrying the empty coffin. In the morgue I was very upset at finding the baby in sawdust and immediately picked it up and brushed the sawdust off its naked bottom and hugged it like a doll. The blue feet were pitiful; I rubbed them, hoping they would turn pink, while Töite garrulously and confusedly arranged the pillow and diaper in the coffin. She had slowly joined her husband in his drinking habits. At the pub entering Bruneck she said she would treat us to a raspberry juice, but Margit and I were ashamed to go in, so she went alone and must have gulped down a couple of schnapps. She said she needed them badly, she was so tired and all in a sweat, and the alcohol went to her head. She spat on her handkerchief and washed the baby's face and twisted a small pink rosary around its hands.

To me it looked like an angel in its baptism frock, and when we were allowed into the women's ward I kept repeating to Mamme: Don't cry, you have a little angel in heaven, it's so beautiful, just like an angel. We always referred to it as

[37]

our *Engile*. Yet, the tears that Tatte surreptitiously wiped off with his crippled hand during the rapid funeral next morning made me wonder about God's fairness. Why deprive these parents of their children? To earn Paradise. Then Hansile came into our family, not only to do a *guits Werk,* but also to earn the pittance the government paid for illegitimates.

At the end of that summer my black ewe came back from the pastures with two lambs of her own. It had been a good summer for the flock, almost doubled and no casualties. There was a tacit agreement between me and Tatte that if I wanted him to feed and shelter my sheep, I must look after the entire flock. I much preferred being shepherdess to helping with chores in the house. It was strenuous keeping the sheep on a small turnip field or on a chewed-off meadow, and then there were the days when sheep were in heat and the rams from other flocks came running to mine and fought with obtuse, persistent determination. *Pfloff* — head-on, the muffled sound for hours. I feared that their bones and brains were all a splintered porridge, but when I tried to separate them, they turned against me. It was hard to chase them off, and even worse to find and bring back our own rams which had strayed. A lonely skipping over stubbles, a sinking into newly plowed ground. It was more pleasant in spring on the soft turf of the communal grazing ground, where sheep and cows could roam at leisure and shepherds play, barter, tell stories and riddles, bet, fight, gather pine cones and heather at the edge of the wood, make May-whistles out of hazelnut branches, or miniature hand-mirrors out of sharp glass blades, which, looped and inserted into the mouth, held a thin film of saliva. This film of saliva we touched — delicately — with the droplet suspended on the torn stem of a milkweed, and myriads of colors, streaked, merged, dotted the film. We called it *Himmlguggn:*

peeping into Heaven, we saw the wings of seraphs, the feathers of the Holy Ghost, the sash of the Virgin.

Le Paradis n'est pas artificiel,
l'enfer non plus.

Once Heaven had reflected itself in the saliva, one had to blow it away and never stick the grass blade into one's mouth again, or one would have died and gone straight to Hell. This milkweed had power over witches. If you had warts it meant the witches were after you. My right hand was full of warts. Saying three times *Hexedruckde*, spitting over my right shoulder and putting three drops of the sticky white milk on the warts for seven days, at sunset, before driving the animals home in the evening, I got rid of them. One worried about witches and evil spirits because they played funny tricks on the animals. One also worried greatly about one's soul and plucked daisies, not to find out whether he loved me or loved me not, but whether one would go to Heaven, Hell, or Purgatory: *Himmlhellefegfoir*.

Every spring there was also the excitement of pulling down, confusion, clearing, rebuilding. The bustle of carpenters, masons, Mamme shouting orders, everyone helping. Mamme was determined to renew the house from top to bottom, to have a room where the Herr and the Frau could sleep, instead of going to that hotel and wasting money. In due course the stable was rebuilt, a new roof put on, the *Stube* and the bedroom above it repaneled and the floors mended. The planning had to be done years ahead because the lumber came from our own woods. In exchange for help at felling trees, Tatte lent his labor and that of his horse. The tiles of the roof were made by hand, at home. We stacked them in the sun and for weeks the stacks had to be shifted, each tile turned over until it was completely dry. Children's chores. Straightening out old nails, handing, holding, fetching. Running for fresh water, carrying wine for the workmen, who lived in the house and had to be served, *wi's do Prauch isch.*

The *Öberstube* was ready, immaculate, smelling of pine-wood. No one was allowed in it. We all still huddled together in the bedroom off the living room. I shared Tatte's bed and was happy to fall asleep with his crippled hand in mine.

It was in the summer of 1934 — perhaps — that the Herr conveyed by letter that he would come for a visit and then take me to Venice. For the first time I remember feeling happy and excited at the prospect of a visit. We painted a rusty iron washstand pea-green; we bought an enamel pitcher and basin, and Mamme, out of a long garment, sewed pale yellow ruffles for the windows; one had an OR monogram in a corner. To us, it seemed a fine ornament, embroidered by hand. I mistook Tattile's puzzled and then amused look for admiration. But the visit caused a great deal of apprehension to Mamme and Tatte. In words and glances they said: This is the end. Now she is grown-up, he is coming to take her away. But why then does he say he wants to buy a field? For some years the Herr had been inquiring about prices: it seemed that he wanted to buy a field. Mamme spent an entire Sunday afternoon writing a letter, explaining the difference between *Acker* and *Wiese*, about the rotation of crops; it was complicated and very uncertain, income was not calculated in terms of money by small farmers. Besides, a field, a single field, be it meadow or arable, was almost impossible to be had. Primogeniture was the law. If a farm was sold, it was sold as a unit, entailed. But Mamme would keep looking and listening, because Moidile had great pleasure with sheep. Tatte frowned about it, it would mean complications.

But he let himself be persuaded to meet the Herr at the

Bruneck station with our four-wheeler. I had my heart set on it, though by the time we reached the station, I was apprehensive. At each bump, Tatte had said, ha, he'll like that, ha ha. Hard to tell whether he liked it or not. No doubt that the driver's bench was too narrow to fit his big beam. He clung to it very earnestly. I sat squeezed between Tatte and Tattile. Tatte handed me the reins to show that I could master a horse and said I was a reliable shepherdess.

At home, Mamme — as though to appease the gods — had prepared a sumptuous dinner, confiding that the outcome of things depended on her ability to please the *Herrschaft*. I had heard her say to Tatte: Perhaps someone envious has written to tell them about the baby, perhaps they did not want us to have another child, perhaps they think I am ill. I sat at the table with the Herr and, since the Frau had not come, the extra bed in the new room had been made up for me.

Tyrolean tables are very low — people have to lean over and reach the pan in the middle. Tatte laughed — the Herr is too tall, but he must eat, eat more — while he watched us from the bench near the stove. No, he would not sit with us, and Mamme kept bringing in more food. Having failed to assemble the rest of the family to sit at the table with him, Tattile said I must get up and clear the table, that was my job. No one must ever expect to be served. Everyone must work, either with his head or with his hands. He worked with his head. Hard work. Much thinking. He spoke in broken German and we listened to him as to an oracle. Tatte agreed: That's how things should be, but are not. Yes, yes, that's how it will have to be. *Arbeit — Geld.*

He was not a rich man, held no important position in government, he was no lord. He did not call himself a poet either, he said: *Schriftsteller,* and spoke of *Bücher schreiben, immer studieren, immer schreiben.* A writer of books. No, not novels.

Not stories for the paper. *Geschichte, Politik. Ökonomie.* And also the Frau Mamma worked with music. Concerts. *Viel Geld?* No, no money in it, good concerts. And I would have to choose between working with my head and working with my hands; everyone must work. What did they think I was best at?

There had been a depression in America. And this required a long, patient dialogue of which I caught only stray words, but I heard Tatte explain it to neighbors *af Teutsch* later on. *Arbeit, Kredit, Gold, Schuld, Jud, Bank.*

Nowhere so well deposited, as in the pants of the people, Wealth ain't.

Perfect agreement on that score. But over the question of the Tyrol, Tatte shook his head. Over Fascism and Nazism there was dissent. Yes, yes, Mussolini was no worse than Hitler, but they both had no manners and no religion. One time he was minding his own business, coming home with a load of turnips, had pushed as far to one side of the road as he could, when he saw the truck in the distance. A truckload of Black Shirts singing and waving the flag. He merely looked on, and two louts jumped off and beat him so that the pipe flew out of his mouth and the hat over the hedge. He should have taken his hat off to the flag. It had not occurred to him, it wasn't his flag. And this forbidding of German in school, and the police and all civil servants speaking Italian so that no peasant had a chance. This Italianizing of documents and all the Balilla nonsense at school. Welfare? That's no good for farmers; it had increased, yes, but it is only *Lumpen* who profit from it, lazy bums and *Huren,* and the small farmer paid exorbitant taxes, contributions to things that did not concern him. No honesty, no *Ordnung* —

for the dog-damn wop is not, save by exception,
honest in administration any more than the briton is truthful

Discontent and rebellion were smoldering in Gais. Herr
Bacher had bought a radio and now instead of *Fairn* as in previous years, Tatte went to listen to the news — although he
said: Nothing but propaganda! Sometimes I was allowed to
go with him. In children's minds, Hitler was synonymous
with Germany and Mussolini with Italy. On telegraph poles
we chalked Heil Hitler, **M** Mussolini. The gypsies were
spreading stories: Hitler is the Antichrist. Gypsies and Jews
were being chased out of Austria. But gypsies were liars. Even
the old *Herzensbergerin* who ranked as their queen — and had
a white horse which she claimed had been presented to her by
the Kaiser — though respected, could not be trusted. Franz
Josef may have been a lousy old bewhiskered sonovabitch —
perhaps, but he came to the front to inspect the troops, he
showed concern and good manners. And the taxes were lower
before the war. True, people were much poorer, but there was
Ordnung and less swindle.

the century-old joke

Well yes, it is all a joke, all a swindle. . . . The *Politiken*
between Tatte and Tattile went on and on. I was told to
spreng — asperge — and go to bed. Dipping the finger in the
holy water by the door and wetting one's forehead before
leaving the room takes the place of saying goodnight. There
was little distinction between etiquette and religious practices.
A *frommes Kind* was sure to have good manners. Mamme explained to the Herr some of the nuances of manners and accent in speech with much sign language. The Herr understood. He was an exception. He had no discernible religion

[43]

but *dechto a Pildung*. A gentleman with an education.

I was still awake when he came up to bed. Mamme carried the kerosene lamp for him and came to my bed saying I should see to the light. As soon as she had left the room Tattile showed great concern over my dirty fingernails. He fumbled in his luggage as though he were looking for something vital. I hopefully thought he was looking for sweets. He found his nail file and scissors and cut and cleaned my fingernails. And what about brushing my teeth? Sometimes I did. And the brush? Well, somewhere. No reproach or criticism, but next day we went to Bruneck to equip me with brushes.

Before starting out he said he had a present. He made it sound important. It was a diapason. I was disappointed. He said it served to set the right tone when singing or playing an instrument. I said Margherita could give the right tone by ear and if we sang at two voices she first started out on my note and then found hers.

And Margherita's voice was clear as the notes of a clavichord.

We walked to Bruneck, like peasants. I had hoped to go on the little train; that would have been a treat. But it had been impressed upon me that we, too, had no money to squander. As we walked through the fields I forgot the train, and grew proud. We passed several families at work, and to all the Herr doffed his hat and cordially said *Grüss Gott,* and the men took their hats off and said *Grioss Gött a —* friendly, respectful. Since my feet were not pierced and my face was not black, the mythical origins of the gift-from-heaven had soon been forgotten in the village. But now the women were clearly curious. *"Des isch mein Tatte,"* I said. And their expression: So it's true that Sâma Moidile comes from *Pessere Lait;* if this

Herr is her father, she can't be a *Schlumpe* like most *Ungi-numm*. *Unginums* means a foster child, someone "taken on," and had, despite being very common, all the connotations of unwanted; outsider and charity.

By now I was able to communicate somewhat in Italian. Mamile said in Venice I must speak Italian all the time and call Tattile "Babbo." Her stern attitude handicapped me more than the language barrier had done. For fear of lapsing into German or saying the wrong thing, I turned poker face. If Tattile now and again resorted to German she knitted her brows: *"Caro!"* So I did not tell her then that twice a week, with the slate hidden under my apron, I went to our neighbors for German lessons. A very exciting secret. The Tyroleans, deprived of instruction in German, had formed an underground movement which, among other things, trained voluntary teachers and provided textbooks. And we were to read and write in the Gothic alphabet. The political motives were obvious, parents and children had to pledge utter secrecy. We took knitting and sewing with us, and the boys carpentry tools. In case anyone entered, we were to wipe the slates and pretend we were working and the book would disappear among the teacher's clothes. The house in which the lessons were held had been carefully chosen, off the road; since the owners were notoriously unfriendly to strangers, peddlers and carabinieri were not likely to drop by.

Between themselves, Babbo and Mamile continued to speak English. All I could do was watch their eyes and facial expressions. For some obscure reason, I was afraid of Mamile. Perhaps I disliked her. An incomprehensible entity with a grudge, a dark resentment as though I were permanently doing her wrong. Mamme's early tears and her complaints that the Frau was *murre, a muddo Sock,* exacting, nagging had probably left its mark on me. I stood as though forever waiting for mercy. One day at the Lido, I cut my toe, and went up to them sitting at a table in the open, waiting for lunch. I saw Babbo's dark face and thought: I should not have cut myself, should not have held up the bleeding toe, a breach in manners; I have ruined their appetite.

Babbo rushed me down to the sea and had me wash my toe, tied his handkerchief around it and carried me back to the table. But throughout lunch he sat furious and ate almost nothing, his face propped up between his fists. It seemed to me that after a while Mamile's tone became coaxing. I thought she might be interceding for me. Years later, when I understood English, the incident was recalled by: "the time he wouldn't eat his lunch and the sprig had cut her toe. Such a rude thing to say to poor Alice." While I was playing on the beach a group of friends led by Giorgio and Alice Levi had turned up, and one of the ladies asked for an autograph. She got an E.P. signature. She insisted for a few lines from the poet, and received:

a lesson that no school book teaches:
some women's b . . . are too big for their breeches.

And it applied to the visitors. Fawning and insistence put in their place, but Mamile must have given him a severe talking-to for him to get into such a fury. It was the first time I had seen him angry. It seemed as though he were visibly fighting a wasp nest in his brain. Quite different from when he was merely pensive. That occurred often, and I knew immediately that he wanted me to refrain from talking. Inherent in his silence was suspense, a joyous sense of expectation, until he broke into a kind of chant that sometimes went on for hours, interrupted and picked up again, no matter whether he was sitting at table or walking in the streets. Hard as I tried to imitate this humming, I never could. No words: sounds bordering on ventriloquism, as though some alien power were rumbling in the cave of his chest in a language other than human; then it moved up to his head and the tone became nasal, metallic. Athena banging in her glistening helmet inside Jupiter's skull, clamoring for release. A hasty scribbling on a piece of paper, a tearing off of newspaper clippings, a frantic annotation in a book. Something had clicked, some truth revealed, a new thought, a new line, a new melody. Le Paradis.

For a flash,
for an hour.

Babbo used to leave the house right after breakfast and briskly cross over the bridge to the other side of the Canal where, at Signora Scarpa's, he had a room to work in, a typewriter and an address. I listened for his return. The tapping of his black malacca cane up the cul-de-sac Calle Querini. A rattle downstairs and a loud, prolonged MIAO. From the first floor; *Miao* — Mamile answered, and my tedium was over. I rushed down the two flights of stairs ready to go out. Shopping, a blissful ritual. It sometimes entailed stopping at the Banca d'America e d'Italia to get some money. If on the exchange or check there were coins, he shoved them over to me and the bank clerk smiled and complimented him on my hair: *Che bei capei, che bei capei.* Also in the streets people sometimes turned to look at us and said out loud: *Che bei capei,* and he would turn too, and take his hat off and bow and chuckle with pleasure in his characteristic hissing fashion. He always carried lots of loose coins in his pocket and we had a little game with beggars. He would pull out a handful of change and let me pick and give what I thought suitable. And then he asked me what I thought of the beggar — sincere? a drunkard? sick? was there really no work available? Eventually I came to the conclusion that the beggars passed word about the generous American who never fails, for we met usually half a dozen on our walk from San Gregorio to La Salute and none anywhere else. When the loafing men who hook the gondolas so that one can step in more easily saw us from a distance, they would scamper, each trying to make it to the gondola first. There usually were two or three hands or caps waiting for the tip.

Depending, I suppose, on whether he was satisfied with the patch of mosaic added to the Cantos during his morning's work — though at the time I did not realize what his work consisted in; "writing" was a vague notion — or on whether he had to mail something urgently or too voluminous to fit into his pockets, we took the short *traghetto* across the Canal Grande or the long one from Punta della Salute to San Marco, which, of course, I liked better. In the latter case the first stop was at the American Bar under the Clock for a small sandwich and an orangeade. Nowhere else in the world have sandwiches tasted so good, in retrospect. A flair for perfection in food as in writing. Frugal but select. Thus, we would proceed up the Mercerie to a small coffeeshop where he would select a mixture of grains and have them ground and the smell was heavenly and lingering, and I left the shop reluctantly. Here he also bought blocks of dark bitter chocolate, and the dainty parcel was handed to me. Thence to Moriondo, the pastry shop with fragrant *apfelstrudel,* cream chocolate and mints. The white-haired man in a brown duster who owned the shop was a special friend and there were long conversations, mostly about politics and prices; Babbo seemed to inquire about such matters with the same care and delicacy that he applied to his selection of sweets.

Back through the Piazza, where he often ran into friends, to the newspaper kiosk near the Post Office for English and French newspapers. To another pastry shop, Colussi's, for cheese straws and crackers. To the baker for pain-carré, croissants and grissini, and more chat with the baker's wife, on *grano, farina, prezzi.* Around the corner the fruit shop where the fat signora was also a special friend — *Che bea putea, che bei capei — a non finire* — and good advice and help in choosing the best melon, peaches, figs, clean crisp and curly lettuce, tomatoes not too ripe. Next door the butcher: careful consultation over the meat for grinding, the thin slices of veal or liver. Then the *pizzicagnolo,* where the choice was a really difficult one between the various cheeses: stracchino, bel paese or mascarpone, olandese or gruyère. Last, and only occasionally, into the *drogheria,* for a packet of mint tablets.

All this shopping was done with great zest and we returned home triumphant, laden with parcels. Invariably the sound of the violin met us at the door, precise, passionate. We deposited the parcels in the kitchen with a hush, but the playing stopped. MIAO. Babbo went upstairs with the sweets and the papers and I could start unwrapping the fruit and the bread and put things in their place until Mamile descended and together we prepared lunch. Babbo put all his care into the choice of food, Mamile put it into details, touches at laying the table. For actual cooking she had no flair:

> 'Some cook, some do not cook
> some things cannot be altered'

If they wanted something that tasted really good, Babbo had to cook it. Usually for supper. A variety of omelets (and the secret lay in adding half a shell of water to each egg, salt and pepper and beat it *very* briskly) lavishly filled with ham, cheese or apricot jam.

There was a passion-flower creeper growing from our neighbor's garden on our wall. We had permission to pick the flowers we could reach from the windows. Mamile told me I must always try and find a flower for the fingerbowls and invariably Babbo was told not to eat it. The meals, apart from enjoying the food, were for me tedious — long conversations I could not follow, a painstaking imitation of their ways of eating — *drink* the soup from the spoon — *never* stick the spoon into your mouth, hold it to the lips sideways — *always* tip the plate away from you — never touch a peach with your fingers when you peel it — and then the dreaded siesta. I was supposed to go to sleep after lunch and could not. I lay listening to the voices downstairs, then to the turning of the newspaper pages and finally deep silence.

During those interminable siesta hours, the studio on the top floor seemed to me a desert. Aside from the open fireplace, the huge gray canvas by Tami Koume and my bed, stifled under a voluminous mosquito net, there was only the long bookcase ending in a desk by the wall, with a tall, square wooden armchair made by Babbo. The two windows, over the narrow garden, faced the gray crumbling backwall of the Dogana, so that looking out of the windows offered small distraction. Moreover, the shutters had to be kept closed to keep out the heat.

Stealthily I would cross the room — the dark boards creaked — and sit in front of the long bookcase fencing off the stairs leading up from Mamile's room. I pulled out one book after another in search of illustrations, or some German or Italian I could read, but everything was in languages I did not understand, and no pictures. Downstairs, on the contrary, there were two or three big volumes at which I could have looked all day long even without understanding what was written in them. But I was not allowed to touch them. They served educational purposes. Out of sheer boredom, one afternoon, laboriously, accurately, I painted Ixotta's face, in the bas-relief walled in by the desk, a shimmering black with a sharp pencil.

Which might be considered youthful levity
but was really a profound indication;

I was rather pleased with the effect. When Mamile discovered it, she looked horrified and smacked my hands hard — very naughty. *Cattiva.* Studiously, tearfully I had to restore it to its original whiteness.

On afternoons, if we did not go to the Lido, Babbo went back to his room at Scarpa's and Mamile would tell me to stretch out beside her on the big velvet couch and would read to me in English out of those beautiful books, then she summarized it into Italian and at the end of the story showed me the pictures; the ogre, Puss-in-boots, etc. Sometimes some frightening ones in *The Ingoldsby Legends:* the head in a bucket a young girl is pulling out of a well, a running man carrying his head under his arm. There were also sweet romantic pictures in the Jean Ingelow poems that made me eager to hear the story. Those were enjoyable afternoons, up to a point: I never felt safe. All of a sudden Mamile might ask me to repeat a word in English, or make me retell the story I had just heard in Italian. My mind stopped. Even if I had understood the story, grope as I might, no Italian word would come to me, and the more I liked the story the more I would assimilate it into my dialect and only German words would come to the tip of my tongue and to a sharp halt. This must have been maddening for Mamile. She was not patient. When Babbo came home, I gathered the conversation was about me, how absolutely hopeless I was at learning English and Italian. I was obtuse and pigheaded. I sensed her disappointment. Her capacity for suffering was great and her forebodings so dark and strong she seemed to conjure them into reality on the spot.

Perhaps Babbo tried to remedy this disaster by getting me interested in learning — or her in teaching me — music. One afternoon, we went to a music shop and he bought a violin. On one of their joint visits to Gais when I was about three, they had brought me a tiny violin. Mamile must have showed me how to hold it, but I probably complied only long enough to have a picture taken. Mamme told me that as soon as I was left to myself I banged it hard on the chicken coop, creating great fracas among the fluttering hens, and she had to take it away from me for fear I might smash it. Now I was being given a second chance. Although I liked the sound of the violin, the tunes were too difficult and alien. On certain late afternoons, when Mamile practiced for what seemed hours, an unexplainable sadness took hold of me. I felt trapped on the steps of the top floor. Mamile and Babbo were strangers. I would never be able to return home. The room downstairs where the sounds came from was on another planet of floating colors and sounds, a choking huge cloud. A wall as thick and impenetrable as the one facing my window — the long, high wall of the Dogana — separated me from Gais, from a ground to stand on. No doubt the oncoming of dusk and the evening bells, which in Venice are particularly sad, added greatly to my melancholy.

Thus I was not particularly happy to receive a violin, though I felt I should be and tried to look it, so as not to disappoint Babbo by seeming ungrateful. If I had been given a choice, I would no doubt have asked for a zither or a mouth organ. I would have learned to play gay and simple tunes — or more likely, I would have immediately given it to Margit so that the boys in the village would have come to sing and dance. Mamile never got around to teaching me the violin because she said I must learn solfège first. That was another failure. All I retained about the violin was what I picked up in the shop from the man who sold it: keep the bow well waxed and loosen the hair when not using. On my return to Gais this violin was put in the glass cabinet together with the tiny one and the diapason. It did not lie idle for long.

Olga, the Herr Lehrer's grandniece, was a good friend of mine. We were in the same class and she often joined me when I was looking after the sheep. Together we thought up a fine device for catching runaway rams. We tied a long rope with a loop on the whip and practiced strenuously. It was Olga who finally succeeded in throwing the loop around a ram's neck. The triumph was short. The animal pulled her down, and since she would not let go, dragged her across the fields. Finally I realized the ram was becoming more and more frantic because it was choking. I was frightened and shouted: Let go. I ran after her and tore the whip from her hand. The exhausted, half-choked ram stopped dead the moment the noose relented. I told Tatte. He roared with laughter and whenever he saw the two of us together he teased us: How about throttling another ram? So we settled for quieter occupations: watching, knitting and telling stories.

Olga had an interesting great-uncle: blind Peter. A familiar figure on the bench in front of their house. The time the teacher could not find the key to the school — the older boys had thrown it in the river to spite Italy — Peter arrived with an imposing ring of keys and hooks. He felt the keyhole with his fingers and easily unlocked the door. Olga told me he also mended watches and could play any instrument. "Not the violin, I bet," and I bragged about the two violins in the glass cabinet. I had to "show" them to Peter. He was delighted and said he would teach me how to play. No way out. He was blind. His hands were fat and white. His body: a big egg with a little egg stuck on, no neck visible and the legs very short. Humpty Dumpty. I was impressed by the theory that his peculiar shape was due to the fact that all the nerves were tied into a knot at the top of his head. A horse had kicked him when he was four. He went blind and his legs stopped growing. In an institution for the blind he had been taught music. But the teacher, a blind man too, had no ear for music. So the pupils whistled to him instead of playing the violin. Peter had picked up a few tricks and was eager to show them to me. He played the harmonium quite well. That I took more seriously; it was played also by the priest. Actually, Peter spent more time telling me stories about musicians than teaching me music, but eventually I did master "O Tannenbaum" and "Fuchs du hast die Gans gestohlen," both on the harmonium and the violin.

I became familiar with the faces of Bach, Beethoven, Mozart and Schubert. They were on four postcards, their names written underneath, pasted under the harmonium lid. All poor, blind, deaf, full of debts and ailments. And sometimes the creditors made off with their instruments. They were geniuses, Peter kept repeating. When I asked him what genius was, he gave me no convincing answer. I did not want to join their ranks, but had to give a concert because Peter was proud of me. I should tell Mamme and Tatte to come and listen, on a Saturday evening.

Mamme would not go to the Herr Lehrer's house in the evening. Margit was scathing about fiddles and harmoniums, music for cats and priests. If ever she got a zither she would show me the difference. Tatte asked Prenn to come with him, to *fairn endodoprugge*, for a change. Although the ex-teacher did not speak to people in the street, his neighbors came to his house in the evening. There were quite a few elderly farmers smoking around the stove and they welcomed Sâma and Prenn. Olga and the two aunts were behind the table, knitting. For a long time it seemed as though Peter and I did not exist. I was getting very sleepy and it was time to go home when Peter firmly opened the harmonium lid and said: now keep quiet and listen to this little girl. And to me peremptorily: "Fuchs du hast die Gans gestohlen." I stuck the violin under my chin and Olga and the aunts came to life. But a man said: "A querulous instrument." Peter paid no attention and we proceeded with "O Tannenbaum," and then the pezzo forte. All I had to do was to draw the bow with extreme vigor over the strings in succession: one, two, three. The easiest thing in the world, a lot of noise and strong rhythm. Bravo! Bis! We repeated the performance with even greater gusto. And then Peter slammed the harmonium lid and roared with laughter. His trick had worked, he had fooled them and was happy.

On the way home I was wide awake. With my entire being I absorbed the crinkling snow, the starry sky and the smell of ice and fog over the river. It is still there. And Tatte's comment: *Öppas konn se schun.* Mamme was sitting up reading all to herself the *Life of Christ.* "*Pa do Frau werschts wo recht sein*" — she hoped the Lady would be pleased if, as Tatte said, I knew something.

Whether by chance, or by arrangement, Mamile's brother and his family turned up in Venice. I was a surprise for them. The surprise was to their liking; they were merry and offered to take me back to Gais in their car. My cousins were respectively one and three years younger than myself. They were told to kiss me on the cheek. I had never before come so close to clean, well-dressed boys. We eyed each other carefully.

They seemed somewhat unreal to me, more like dolls than boys. Peter and John. John said something and everyone laughed. Years later I learned that he had asked: Is he the Ogre? He meant Babbo.

A wicker case on the floor of the car was cutting into my legs. I tried to convey this without too much fuss, but failed. A strange sense of helpless rebellion seized me as I endured the torture for hours. When we finally stopped for a picnic lunch, my uncle was distressed by the marks on my legs and rubbed them and rearranged the luggage and tried to explain that I must not be too shy to speak. It had not been shyness. For the first time I experienced a feeling of discontent. Aunt Jane was jolly and loud like Mamme, a beautiful lady who hugged her children and was expansive with her husband. Tatte was delighted when she asked him to scratch her back. Putting on no airs. A bit of straw must have fallen down her neck as they were taken to see the stable and the barn. Tatte apologized. Oh no, it was the mosquitoes in Venice. Ha Ha! They spent the night in the Schloss Hotel in Sankt Georgen; in their opinion the Öberstube was too small for four. Mamme feared it was because of the open latrine. Next morning uncle Teddy came to take me for a ride. In Bruneck he bought me a bag of sweets and a German edition of Thackeray's *The Rose and the Ring*. A book I could read. And I loved it. When they departed and the cheerful waving was over, I felt left behind. Not that I had wanted to go with them — such a possibility had not entered my head; and we could not understand each other. And I was glad to be back home. But something no longer clicked. I had outgrown the swing in which I sat musing and munching sweets while reading of Prinz Bulbo and Angelika. Margit seemed hostile. Who did I think I was! I had been home since yesterday and had not done a stroke of work, *du vinediga Soafe!* I suppose she used the term

'Venetian soap' to brand me as soft and delicate. The kitchen seemed all of a sudden too small, too smelly, too dark. I almost longed for Mamile's scent. *Iz schleinde la.* No time for dilly-dallying or longing for refinement. I soon fell into step with the tone and the pace. But I did not want to sleep with Tatte any longer, so for the winter Margit and I moved into the new paneled *Öberstube.* And I started to make plans for a room of my own. Probably Babbo had realized during his short visit during the previous summer that I needed a room more than a field. I had to write to him about how much it would cost — a door, a window frame, and so on: *Adesso non stanno le mura perchè c'è troppo freddo* — the heavy frost would certainly spoil the job; the building had to be done in the spring.

3. By now I was Tattile's partner — or rather, he was my partner in the sheep business. He also sent the money to buy a sheep for himself. I had to send accounts and explain how much it cost to feed a sheep, to house it, to take it to summer pastures, and in taxes: one lira per sheep nel Tirolo. To Tattile I tried to explain, with Tatte I discussed these matters and together we made the decisions about buying and selling. I had a ram ready for the butcher. The offspring of my black lamb was as prolific as her mother. Even by keeping my flock down to five, my services as shepherdess were highly overpaid. We had six rams and one sheep to drive to All Souls

market, and there was a heifer, too, that Tatte had to sell.

He would never have sold any animals, were it not for Mamme's reasoning about the expense and the shortage of fodder and space. She usually went to market with Tatte, but it was decided I was now big enough to go in her place. A good three hours to reach the market. It was dark and very cold when we set out. Tatte wanted to be there early. The going was hard with straying rams and a reluctant heifer. Tatte led the heifer on a chain and pushed his bicycle — if all went well we could ride home. I drove the sheep in front of him. We had to help each other out: anything ahead of us frightened the sheep and they turned back. Or the heifer now and again just would not budge, so I had to run behind and prod her. The corrals for sheep and cattle were quite a distance apart. I was stationed with the sheep. Tatte found a good place to tie up the heifer on show. We would deal with the sheep first; they were more difficult to get rid of and absolutely unwanted, whereas if the heifer found no buyer we might console ourselves by speculating that prices would be higher in the spring.

Schmalzl, everyone knew Schmalzl, came straight up to me. He was a rich cattle and sheep merchant, with a butchery and an inn in Sankt Lorenzen, and a huge silver chain across his stomach from which dangled a row of silver *Theresiethaler*. Whenever he moved, and especially when pedaling on his bicycle, a tinkling sound went with him. Mamme said each time he cheated some stupid farmer, he added a piece of silver to his chain, and since his waistline grew bigger and bigger, the chain had to be lengthened from time to time, and his cheating grew heavier. He was not liked — *do Ponzate* — but feared and needed. He asked me to whom I belonged. "Sâma." All rams? As though he did not see for himself that there was also a sheep! *"Wo a Gherre a!"* I was not afraid to

talk to Schmalzl. He started fingering a ram: *"durre, durre"* —
thin. "Try and lift it!" And he couldn't lift it. I kept him at
bay and yet amused until Tatte arrived. "A nice little girl you
have, how much do you want?" "How much do you pay?"
"Twenty-five." "You had better take them home again." Tatte
said this to me, and Schmalzl: "They belong to her?" "Some
do, and under thirty she won't sell." Schmalzl walked away
and we waited. Tatte went around listening to what people
said and I kept a watchful eye on our flock. The morning
dragged on, fun and excitement turned into weariness. Slack,
slack.

Mamme's older brother, who was also a cattle merchant,
passed by and asked me what we had to sell. "Tell Tatte not
to let go under thirty-five, things are picking up." But no one
came to bid. Shortly before midday Tatte sold the heifer. Not
too bad. Schmalzl came back, redder in the face and perspir-
ing. He had worked well. He nodded at the rams. "Can I
have them now for twenty-five?" I rang out, "Thirty-five." He
was amused and taken aback. "All right, thirty." That is the
best we could have expected. I think the brother-in-law had
said thirty-five because he knew Tatte was not a hard bar-
gainer, and since he was not buying from him he might just as
well give him good advice. The sheep remained unsold, but
Tatte gave me two lire and told me to get myself something
to eat and look around. I wandered over to the part of the fair
where the fun was and bought myself a hot sausage from the
cook-stall. I was all set for the merry-go-round, but got side-
tracked by music coming from a nearby tent. A small circus.
A clown shouted wonders: for fifty centesimi you will see a
dwarf, a giant, a serpent, a monkey and a bear.

The previous spring a gypsy and a female acrobat had
camped by the river, with a dancing bear and three poodles.

In the evening they gave a performance at the pub and Tatte had taken Margit and myself to see it. We were thrilled by the bear dancing, with a plate in his mouth, nodding when anyone dropped a coin into it. But the woman in the scanty bathing suit was shocking, we thought. Still, how else could she glide through a succession of rings? The performance had ended with herself arched to a circle, head on the floor and the biggest of the three poodles kissing her face. A middle-aged farmer leaped over the table and, smack, kissed the woman on the mouth. "Better than a dog!" Everyone laughed and the woman burst into tears and ran out of the room. The gypsy was angry and swore at the spectators for being such rascals. I left disappointed.

Surely a real circus would be different; people would behave. My curiosity was great and I bought a ticket, pushing ahead with the throng. It was dark inside the tent. I groped and stumbled over wooden planks. A buzzing of voices and instruments, noise, rank air. The crowd grew and kept pushing. Whenever the tent flap opened I caught a glimpse of the interior and found myself near a cage with a decrepit monkey. I felt sick and panicky. Would the show ever begin, people sit down and keep quiet, and the tent be lit up? How long had I been gone, and what if Tatte had sold the sheep and was looking for me to go home? He would never find me here. I had no business to enter. Dwarfs and giants were surely evil. The trumpets blew louder. I must have experienced claustrophobia. Danger loomed in every shadow and I made blindly for an opening in the tent. Once outside I felt an utter fool. To have been lured into a circus, wasted time and money hard-earned. All for nothing. Never again. I hurried back to the sheep corral, downcast. Tatte had not yet gotten rid of the sheep, but a farmer who had done well on pigs was nibbling.

I was dreading the walk home. If we were not empty-handed, no bicycle ride. And I resolved there and then that as soon as I had enough money I would buy myself a bicycle and be independent. This I did the following summer, a Perla bicycle for 200 lire, all on my own and against Mamme's wishes, since she feared I might take to wandering too far away from home and get run over.

I think Tatte lost a bit on that last sheep, but he, too, was tired and probably dreaded the walk home as much as I did. He gave in and got rid of the sheep, bought a big carton of roast chestnuts to take home, and off we went. When I was safe on his bicycle frame, I confessed my foolishness about the circus.

There were three or four houses in the village sought out by peddlers and beggars for night shelter. Ours was one of them. The others were big farms with lots of stable and barn space, where a loaf of bread and a bowl of milk for the needy was a duty easily discharged and meted out rather indiscriminately. Mamme on the other hand had her special protégés, characters with a story or a distinctive trait. They were not asked to sit at the table with us, but were handed the food in a bowl — by the stove in winter and on the bench in front of the house in the summer. A number of well-to-do peddlers were treated as paying guests and instead of being sent to sleep in the hay, they spent the night in the *Stube*. They would leave a packet of hairpins, a few yards of rubber band or something similar in return.

Each spring brought an old couple dressed in clothes of a previous century, the man in faded green, the woman in dove-gray. Baucis and Philemon still walking the earth. Wizened, reserved, and serene. Mamme said she had known them since childhood. Always the same age, the same clothes, the same story. Not that I have ever heard them tell it; one just knew that they were on their way to revisit a castle of which they had once been the keepers. Or the owners? Where? In their minds or over the frontier? How did they get across the mountains? They were never seen on their way back. Short of disappearing into a cave, they must have drawn a wide circle. I stood in great awe of them, and even Tatte tipped his hat to them. When they appeared in the doorway, smiling and bowing, they were immediately led into the *Stube* and told to sit down and we took food in to them on good plates. After breakfast next morning they again smiled and bowed and mumbled thank you in a German not spoken in Gais, and tottered off, the man carrying a small leather bag of the kind doctors used a century ago.

A contrast to them was an old woman who also came regularly, clutching with one hand a dirty bundle under her arm, with the other beating on her head — because it hurt so, she said, and she must not stop beating for a moment or it would fall off. Raving and haggard. Clinging to her bundle and continuously beating on her head made it impossible for her to eat and sleep, and for us too, since the beat was heard throughout the house and, what made it worse, we knew that the pain was caused by the banging and the banging by lice. Whenever a civic-minded person or institution tried to help her, to rid her of lice, she ran away screaming. All her movements were shifty and distrustful as though in constant terror of being seized. Relief came to her eventually, as to most of our tramps, through "painless death" at the hands of the Nazis in 1940 or thereabouts. An end foreseen by the blind harmonica player? He was a Ladin from Val Badia, an enclave where Romansch is spoken. A minstrel going from village to village, led by his mother, playing and singing in a butter-and-honey voice. In the street he played like any other musician-beggar, but when offered food and shelter in our home, he and his mother seemed to sing for their own pleasure. We did not understand the words. Bertrand de Born and Arnaut Daniel might have sung that way:

can chai la fueilla . . .

During the political options of 1938, when Tyroleans were compelled to choose between Germany and Italy, he hanged himself. The mother came back once, to tell of her gay blind son's death and of her forebodings. But she had never learned German, and *Krautwalisch* sounded too much like Italian for the by then propaganda-sodden Tyroleans to pay any attention to her. But Mamme said she understood her prophecies and wept with her for the loss of her son and his songs.

On a cold November evening a *Kornarin* dropped in as though on her ordinary errand, begging and seeking shelter. Later we realized that she must have gathered information and was carrying out a well-studied plan.

Korner are immediately recognized by their slovenly way of dressing and their sluggish walk. They lead the life of gypsies, but have none of their romantic connotations and are usually blond. This young woman even held her baby sluggishly, its spindly blue legs dangling down her flanks. Mamme immediately took the baby from her and scolded her: was she too lazy to wrap the blanket around the creature's feet! Frozen up to the knees and so pathetic, it did not even cry. The blue feet reminded me of our "angel" and I cuddled and fondled it all evening. Slowly a web of woes unfolded. She said her husband, the father of the child, was in prison. He was drunk and had beaten her and the baby in a pub and someone had tried to interfere, so he became jealous and started to smash the furniture and the police came and led him off. But she must find him, she knew he had some money and besides he was a good man when he did not drink. Would Mamme keep the baby until she found her husband with the money . . . ? "That might take you ten years or a lifetime" was Mamme's experienced answer. But there were promises and tears and flattery and I was so taken with that baby that I joined in the pleading and promised I would take care of it, do all the work, buy things with my sheep money, until Mamme gave in, against her better judgment. She knew I did not care for my milk-brother Hansile, he was such a loud and rough little boy. But this baby was so fair and frail, and rolled his blue eyes ecstatically while he sucked the thin porridge from the bottle we had prepared for him.

A few weeks after the *Kornerin* had gone off, a letter arrived saying she was in the hospital, that her man was still in prison, and that since they were not actually married, Mamme should claim the illegitimate's subsidy. Mamme knew what this meant: keep the child for good. Loisl became my special charge, and I took my motherly role very seriously. He was a sweet child. Unfortunately with the passing of years his docility became a burden; he had no willpower, no initiative, and during adolescence he suffered from, fits of epilepsy. "*Schlechts Bluit,* a sickly mother and an alcoholic father . . ."

Mamme was forever blaming character traits on heredity and with her unshakable convictions took every new burden in her stride.

"I thought our girl-child would be of no use to us," said Kagekiyo. But in my case it was not as simple as that. The image of my Tattile always presented itself as a huge glowing sun at the end of a white road, but I never dared look at it for too long because I knew that after a while a dark cloud of dust would enfold it. *Die richtign Elton* — the real parents — were still unreal. I thought of them as little as possible: because of Mamile's resentful, disappointed eyes; their forceful impact overclouded the beaming sun. The light and the dark never merged, casting a ring around me which made me feel powerless, deranged in feelings and reason. God's eye art 'ou. The triangle with God's eye in the middle was less scorching. Pegging on to the Bible had become an unconvincing device.

The end of another September. Another visit to Venice. I went reluctantly. It seemed to me I was too busy, full of responsibilities and needed. This playing at being a *hearrische* in Venice was a waste of time. Who did I think I was when I came back? The more spiteful made fun of me, if in my dress or manner they detected something foreign. And it vexed me to be dragged out of my world, made to wear clothes and assume manners that in real life were of no use to me. Time I was taking care of myself. The Herr had said everyone must work, be self-sufficient, either by one's brain or one's hands. I decided I preferred working in the fields with Tatte to studying. I was following the general trend; propaganda against Italy was infiltrating every plane, and what they taught us at school was at home considered nonsense because the teacher was Italian, hence a fool.

And so, once again, I felt I had disappointed Mamile. My Italian had improved very little, why did I not study it more? The clothes I had brought with me were all too long. I was grown-up; in Gais I could not possibly wear short skirts! Nonsense — Frau Marcher had bad taste. And I was given two dresses — in retrospect very pretty — that made me feel like a doll, and an indecent one at that: too short. And I was told to go skipping on the Zattere. I was too heavy and clumsy and must practice being light and graceful. Nonsense! — *tumma Tanz* — at home weight was the thing to have, weight behind the work. So, I was growing into a problem: a clumsy pigheaded peasant instead of a graceful bright sprig. Not, at any rate, definitely not, ". . . *a victim — beautiful perhaps, but a victim; expiring of aromatic pain from the jasmine, lacking in impulse, a mere bundle of discriminations.*"

One afternoon Babbo and I went alone to the Lido for a swim. He smiled and blinked, and I was happy and off guard. At this stage it was always he who put questions to me. When I grew up he insisted I put questions to him. He must have inspired me to prate about Gais, for suddenly he asked: And when do you want to go home? He said *a casa*. I was not sure whether he meant Calle Querini or Gais, I did not think I had a say in such matters. I replied: *Presto*. So he knew I meant Gais. "Why?" I must take care of Loisl, I miss him. There is so much work at this time of the year, they'll miss me. *Heimweh*. When we got back, Babbo and Mamile talked for what seemed an interminable time. Finally she turned to me: So you want to go back soon? "*Si.*" And this was all I managed to say. The room filled with repulsion and hostility. A solid blackness. She started to cry. Babbo took her on his knees and tried to soothe her. It was pitiful to see a great goddess cry in her anger and hurt pride. Or was she a mortal woman hankering after her child's love? I sat on the floor feeling miserable as the cause of all this misery and began crying too, like a grown-up at first, silently. Then, loud sobs, clamoring for attention. Babbo told me to come over to them, and sat me on his other knee and patted us both until the sobbing ended.

Then he handed me his big handkerchief and dashed out of the house; he found out about trains, bought me a ticket and sent a telegram to Mamme asking her to meet me in Bruneck next evening.

I had no way of knowing who, of the two, took the decision of sending me back immediately. And why? *Perchè?* Nothing was ever explained. Or perhaps I was not able to understand then that in life one gets what one asks for. All I realized was that among *Pessere Lait* one had to choose one's words very carefully and use *yes* sparingly. As for tears: I had seen them provoked by real pain: losing a baby, physical suffering, cold and hunger. What were these deeper bruises from phantoms and feelings? *La Machine Infernale.* A tricky world, this floating Venice-world. An uncomfortable inkling that my trust had been betrayed. Why did not Babbo smooth out my blunder and prevent futile suffering?

To regain balance, to feel safe, I would have to keep my feet firmly planted on Gais-ground. There, if words got you into trouble, you could get out of trouble with words. Mistakes were met by charity, or by punishment. And sins were sins, and one went to confession and repented and trusted in God's justice and in the power of one's Guardian Angel. But in Venice I was not allowed to wear my blessed *Pfennig* to protect me from evil. — A cheap aluminum medallion on a dirty string. — Aesthetically I already saw it in that light, but the priest and Mamme were hollering inside: heathen!

All these worries would be over soon. Mamme and Tatte would welcome me back — so much the better! — once I reassured them I had done nothing disgraceful, had taken pains to say please and thank you, to give precedence, open doors, carry parcels, hand hat and slippers . . . I was, by nature, eager to do the right things, to please, and seek affection, but

I also had to prove that in Gais too we had a *Pildung*. A question of loyalty. Please may I go back there . . .

"Man perambulates triplex, seeking the USEFUL (this he does in common with vegetables), the DELECTABLE (in company with the animals) and the HONESTUM (where he ain't got no company unless it's the blinking hangels)" — About this time Babbo wrote *Laws for Maria:*

1. That she is not to lie, cheat or steal.

2. If asks inconvenient questions, to be told
           All countries do not have the same customs.
That her father was like that, or that such was HIS custom and that she can discuss it with him when she thinks she has arrived at suitable age.

3. That if she suffers, it is her own fault for not understanding the universe.
       That so far as her father knows suffering exists in order to make people think. That they do not usually think until they suffer.

4. That she is not to judge other people's actions save from two points of view:
       A. objectively as elements in a causal sequence i.e. as effects of causes (anterior) and causes of subsequent effects.
       B. as to whether such action or course of action is one she wd. LIKE for herself. A preference which
       has NOTHING whatever to do with its being suitable or likable for someone else.

5. In case of disliking things, to blame 'em either on the universe or on herself. The former course is in some religions considered presumptuous.

LAWS FOR MARIA (passage from vegetable to animal life).

I. First thing to learn is: NOT to be a nuisance.
       I think you have learned this.

II. Autarchia personale. To be able to do everything you need
   for yourself: cook, sew, keep house.
                (otherwise unfit to marry. Marriage: a partner·
                ship, mutual help.)

III. Autarchia. The ideal is that everyone should be Bauern-
    fähig.
                The moment a family is separated from the land
                everyone must be able not only to DO something, or
                MAKE something, but to sell it. When the land is no
longer there, nothing will WAIT. People not peasants must
think QUICKER than peasants.

/ / /

Curriculum: I. Typewriting (dattilografia)
             II. Lingua Italiana without which you will not
be able to sell what you write in Italy.
             III. Translation.
             IV. Inventive writing? first simple articles, then
the novel
      That is to say, I can only teach you the profession I
know.

Passage from vegetable to animal life. I don't remember being shown them, nor could I have read them since I knew no
English, but the gist I knew. More serious rules of ethical
conduct had been put into writing for me years earlier and
they have come to mean much more than *Die Zwölf Gebote
Gottes, Die Fünf Gebote der Kirche* and *Die Sieben Haupt-
sünden,* — the laws of God and the Church, rattled off every
year at every interrogation in *catechism.*

At school, back in Gais, I was made Capo Piccole Italiane.
It was not a matter of choice or of merit. All schoolchildren
were registered as belonging to the Fascist party, Balilla the
boys, Piccole Italiane the girls, but almost all refused to pay
the five lire for the *tessera* — the party card — and only a hand-

ful wore the uniform. When I came home with the circular requesting that schoolchildren whose parents had sufficient means be provided with a Fascist uniform, Mamme merely said: *Tumma Tanz* — nonsense. And, anyway, she had no money to throw away and it couldn't be made out of some old dress. I forget whether she sent the circular to the Frau or whether she made me write a letter to ask what I was to do. "If she thinks you should have one . . ." — thus for the first time declining responsibility. In due course, a parcel with the complete uniform arrived. *Tumma Tanz.* And Tatte: *Iz wern si de wo auslochen, a sella lopparai!* — people will laugh at you, such a farce. To be quite honest, I was pleased; after all, it was a new dress, and the white blouse and the black pleated skirt had a certain flair. Others who *had* to have uniforms were the daughter of the postmistress, the two daughters of the train conductor, and Romana, the orphan of an Italian land surveyor: people who drew their salaries or pensions from the government. Of the boys: Romana's brother and the Dal Rio gang. Their parents had to choose between complete indigence or government subsidy. In exchange for a shack near the railway and food-cards they consented to Italianize their name from Bacher to Dal Rio. From being merely "poor," they became pariahs. The five boys loathed their Balilla uniforms and did their utmost to wear them out. Of this ill-assorted group, I was the Caposquadra. I did not take my position very seriously. We had to stay on after class on Saturday to learn the *giuramento fascista* and songs, "Giovinezza," "Sole che sorgi" — the oath and the anthems. But we had learned at catechism — the only lesson still held in German by the priest, thanks to the Concordat in which Mussolini had granted the Church freedom and autonomy — that to swear a false oath is deadly sin. So, sly brats that we were, we slipped in a *non* as a private reservation. *"Nel nome di Dio e dell'Italia giuro di* NON *servire fedelmente la mia patria."* — In the name of God and Italy I swear *not* to serve faithfully my country . . . At the *non* we gulped, looking the teacher straight in the eyes. We considered it daring and fun. We also had to learn how to march and to command the rest of the school when marching. *Attenti! Riposo! un due, un due, dietro front frònt.* This was called physical education, two hours, twice a week, back and forth in front of the school and, when, in spring especially, grown-ups passed by, they fumed: such nonsense, wearing out their shoes instead of letting them go home and give a hand where they are needed.

But time was never grudged for Church activities and we had grand processions and parades when the Bishop came for the confirmation ceremony or when one of the village boys came to officiate at his first Mass. No greater blessing or honor could have befallen the village; the grown-ups rejoiced and we children were wildly excited.

'. . . The priest here
had una nuova messa
     (dodicesimo anno E.F.)
bella festa, because there was a priest here to say his
first mass
and all the mountains were full of fires, and
we went around through the village
     in giro per il paese
2 men and 2 horses
and then the music and on the sides
children carrying torches and the
carrozze with the priests, and the one that had to say
the new mass, and the carrozze were full of fine flowers

and there were a lot of people. I liked it,
all the houses were full of lights and
tree branches in the windows
covered with hand-made flowers and
the next day they had mass and a procession
Please may I go back there
and have a new pair of Sunday shoes?'

The new pair of shoes I needed when the Bishop came and I
had to recite a poem: *"Festlich die Glocken klingen willkom-*
men!" Mamme made over her Tyrolean costume for me. She
had not worn it since the war and kept it hidden at the bottom
of a drawer — lest the carabinieri might find it and confiscate
it. These fears were more a reflection of guilty conscience than
real danger. The carabinieri, it is true, did sometimes search
the houses for saccharin, flints and tobacco. These items were
smuggled over the Austrian border. A form of economic as
well as political sabotage. Besides, who could afford real sugar!
That this smuggling was carried on was an open secret, but
to look for a tiny box of saccharin or flints in a haystack was
no fun. Little wonder that the Italians sometimes lost their
temper and seized any odd item that hinted of nostalgia or
hostility.

The clergy had not only kept the prerogative of the German
language but they also encouraged the wearing of costumes,
and assured protection to anyone who wore them to church
and at processions. There were very few national costumes
around, and as yet no one could afford to have new ones made.
Mamme was very proud to be able to fit me out with all the
accessories, except shoes. The red and white feathers on the
hat were the most daring touch, a defiant hoisting of the
Tyrolean flag. Tatte sniggered: They'll pluck you! But I made

my bow to the Bishop and recited my poem undisturbed in the center of a half-circle of little girls dressed in white with their long hair loose and curled. The carabinieri looked quite harmless and unprovoked. For the occasion they wore their high Bourbonic uniforms, the fluffy tricolor feather duster on their foreheads a worthy contrast to my two long feathers on the nape.

I was, from then on, much in demand at festivities and my Tyrolean costume was given prominence at processions and parades, as it lent a touch of patriotism and protest. Until then, I had carried a big silver-paper lily stuck into a purple wooden heart — for a handle — like all the other little girls in procession. But now I walked empty-handed, proud and lighthearted, right behind the priest, between two girls in white dresses carrying the silver lilies.

Being jerked between the two factions — Italian Fascists and Tyrolean nationalists — because I owned their respective uniforms, did not disturb me. I don't think I ever gave it any deep thought, since my loyalty was undivided: it was everything Tyrolean that made me bubble over with enthusiasm and excitement. The rest was politics, not oppression.

I forget at what age I spent three days in Meran. Mamme, on receiving a letter saying she should bring me as far as Bolzano, where the Frau would relieve her of her charge, had the usual fright: this is the end. Judging from snapshots it must have been a year or two after the family's converging at the Hotel Greif in Bolzano: the Herr and the Frau and the Herr Grossvater. I have most pleasant memories of an outing to Oberbozen on a funicular railway and I was allowed to take my shoes off and there were cows that seemed bigger and more beautiful than the ones we had. And grandfather kept saying I had grown so tall he could not lift me any more, but whenever he sat down he told me to stand on his foot and swung me up and down gaily.

Grandfather inspired trust and joy. I don't think he was smaller than Tattile, but since he had no hair in front and was clean-shaven and his dress very sober, he gave the impression of being half Tattile's size — a *shmouldo* — narrow. When he was not swinging me on his foot, it seems to me we were always hand in hand; swinging our arms, taking big steps and hopping. And yet I know that he walked with a stick. That was later, perhaps. Anyway, we always had fun together although we did not understand a word from each other. He drew funny faces on our breakfast eggs and produced the most vivid animal shadow plays with his hands on white walls. Meran must have been after my bow to the Bishop. On the train from Bolzano to Meran, Mamile told me I must curtsy to her friends. *Fare un inchino*, did I know how? Of course. Not only had I made one to the Bishop, but at a school recital at which I personified the Cornflower, I had practiced a swooping gesture of welcome. And this is how I greeted Renata Borgatti at the station platform. She seemed very amused, and Mamile laughed for a long time, but I did not see what was so funny. Renata had an imposing figure, her hair cut short like a man's. I believed her to be my godmother. Mamme's secret worry had always been: Is this child baptized? Yes, the midwife had said so. But who was my godmother? Godmothers are important. The *Töite* was only my *Firmtöite*, had taken me to confirmation. What counts most is baptism. To appease Mamme's concern, Mamile had sent me a picture of *la madrina*: a drawing of Renata Borgatti by Sargent on a concert program. It was all a bit vague and confusing. However, I took a great liking to Renata, who spoke German — and was considerate to the horse.

In the hotel room Mamile changed me into a lovely dirndl. It was the first time I received a dress I really liked. I let her do my hair differently, and when she explained to me how one did curtsy, just a slight knick of the knees, I felt glad for the correction. She was cheerful, no rancor or tension. I was thrilled with everything and put up no stubborn resistance.

Frau Langenham was a live wire of an old lady, very frail, dressed in white, with short, crisp red hair and a pair of fiery black eyes. She waved and extended thin long arms. I was afraid to take her hand: she seemed made of porcelain that might crack at the slightest contact. Yet the grip of her hands and the brio of her voice contradicted her apparent frailty. Mamile told me that the old lady, despite her rheumatism and other ailments, directed a music school at Schloss Berg in Thurgau and that Renata was her favorite pupil. I almost wished I could study music and go and live with them in a castle in Switzerland, and Mamile did not seem to exclude the possibility of such a thing in the far future — if I was very good. But now we were all on a holiday and enjoyed playing cards. Frau Langenham, every time I beat her at Schwarzen Peter (I think she allowed herself to be beaten), put on a fascinating performance. I had to hold up her hand mirror and close my eyes; when I was allowed to open them, the most clownish, yet tragic, mask was painted over her wrinkled diaphanous face.

Among vineyards I trailed after Renata and Mamile, insisting on carrying her violin, to a little house where there was a piano. I was told to wait outside while they practiced. I sat down and listened. What storming sounds, what tempo! I decided that my performances with blind Peter were awful, a farce, I would never go back to him. Had I then been more humble and enlightened, I would not have allowed myself to be discouraged, but the beauty of that music seemed something out of this world, unattainable by mortals like blind Peter and me, and I knew that *that's* how music should sound. I was moved to stomp and dance to it until I felt quite exhausted and a bit ashamed: what if someone had watched me! I wondered how long they could keep up the tempo, which seemed too tempestuous for angels. I wonder now what they played.

For three days Mamile seemed carefree, and as capable of laughter as her exuberant friends. I felt relieved that in her world too, people could be gay and I returned to Gais a little less skeptical of that world. So far, leaving Gais had always seemed an unavoidable penance for some unfathomable crime, with Mamme weeping and sprinkling me with holy water and Tatte with shiny eyes: *Pfiote Moidile wenne hot nimma kimpsch* — goodbye for good. Naturally I felt triumphant and happy when I saw them again and could say: See, I always come back. And yet, a curiosity, a desire to fit into the other world started to nibble in me.

And it all of a sudden seemed as though my connections with the outer world were more of an asset than a hindrance. For Christmas I received a parcel from my English uncle: a little red projector with half a dozen Mickey Mouse films. A *hexarai* no doubt — a devilment — but it created a great sensation. After dinner and rosary, Tatte was the first to clamor for a show and to pin the white sheet on the wall. All my friends came to watch and even grown-ups, with the excuse that they "wanted to see how it worked." Almost as bewitching as Bacher's radio and Moar Zenz's phonograph, things one simply could not comprehend. Thus I may claim to have introduced the cinema to our valley — people had heard of it, but the two neighboring towns had no movie houses yet, and even when they were built, people did not go because the films were in Italian — and very sinful, it was said.

As soon as spring came Mickey Mouse was forgotten because Tatte was finally getting round to keeping bees. For years Mamme had been pining for honey, never tired of repeating how Margit and I were cured of the whooping cough by a pot of well-seasoned honey — and now with two small boys permanently in the house and a continual coming and going of little nieces etc., etc. Tatte had smoked over these remarks for a few years, but now he was as excited as Margit and myself, we too longed to keep bees. Tatte bought a secondhand bee-house and borrowed this and that from Prenn and other beekeepers, and Margit and I scraped and scrubbed and painted, and Mamme planted a Goldrute because honey from its pollen was supposed to be especially medicinal. The trouble was money. Margit had managed to save enough from the sale of her sheep. I was short. I used to keep my money in a little white cardboard box and Mamme locked it up in the glass cabinet. But I knew where the key was, so I would rob myself whenever the other shepherds said: Sâma Moidile, why don't you get us some candy? Or some special friend at school: Haven't you got a sweet? Or, if we played at our favorite game — saying a First Mass — we had to stage a miniature banquet, and only sweets could give it some festivity, and only I could provide them. Although I knew it was bad to spend money on sweets and was full of "penny-wisdom," I couldn't resist the self-indulgence of making the others feel grateful and like me. So I would sneak past the kitchen door

. . . I think Mamme knew what I was up to, but she did not seem to mind.

It was the usual kind of letter: Caro Babbo, could you please help me to buy a beehive and when I come to Venice I will bring you the honey and there will be enough for grandfather too, and for la mamma, etc. And the money promptly arrived and Babbo and I became partners in bee-raising as well as in sheep-breeding.

When that summer — 1935 — via Salzburg and Wörgl —

a nice little town in the Tyrol in a wide flat-lying valley near Innsbruck

— the Herr and the Frau arrived in a car driven by the tallest young man in company of the handsomest young man anyone had ever seen, the first thing we proudly showed them were the beehives and the goldenrod in full bloom. One of the swarms decided to fly out that very minute and there was much scampering with hands clasped over heads, and laughter and flutter. Mamme and Margit and I were torn between the desire to welcome the guests and set the table and just to gape at the two handsome *Amerikaner,* incredulous that anyone could be taller than the Herr. Eventually Margit followed the flight of the swarm, and I the summons: "Quick quick quick get dressed." Once again — to Venice. Bùt first Mamme insisted I must show off my Tyrolean costume and have pictures taken.

I was given an enormous pair of goggles to wear in the car, and it seemed to me that the young men were making fun of me. Their names were Jas and Jim. Tatte had wanted to know what the names would be in German. They were somehow turned into Johann and Jakob. Yes, just like Hanne and Joggl. We were all pleased to hear that in America people had the same names as in Gais. I sat in front with Jas and Babbo, it was all very jolly. We stopped for lunch at the Hotel Greif in Bozen. While we were waiting to order, Babbo, pulling me by the hand, dashed across the Walterplatz (at that time called Piazza della Vittoria) to a sweetshop. He bought a great variety of sweets, lots of mint chocolates and he handed me a Suchard roll, and I was thrilled because I remembered that those sober-looking mauve rolls were packed with chocolate money wrapped in gold. Outside the shop stood a girl. I was struck by the look of longing on her face, she reminded me of Margit. I said to Babbo: *Sembra Margherita*. He threw her one of his quick glances and said: Perhaps she would like some chocolate. The look of longing turned into one of incredulity when, coming out of the shop, I handed her my Suchard roll. Babbo rushed on and did not give her time to say thank you. The incident puzzled me all through lunch, while the grown-ups chatted in English. I thought: This is how life should be, if a girl longs for sweets a stranger should appear and just give her some. But had I interpreted Babbo correctly? Wasn't that roll of chocolate intended for me? Did it mean that if I had pity on others I must carry out my impulses at my own expense? I had interpreted his comment as an order; still, I wished he had bought her another Suchard roll so that I could have kept mine.

We drove over mountains. The engine started to steam. While Jas looked for water Jim looked for flowers and when we all got into the car again he gave Mamile a little bouquet of wild flowers. This, I thought, was very romantic. Next morning in Venice the two young men came to our house for breakfast. Whenever there were guests, a Venetian cook all dressed in black with a white apron took over. Everything seemed beautifully arranged and served. A row of eggs *à la coque,* laid out just as in the first picture of *The Rose and the Ring.* And I fancied that Babbo was the King and Mamile the Queen, so I would be Angelica and one of the two young men Prince Bulbo. The choice fell on the tall one; he seemed more friendly and tried to talk to me in German and in Italian. The other seemed too proud and had given his flowers to Mamile; anyway, he soon left, whereas Jas went with us to the Lido and carried me on his shoulders into deep water.

My fantasy about the prince — the British humor having naturally completely escaped me, or perhaps to some extent escaped the German translator — came to full bloom the following winter when I received a parcel from America. Two big black books: *Celtic Legends* and *The Arabian Nights.* I pored over the beautiful illustrations, and even Mamme and Tatte agreed that the stories must be wonderful — too bad no one could read them. And the accompanying note — "Dear Princess" — and then in Italian: "When I was young I liked these books, I hope you will like them too. — Love from Jas."

Babbo had bought me a tiny red Italian-English — English-Italian pocket dictionary. I was delighted when I received it, but had made small use of it. My English was still limited to two nursery rhymes. It had taken me days of anguish to learn them by heart. I could have looked for hours at the illustrations in Mother Goose, but I was allowed to have the book only when studying — the notion being, I guess, that one's pleasures must be earned. I had mastered "There was an old woman lived under a hill . . ." and "Mary Mary quite contrary." Mamile had said I must learn some by heart and I chose one for its brevity and the other for the name, but over the cockleshells I invariably stumbled. My resistance to the

English language — and to the things this language would disclose to me? — was still strong. I probably never tried hard enough to overcome the cockleshells because I knew I would then have to learn yet another nursery rhyme. Much as I liked looking at the picture book, I disliked the sensation of being lured with carrots.

But the "dear princess" and "love from Jas" was different and I resorted to the little dictionary with great eagerness. Sure enough, it meant: *Cara principessa amore da.* I fancied the letter and the books were a key to my future, perhaps to my origin. Also intriguing was J.L.ɪᴠ on the wrapper. At school, in history, we had reached Vittorio Emanuele III, and he was the King of Italy.

The busy, practical life in Gais made me forget these vagaries soon enough, including the resolution to learn the red dictionary by heart, but when I went to Venice the following year I took the letters and the books with me. Mamile showed great pleasure over the books, but when I timidly asked about the meaning of "dear princess" she said it was the usual way in which American boys addressed small girls. And the J.L.ɪᴠ simply meant that there were four generations of James. As for "love," she laughed, it means "affettuosamente." So this, like Calle Querini, was a blind alley. No easy fantasy would solve riddles and open doors.

Uncle George. Another uncle? No, another American habit. Just a friend of Babbo's, a great man. How his dirty fingernails and his smacking the waitress's young fanny were compatible with being a great man and a friend of Babbo's I could not quite figure out. Nevertheless, I thoroughly enjoyed our trip to Monte Grappa and recorded it in pidgin-Italian. *Venezia: 21–9–1936. Ieri io e il babbo avevamo un invito.* . . . We first drove to Pieve, to see the place where he had opened fire. When America entered the war to help Italy he had been the first to shoot a cannon. And the cannon is now in Rome in the museum. And although he had been around the world twelve times, this was his first visit to the battlefields — where his car had turned over and the other three men who were with him were killed.

We climbed to the top of a campanile and drove to the top of the Monte Grappa where the War Memorial stands. And a big telescope, and a map with arrows. I recognized the names wrapped in the myth of Tatte's heroism, the mountains conquered and lost inch by inch. My mind must have been in a turmoil, for here I was with the enemy, a great man. I looked through the telescope: "I have seen as far as Campo Tures, not the houses but the mountains behind them. *Mi ha contentato molto di vedere fino a casa era magnifico.*" I was happy thinking I had seen home from that distance.

Il signor Tinkham was such a jolly mimic, very concerned lest the signorina should get bored while he and her papa talked relentlessly in the back of the car. He wore a conspicuous black hat — to hide his baldness, he showed me, laughing. He pulled out a pack of photographs of the animals he had killed, mostly in Africa. My amazement pleased him, and my laughter too, when he told the story about his being scared by an eye looking at him as he woke up one morning in his shelter on a tree. He reached for his gun, but stopped himself in time, the eye looked too tame and sardonic. He realized it was a giraffe and felt like a fool, for he was after leopards. Yes, he had killed lions and leopards and elephants, crocodiles and wildebeest and serpents too. Twelve times he had been around the world, but this was the first time he had returned to the place where he himself might have been killed, killing Austrians. All this did not seem to concern Babbo very much.

[83]

Wasn't he a great man because he had traveled and killed so much? No, but because he was an American Senator, which at the time meant nothing to me.

And in the cage, in Pisa, Babbo remembered:

    (Unkle George cd/ not identify the place on that road because the road had been blown off the side of the mountain but he climbed about 200 steps of the tower to see what he had seen through the roof
      of a barn no longer standing
                    sul Piave
where he had fired that howitzer
and the large eye that found him
at its level was a giraffe's eye
        at dawn, in his nest, hunting leopards.

'The pose' he said 'is a taxidermist's fake
        the cobra is not a constrictor
and would not wrap itself round the mongoose'

This Babbo and I had shared, but Uncle George in Brassitalo's abbazia, his meeting with Princess de Polignac and

    . . . observing Ct/Volpe's neck at the Lido
    and deducing his energy.

I did not witness and it would have been lost on me anyway. But I did participate, almost like a grown-up, trying to remember the names of people I met, though I had little inkling of who and what they were. Most of them seemed old people to me, so that when finally I met a girl of my own age I could hardly believe my eyes.

I was alone in the house one late afternoon and knew I must not open the door to anyone, ever. But the bell rang and rang. I peeped out of the window and recognized Maria Favai, but withdrew instantly. She knew I was in the house and called out: *April!* I stuck my head out and said firmly: "No one is at home, I can't open." Maria laughed and said: "You are somebody; I have brought a friend for you." "La mamma has said I must never open the door to anyone." It was difficult to strike a balance between my utter freedom and self-reliance in Gais, where no door was locked during daytime, and the restrictions and my insecurities in Venice. Blind obedience seemed the only safe course. But Signora Favai insisted that she was a friend and that she would explain to la mamma. So I went down and opened the door but did not ask them to come in. I spoke with one foot in the door so it would not close on me.

I liked Henny immediately. She was a Norwegian girl my age, spoke German and Italian and was also studying English. Above all she was fair and friendly, but I saw her only once again at that time. Soon I went back to Gais. Babbo accompanied me halfway. We stopped at Cortina for a few hours to see some friends in a villa rather far from the station. A hurried climb, a most warm and loud welcome, and since there was no time to stop for a meal they stuffed my pockets with candy.

My last winter in Gais was rebellious, yet conventional, full of marriages and deaths that concerned me closely. Johann Passler, the priest, died. He had once beaten my right hand so hard with his rod that it was swollen for days. He had found me intent on drawing a house on the bench instead of paying attention to the *Religionsunterricht*. Once I arrived late in class and had to kneel on a triangular log, and he invariably made fun of my short skirts, though they were not short at all. Still, he was the caretaker of our souls, our immediate "superior." We prayed for him and loved him as a matter of course. Someone who was always there, at the altar or in the side bench. Or else behind the green curtain of the confessional. He had never missed saying Mass once. And now we felt lost, loitering in front of the church at seven o'clock in the morning; there would be no Mass for the schoolchildren that day.

Olga, being the niece of the churchwarden, knew all the details. He had died a few hours ago. Did I want to see him? I forgot how frightened I had been years ago when I had peeped at a dead old woman. She had the reputation of being a witch. She took snuff and smoked a pipe. She was "grandmother" at the shop, where in order to get in one had to pull the doorbell and wait. Once I got so bored waiting that I put the coin in my mouth and when she appeared at the end of the dark corridor and asked what I wanted I swallowed the coin. I wanted sweets, but the money had slipped down my throat. She would not believe me and got very angry. I had good reason to cry and run away. When I peeped under the sheet I half expected to see the Devil, but the shriveled face of the old woman was more frightening than I had foreseen, completely black — or so it seemed to me.

When anyone died, the corpse remained exposed between candles and flowers for two days in the living room, and at midday and in the evening the village gathered to say rosaries in front of it. The children thronged around the catafalque so as not to get crushed by the adults. Only when someone was very disfigured did they cover him up, but it was considered rather a disgrace to have an "ugly" corpse in the family.

The priest was not yet laid out among flowers and candles. He seemed enormous in black pajamas, bare feet, disheveled and unshaven, stretched out on the dining room table. It was indiscreet to look at him in that state; nevertheless, I kissed his hand as though he were still alive. Five years earlier, at this same table, he had offered us our First Communion banquet. A unique and festive experience in everyone's life: a white tablecloth and lots of hot chocolate and *Gugglhupf*.

And because he was our priest, all the children wanted to carry flowers. A few of us went to Bruneck to buy carnations at the florist's. The poorer ones made beautiful fir-wreaths dotted with paper flowers.

Children looked forward to carrying flowers at funerals. It often meant an invitation to the banquet that followed. One listened attentively to the announcement the nearest male relative would make before leaving the grave: in the case of a wealthy family, all those who had attended the burial would be invited, and the announcement made in a loud voice. In other cases, the voice was more subdued: only the relatives, neighbors and wreath-bearers were invited. Sometimes an invitation was whispered only to the nearest relatives who had come from afar: Have a bite at home. There was no banquet after the priest's funeral, but we were all impressed by the great number of Masses that were held for him.

Shortly after the funeral his furniture was auctioned. A furniture auction was a novelty; everybody went to see it, but there was not much to bid for, mostly souvenirs that devoted parishioners bought to help out the Pfarrer's sister. A small table caught my fancy. The furnishing of my own room was at the time very important to me and that table was exactly what I wanted. So I put in a bid. The grown-ups were amused; a man to my "Seven" said "Eight." I tried to catch

Tatte's eye, but he seemed uninterested. I said "Nine," determined to get the table. The man said "Ten" and everybody laughed. I was lost; I knew I did not have more than ten lire. Someone else said "Eleven." And then to my amazement I heard Tatte's voice: "Twelve." He got it and carried it home on his shoulders like a trophy. He said: You were right, this is a very handy little table, it even has a drawer. I said: Can I have it if I give you ten lire? Yes, yes, and added: "That man had no business to tease you."

Ghost stories were popular. Some people claimed the priest had announced his death through knocks and eerie calls. The spook was felt for weeks. By St. Nikolaus eve fear of Death and the Devil had reached a climax,

> where the masks come from, in the Tirol
> > in the winter season
> > searching every house to drive out the demons.

On the seventh of December about twenty masked young men race through every house they find open. In certain houses the neighbors gather and there they perform the Nigglas play, in the center of the *Stube*. A *Bajazz* somersaults into the room and with great jingling greets the assembly and tells them to clear away the spinning wheels, to get behind the table, and to remain close to the wall — for the Devil is coming to pay them a visit. Then a second jingling buffoon joins him and announces the order of the play. Sometimes a few more *Bajazzer* tumble into the room and they all somersault until the spectators are virtually nailed to the wall. Then the jingling suddenly stops and, in deep silence, enters an Angel, dressed in a long white tunic, with drawn red sword and huge cardboard wings. He speaks of the battle between good and evil and exhorts everyone to be *fromm* — pious. Then he calls Saint Nikolaus: *"Heiliger Nikolaus, komm herein."* Enters the bishop, solemn with the miter and crosier, followed by two small angels: one carries a basket filled with apples and nuts, the other a whip. *"Ich bin der heilige Nikolaus und frag die kleinen Kinder aus . . ."* He asks the children questions about God and the Commandments. If they reply correctly they get an apple or a few nuts, otherwise, the whip. The bishop then retires to a corner and . . . in bursts Lucifer, in black fur, a frightening mask, horns, hoofs and tail! Two small devils hold him back with a chain, but he threatens everyone with his pitchfork and seeks out Saint Nikolaus, spouting at him the most foul insults. When the little devils can no longer cope with the satanic fury, the angel intervenes with his sword: *"Vade retro!"* It is not easy for him to banish the devils from the room; sometimes there is a veritable fight and his cardboard wings are put in danger. Then enters Death: tall, thin, wrapped in white linen with a skull on top of his head and a scythe. Stooping he dogs, clockwise, the steps of a little old Everyman who begs to be spared. The dialogues, except some of the devil's rantings, are in rhyme, but it is all oral tradition — though with a fair amount of improvising, since character traits of the spectators or some recent events in the village are woven into the play, especially in the comic acts that close the show: sketches of "peasant and doctor," "goodwife and peddler," etc. The buffoons, *Bajazzer,* are present in the room all the time, sometimes interfering in the dialogues, reciting long rigmaroles during the entr'actes and above all, harassing and necking with the girls, young and old. When the show is over, the players are offered *Glühwein* and *Krap-fen,* and the head of the house opens his purse.

Fun and fear, sacred and profane elements were blended promiscuously in these masked plays. And even the grown-ups sometimes got frightened if a devil or Death came too close or spoke too plainly. Since our house was one of the last in the village, the players seldom arrived before eleven o'clock, though one started to listen for the jingling of the *Bajazzer* and the chains of the devils as soon as it got dark.

Herr Bacher's three nieces came to watch at our house, arriving early, for fear of being caught in the street and thrown in the fountain — for this is what happens to girls caught outdoors after dark on St. Nikolaus eve: skirts knotted over their heads and *ploff!* into the water. The four of us kept running up to the road to listen for the approach of the Nigglas.

As we were standing, tense with apprehension, by the sheep stable, we all distinctly heard a knock. We ran back to the house and stumbled into the *Stube,* one on top of the other, white as sheets. For a while we could not even explain what had happened. A knock by the sheep stable? Roars of laughter. Obviously a sheep scratching. It had not occurred to us. I felt very foolish and stopped being impressed by ghost stories. When later on I told Babbo about this incident, he seemed pleased that I did not take ghost stories too seriously. Uncle William — he said — had tried to convince him about supernatural phenomena. In Ireland there is a story of a priest who had married a couple who had been dead for a long time, and in Japan there is a similar legend. Such things are possible. But knocks and the like are all hokum. I had to patch all this together years later, when I realized who Uncle William was.

In Gais they believe that every deceased person may, within

the year, return to fetch two close relatives or friends. A priest may call for as many as seven of his parishioners: he is expected to do a final good deed by releasing the long-suffering or the very old whose souls he knows to be without mortal sin. But Johann Passler did not conform. The first to follow him was a young girl of fifteen, Genoveffa, the youngest daughter of the Schloss Neuhaus innkeepers. Beautiful and gay, a good dancer and harmonica player. It was whispered that she had too strenuously entertained her father's guests, yet as she lay in state in the Schloss chapel — more appropriate than their living room, which was the pub — everyone said she looked like a saint. Long blond tresses loose on her bosom, a wax image of innocence dressed in white.

The second was Moar Tondl, who I fancied was my sweetheart. The Moars were Mamme's neighbors before she married and still her best friends. I used to spend a great deal of my time at their home, a strange house, squat, sunk deeply into the ground. The smooth stone slabs in the hall were big and black, shaped like a man's open umbrella. Small arched doors led into many dark corridors and cellars — unpaved, smelling of dampness and mold, rotten potatoes and spilt wine, earth that had seen no sun for centuries, crossed by currents and whistling drafts. The first floor, in contrast, was all green and light and smelled of newly baked bread and cakes — and of camphor, when mother Moar had a headache. Tondl had been called up to do his military service. Before leaving he had offered me a couple of rabbits. Because I was 's Sâma Moidile the terms were a bit vague, but sounded most lucrative. For the trouble of feeding and housing them I could keep all the young ones and when he came back, return either the old couple or a young one. Tatte shook his head and said it was not worth the trouble, there was no profit in rabbits unless they were angora and you had the patience to comb them regularly. That's what Margherita did, joyfully:

And Margherita's voice was clear as the notes of a clavichord tending her rabbit hutch

I did not heed Tatte and was delighted with my rabbits. They multiplied rapidly. I kept them in a small shed by the sheep stable, and fed them lots of cabbage. Margit protested, she said it was a waste. I claimed the contrary, saying it did not matter whether angora rabbits were fat or thin, but I had to achieve weight. Then one morning my rabbits had vanished. No trace. The door was bolted. Theft was excluded. Eventually I discovered under the old manger a very small hole and as far as my arm and a stick could reach, a tunnel. A masterpiece to which I never found the exit. Tatte laughed. He said he had always suspected that Tondl had me *pittagglt* — cheated — and had given me a pair of wild rabbits instead of tame breeders. I moped for a while. Then the news of Tondl's death changed the nature of my sorrow. He had eaten an ice cream and died of it. An act of Italian cruelty: sending a boy from the mountains down to Bari! We prayed in front of an empty catafalque, a service was held in absentia and his photograph put on the family tomb. I thought he was very beautiful. I felt completely grown-up.

Then followed a very gay wedding feast. Mamme's youngest brother, the saddler, had finished building his house and he married a woman who had enough money to furnish it. I was the youngest member of the party and did not miss one dance. A sour spinster said out loud: Who is that little girl; they should stop her from dancing or she won't grow any more. She meant it seriously, but no one heeded her.

*Il maestro ha detto che ora dobbiamo comprare un altro
libro cioè il susidiario di quinta . . . li ci sono dentro le cose
principali cioè tutto, religione, storia, geografia, conti scienze e
la vita del uomo . . .* (E. P. Guide to Kulchur)

Thus I wrote for a new schoolbook. I had reached the fifth
elementary, the end of schooling in Gais. But I was not really
interested in studying. Once I was even suspended from
school. The entire class had decided to go and look at the site
where they were laying the foundations for a new school. The
idea had not sprung from me, but I was game. At two o'clock
we returned to the school, an hour late. We pretended it was
one. The teacher, a thin, dark, spectacled Sicilian who always
wore a black shirt — and we said it was because he could afford no other — was naturally furious and kept shouting:
"*Bestie, bestie!*" I said: "What's the matter; it has just struck
one." He did not think this funny. I of all people, a caposquadra. "Go home immediately and come back accompanied
by your father in two days." I said this could not be done because my father lived in Venice. I was still in a teasing mood.
"*Tuo padre putativo!*" he shouted. Everyone laughed: *padre
putativo* was St. Joseph's designation. He ushered all the children in and left me standing. I did not want, or dare, to go
home. This was unfair, I thought. An injustice. I would report it to the carabinieri. I felt a bit shaky as I climbed the
long wooden stairs to the police station, but some devil pushed
me on. The *maresciallo* looked surprised, then amused. "If
paying five lire for the Fascist *tessera* makes me responsible for
the whole school and means that I am the only one to get punished, I want my money back," was my final outburst. The
maresciallo seemed to think I was right, he would talk to the
teacher. The following morning the postmistress brought an

[93]

ominous orange-colored envelope. On official Municipio stationery, I was being suspended from school for two weeks because of insubordination. Mamme and Tatte were very upset. What if the teacher chose to write to the Frau! What a *blamage* that would be. How could I be so *tum* — idiotic, and turn to the carabinieri for justice! Yes, it had been a mistake. Dummheit, nicht Bösheit.

Mid-June brought an end to all that. I was carefree and in the fields all day. One warm afternoon I was trying to get Loisl to sleep. Margit called me. I answered rudely, she had awakened Loisl. She called again: a *hearrischa Ghitch,* a city girl, wanted to see me. And there stood Henny. She seemed surprised: a disgruntled, barefoot brat in place of the well-groomed, shy little girl with such fine parents and such an elegant house. Her family had rented a small villa near Bruneck for the holidays. Would I come and play with her; her mother had asked me to their house. In a second I put on a clean dress, washed my feet and was ready to follow her. Mamme frowned — it was a busy afternoon; now she had also Loisl thrown on her hands. But she knew that this blonde girl was a messenger from that other planet, stationed in Venice, and I had to go.

Henny and I grew very fond of each other, and Mamme came to like her too, for she appreciated plain bread and butter, was well-mannered, and put on no airs. But I came to spend more time bicycling to and from her villa and less and less on the fields. For my birthday — and it was the first time I remember it having been taken notice of — Mamile sent me a book on Giotto in Italian, with the suggestion I make a short summary of each page and have it ready when I came to Venice. It was an order. I liked the story well enough since Giotto had started out as a shepherd, but writing a summary was a bore. Henny helped me. She was a gentle, natural link between Gais and Venice. When we met again at the end of September we had much to talk about during our long walks on the Zattere and I could mention *Heimweh* without being misunderstood.

4. I don't remember any special anguish at leaving Gais
for good or whether it was clear it was for good. Babbo
met me at the station in Bozen and filled the day so that, in
retrospect, it remains one of the happiest and most eventful
of my childhood. He treated me like a grown-up. And showed
me Verona. Perhaps I might remember more of the Arena and
S. Zeno if I had been taken there first; as it is, the image of
Babbo dims the monuments in the background: it is he standing on the circular stone steps, he looking at the bronze doors,
and explaining, explaining, focusing his attention on some detail, wondering out loud. I was too thrilled with the presents

he had bought me: a tiny wristwatch and a pair of new shoes. The wristwatch he chose. In the shoe shop he sat back and told them to bring something beautiful for the signorina. And when I picked a pair of brown suede with a bit of heel, he gave me an approving look and paid and told me to keep them on if I wanted to. After which, how could I keep my eyes off my wrist and my feet for very long!

Until, that is, on arriving at Calle Querini, Mamile· said those shoes were not suitable, too grown-up. She would keep them for herself and get me another pair.

Maria Favai had not only found a friend for me, but also a school. The Favais were, like the Levis and Dazzi, part of Venice. Always there, and Babbo seemed very fond of them all. He sometimes made fun of Maria, puffing up his cheeks and drawing an ample bosom with his arms: *"Povrina, povrina,"* he'd laugh. Maria had a very heavy figure, always clad in black, and a very heavy Dutch accent. She was a poetess and her husband, Gennaro, a Venetian painter — a striking contrast: tall, thin, vivacious, in a dazzling white suit and with an enormous white beard and crinkly hair standing upright. His black eyes and his tongue were always active, except when he and Babbo played chess — absorbed in their game for hours on a rainy afternoon, or evenings. I loved going to their house with Babbo, a big studio in Campo Sant Agnese, filled with heavy furniture, books and his own curious paintings: pale-colored, misty landscapes, mostly views of Venice. I would be given art books to look at, and shown Maria's wonderful collection of teaspoons: the handles were topped by lacy windmills. Gennaro always greeted us loudly in Venetian at the top of the stairs and as soon as I was within reach he kissed me on the head: *Che bei capei che bei capei, che bea putea.* The usual Venetian refrain.

I do not know whether Babbo approved of the school Maria had helped get me into. He certainly did not think much of the education I got there, and only once during my four years in Florence did he come to see me. At present he seemed very eager to educate me himself. The ban on the German language — now that an Italian school had been decided on — was lifted. Babbo gave me a red Insel Verlag edition of Heinrich Heine's *Buch der Lieder*. It was the first book he ever bought me. He would take me on his knees and make me read to him for as long as he could stand my halting stammerings. Then he would take over: "*Und sieh und sieh, auf weisser Wand . . . Buchstaben aus Feuer*," made me *see* the fiery letters on the wall so vividly I was afraid. I learned "König Balthazar" by heart without the slightest difficulty, so powerfully had its rhythm been drilled into me. The previous year he had given me *Märchen aus Kordofan* inscribed by Frobenius and now he said I should write down all I knew about Gais. As simply and clearly as Frobenius wrote about Africa. Although I was by now able to make myself understood in Italian, spelling, grammar and construction were beyond my reach and my vocabulary was extremely limited. Whatever I wanted to describe had no name in Italian, it did not exist in Italy — or so I thought. In Gais we used to say to the Italian teacher: "God does not understand Italian," when made to study the Lord's Prayer in that language. Babbo did not accept ignorance as an excuse for not doing. It was the content that mattered, and if I had no language to express myself in, he remedied by translating the "Storie di Gais" into English.

An attempt was also made to read the Bible to me in English, but I think it was more for the sake of ritual that Babbo would take me on his knees and read a few pages before sending me to bed, for although I knew the "story" I grasped nothing of the English text. There had been some perplexity about which version to read to me, since I was a Catholic; it seemed a very serious matter, but I did not understand why. Babbo seemed to have gone to considerable trouble to find four black, soft-covered booklets, and he started with the one entitled *The Gospel According to St. Luke*.

And he tried to broaden my mind by taking me along wherever he went. Often it was to the Quirini Stampalia Library of which his old friend Manlio Dazzi was the director. He always welcomed us smiling from behind a huge desk and while Babbo was engrossed in some book, Dazzi would whisper to me: "*Il tuo Babbo è un fenomeno*" — looking dreamily towards the phenomenon. I did not understand the word, in fact I understood almost nothing of what Dazzi said, but I knew he meant something huge and beautiful and I felt very proud. On top of the small bridge outside the Quirini Stampalia, I took Babbo's hand, as unobtrusively as possible, and presented him to the world enacting a grandiose inward pantomime. I fancied that all the passersby applauded and bowed to the hero. The hero was unaware, rapt in his own visions or problems, and would, as often as not, continue the search after some particular book or information in a long, narrow second-hand bookshop at the end of the Calle Larga.

Then, on the way home, to amuse me we would stop by the printing press in Piazza Santo Stefano to listen to the clatter of the machines: like the clacking of cooped-up hens, we thought it very funny. And in the evening we would return to Piazza Santo Stefano for ice cream: the best in all Venice, Babbo declared. Mamile soon gave up trying to convince him that the only place fit to be seen at was a caffè in Piazza San Marco — so and so would be there in such and such a dress.

No, the ice cream was bad and expensive and so and so a chicken-head without historical interests.

In Piazza Santo Stefano we were often joined by Aldo Camerino and Carlo Izzo. Izzo, roundish, reddish, with spitting protruding lips, was a jovial professor of English and American Literature, interested in translations. Camerino, dry, lean, tall with a prominent nose and shiny black eyes, was the director of the Venetian newspaper *Il Gazzettino*. Both wore spectacles, as part of their face, whereas Babbo was constantly changing his three sets of rimless pince-nez. Sometimes Izzo brought some shy young man interested in poetry. Babbo would immediately challenge the newcomer by pulling out a ten-lira note and telling him to look at it carefully, to read the fine print. What did it mean, what did it say, what did he know about the nature of money? Nothing. Unless he understood the nature of money he could not understand or write good poetry. Then followed a list of assignments. The young men seldom came a second time.

Now and again Dazzi, Izzo, and Camerino came to Calle Querini after dinner to hear Babbo read the Cantos. The sound of Babbo's voice, the atmosphere and the tableau that repeated itself for years is still vivid: the audience grouped in a semicircle around Babbo in his big, straw-bottomed, wood-framed armchair by the green reading lamp; Dazzi in a similar chair, except for size — man and chair were half the size — facing him; Izzo and Camerino on two stiff plain *careghe* or Chiavari chairs painted dark blue, facing the big velvet pearl-gray couch, upon which lay Mamile, dressed in black with a multicolored sash around her very narrow waist, in a Duchess of Alba pose with me beside her, equally dressed up, my hair loose and shiny after the obligatory hundred *coups de brosse*, held off my face by a shiny black ribbon with a huge bow to one side. I liked the preparations and the careful dressing-up for these evenings; moreover, there were the sweets bought in the morning at Moriondo's to look forward to, and the orange juice. It was my job to squeeze lots of oranges, enough to fill a big green glass jug. The guests were never offered anything alcoholic.

While Babbo read out loud no one stirred. A sort of tinkle hung suspended in the air, threatening to explode if anything moved. Since Dazzi understood no English, at the end of each Canto, Babbo would translate for him; then followed questions and long arguments. This bored me, so I would retire to the bathroom and there try out Mamile's rouge and powder and creams, scrubbing my face violently and resuming my place on the couch as soon as I heard Babbo's pince-nez case click: I knew he was on the point of resuming his reading. Silence.

Cantos in the evenings. Afternoon concerts at Giorgio and Alice Levi's. At the entrance of their large drawing room stood a collection of sticks which Babbo and I greatly admired, as well as some of Alice's paintings in the adjoining studio. Both Alice and Giorgio limped, but it seemed to add to their charm: always gay, enthusiastic and full of curiosity and interests. Giorgio teased me and Alice defended me, it was a great game which invariably ended in some little present. Once it was a 5-centesimi coin with a hole in the center: for good luck, Giorgio said. I loved the Levis, and so did Babbo and Mamile. It was to see them that Babbo stopped in Cortina the last time he accompanied me back to Gais. A long walk from the station just to say hello and give them time to stuff my pockets with sweets. Giorgio was a very good pianist and Babbo told me he had saved a friend from despair, while he was laid up, blind for months, by playing the piano to him. Later I learned from Mamile that the friend was Gabriele d'Annunzio.

At these afternoon concerts — sometimes they were rehearsals — the second violinist was Mr. Nixon, a jolly, red-headed American with a very frail, shy wife. Puppets were their hobby and they were training cats to dance, for a show. But all this may have been said to keep me amused. What is certain is that these were the first Vivaldi concert revivals and Giorgio was full of enthusiasm for these Americans who had brought to life Vivaldi in Venice.

I never was taken to the concerts of Princess de Polignac's. I knew they were important for Mamile because of her intensive practicing beforehand and the elegance of her clothes. Babbo looked at her with pride, and I admired them both when they went out in the evening — that year Mamile in a long black velvet skirt that harmonized with Babbo's velvet dinner jacket. I was fascinated by his patent leather shoes and the broad silk cummerbund. Once they took me with them. No, not Mamile playing; friends. In a beautiful place. Some palazzo, or the Fenice? I was too dazzled by the preparations and all the glittering lights and people to remember much. Except that I had a short gold cloth dress to match my hair and a big white gauze starched ribbon and before going out was stood on a chair for inspection or maybe that was a previous year, probably when the Hungarian Quartet played in Venice. The future king of Italy attended. And I was again stood on a chair to catch a glimpse of him.

The best part of the day was still spent at the Lido. We always came late in the season. The beach was almost deserted and we had the full attentions of the lady renting the towels and the *bagnino* renting the *pattino*. Each year they greeted Babbo like an old friend. Babbo loved to row. He and Mamile would get into the water when we were way out and I was left in charge of the oars. I was a coward and never learned to swim properly. Often Mamile and I would cling to the two points of the *pattino*: mermaids towed along with great delight and vigor. No loafing around on the beach; we were there to swim and to row and it was done with zest and speed. One could idle on the *vaporetto* on the way back and forth. If Babbo and I were alone, he would engage in conversation: if Mamile was with us they talked together or read the papers while I roamed around the boat.

In October preparations for my school outfit started. Babbo bought me a handsome leather suitcase, a real, hard suitcase like his own except that it was smaller. He had my initials stamped on it and I felt very proud. Then he left — suddenly, it seemed to me — and Mamile and I were alone in Venice. She went to a lot of trouble for me and gave me her own silver spoon and fork which she had had at school and had my name engraved after hers. I now was "Mary," also on the silver goblet. I was looking forward to school. I had no clear idea what it would be like: surely a fantastic place if one required silver service and dozens of white linen knickers and shifts and long nightgowns bordered with lace. Whenever I saw Henny we still talked mostly about Gais, which in our fantasies started to assume the aura of the country house where I would go and spend the summer. I imagined I was heading for a school that was not a convent, but an assembly of noble ladies, devoting themselves to education of Italy's choicest blossoms.

To do justice to the Regio Istituto delle Nobili Signore Montalve alla Quiete I would need a Proustian mind — which I don't have — and no sour grapes. Some woman had actually written a novel about her school life there. When I read it I recognized nothing except the big chestnut trees of San

Cresci, Mugello, where one spent the summer. The subtle relations among the girls and the nuns and the priest and the teachers which she described had all escaped me.

At first I tried to make sense of the enormous staircases, the high ceilings, the long halls. All the windows were doors and the beds had white curtains around them. A Medicean villa above Florence with a suite of parlors hung with Della Robbia ceramics and Carlo Dolci Madonnas, cloisters and walled-in gardens, terraces and roof gardens overlooking an immense Renaissance garden with fountains, baroque statues and hedges and trees cut into strict geometrical forms. At the back was a park with huge trees, a tennis court and a croquet lawn and a turkey farm which served to stuff us on Sundays. The Lady Mothers wore Seicento Spanish costumes and a golden ring in the shape of a cross: Sponsae Christi. The structure of the silk headgear must have been modeled on buffalo skulls, covered in ample black crepe, the tip of the wide horns turned inward on the shoulders, so one wondered how they could sally with all that wind bagged in behind their necks.

The evening I arrived my being a "foreigner" held some attraction: the girls thought my mistakes in Italian cute, but the novelty soon wore off and I spent the first three months huddled up behind the grand piano, crying. I mean the recreation hours, for during class I had to pay attention because, as it happened, I was the only one in my class. A stroke of luck. I could not have kept up with sixth-graders. *La prima ginnasio*, almost like private tutoring; so that the following years I was prepared for the regular courses in Italian.

Heimweh — all I felt was homesick. Sundays we had to write letters home. I wrote formally affectionate letters to il Babbo and la Mamma, and then poured my heart out in long long letters to Mamme. Shortly before Christmas I stopped

[104]

crying because "the Frau has written you can come to us for a week. But I must not let you know, only stop crying immediately." To me Mamile wrote: We shall take you skiing to Siag.

In the train I kept writing on the window panes: Siag Siag Siag. After Franzensfeste — Fortezza — feigning great surprise, I said: Funny, if one reads it backwards it is Gais. Mamile did not let on: it's a secret, you'll see when we get there. It was dark, I pressed against the windows to look at the landscape inside me: I knew we were coasting along the river Rienz. In Bruneck I could pretend no longer: *"Mamme! Margit!"* *"Schau schau 's Moidile!"* On the little trolley car to Gais, Mamile repeated for my benefit what she had already explained to Mamme by letter: she was going on to Taufers, she had reserved a room for herself at the Hotel Elefant because she had much work to do and needed a warm room. We naturally expressed regret and Mamme said she had prepared the *Öberstube* and heated it, etc., etc. No, no, it was better for me to be alone with them and then in the afternoon I could go and see her and do some skiing. I could hardly listen. Margit and I chattered away; I wanted news of everyone at once. *"Soug guita Nocht,"* I had jumped off the trolley forgetting to say goodnight to Mamile and had to jump back on. I saw she was hurt; Mamme tried to cover up and excuse my exuberance. I was bursting with joy: the smell of the snow, the sharp air, the gurgling river, although so very familiar, were all of a sudden new.

But inside, the house seemed too small and stuffy. The low paneled room spun around my head. Tatte, on the bench by the stove, seemed tired and shrunk; to his *"Iz dozeilmo la"* — tell me, tell me — I had little to say. And the horse, and the sheep, and the cows and the bees? The *Krapfen* were as good as I had remembered them, but I felt embarrassed when Margit caught me reaching for the napkin that was not there, and laughed: "*Aha du hearrisha.*"

In the polished vastness of the school I had felt lost and cold. Now this coziness and warmth seemed stifling. Still, by next evening I was glad to get back to it: the afternoon in Taufers had bored me to tears, and possibly also Mamile. I found her in her hotel room copying music. She tried to get me interested in what she was doing: deciphering and transcribing scores; she was doing the work for Babbo. They held concerts in Rapallo. I must make an effort and learn some solfège at school if I wanted to understand music.

She was heroic, she limped to a nearby slope with me. She had badly sprained her ankle the previous morning at Rapallo as she was rushing to catch the train. The long journey and the cold had made it swell up. Now she sat huddled up on a tree trunk taking pictures of me while I pretended to enjoy myself sliding down that stupid slope, invariably falling the minute I heard: Bend your knees instead of sticking out your bottom!

Thus the week passed. The going back and forth between Gais and Taufers had turned out to be an unrewarding compromise. Lonely skiing instead of riding sledges with my old friends and Loisl. They assumed it was because I now gave myself airs. No longer one of them. On New Year's I heard the voices of all the village children. Some I recognized. Instead of going *noijour schrain*, I stayed at home, although one was entitled to make the rounds until one was fourteen: going from house to house with a big bag, shouting in the hall:

I winsch enk a glickseligs nois jour
Chrishkindl in gekraustn hour . . .

Some ditties went on for several strophes, wishing the farmer luck in the stable and the housewife luck with her hens, and the maid luck in her chamber . . . and for the children plentiful gifts. To be answered by a voice saying: "Come in, hold up your bags," and one received a small bread roll, an apple, a handful of dried figs, a few walnuts, sometimes also a coin, sometimes only coins. By evening one was very rich.

I was miserable leaving my Gais home, but probably because I felt I had not really been *home*. I was also worried lest Mamile had "sacrificed" herself on my behalf. *Fare un sacrificio* was the most recurrent phrase at the Quiete. A new attitude to life: in Gais no one had ever mentioned sacrifices, people did things naturally, according to their instincts or nature. Now it seemed as though parents and teachers were constantly hating to do things, anything, and only the love of God — a God that was represented by Suffering or Duty — could move them from inertia. All this seemed wrong to me. Fortunately I really believed in God and in the Saints and in Angels, in Heaven and Hell. I became more and more pious. The chapel was the only place where I felt at peace: I could say rosaries and talk to God in German.

Then a huge fuss broke out over a missal. All the girls had Latin-Italian missals, it was part of the outfit. I asked: Could I have a Latin-*German* missal? The request had seemed reasonable. The nuns ordered one from Brixen because none was to be had in Florence. It cost almost three times as much as the Italian ones. But I do not remember having been made aware of this fact. I was given a beautiful Missal, charged to Babbo. Who wrote to the Superior:

Dear Madam

I take a very grave view of encouraging a child to spend money out of proportion to its probable expectations. Maria did not receive an authorization to spend 87 lire on a Mill Missal. There was talk of 30 lire.

The child should not have been tempted to spend more. Naturally I have no interest in text books other than required for the state examinations.

I think it silly to study Latin via German. Especially as the child knows quite enough of the latter language.

A book at this price is a luxury even for university students in advanced courses.

I shd/ be glad if you will exchange it. Naturally the child desires a handsome object, but the lack of precise statement will do more to destroy any morality than mixing it up with piety, which is of all places the field where honesty is or should be most emphasized.

There is no beauty in inexactitude, and the church was most holy when its theologians attained the greatest clarity of expression.

I am thoroughly displeased with her letter in which she leads the attention away from the point of my question. You will destroy any respect the child has for religion, if religion or the religious object is associated in the child's mind with an action not scrupulously honest; with an indirectness or evasion. That is not a small matter, either from your point of view or from mine. . . .

And so on. I was utterly confused and miserable: "*Caro babbo mi dispiace tanto di aver fatto questo sbaglio che ti fa gran dolore e mi pento e ti prometto . . . purchè tu mi perdoni.*" And then I fell back on Gais arguments: It is a very strong missal and it will last me all my life, and again I repent and beg for forgiveness and promise, etc.

The Mother Superior had to send a second explanation:

. . . regret that the previous explanations have not satisfied you. We appreciate your point of view, and agree that Mary should not have spent more than the sum she had mentioned to her mother without permission. As for this we are partly responsible, we will not ask you to pay more than the 30 lire which Mary had received permission to spend. The book cannot be returned as it has already been used for several weeks. When it was ordered no one had any idea that there would be more than a slight difference in price for the German edition. . . . We should have referred the matter to the Signora before allowing Mary to keep the book. I regret this was not done. Mary was so pleased with the truly beautiful book and her argument that it would serve her all her life and would be a textbook as well as a prayer book for her, helping her to keep up her German seemed to us reasonable and we thought that you would not consider it a foolish or unnecesary outlay.

We have talked everything over with the child; she is very sorry for her fault and wishes, if you permit, to pay something herself when she has a little spending money, so as to atone. We will settle for the book and she can pay a small sum, 10 or 15 lire, gradually, should this seem to you just.

A good prayer book is required for each child, some have quite handsome ones, but Mary had only wanted a *good one* such as most of her companions have. . . . Please do not insist on its being sent to you, as it is required for *daily* use and especially during Holy Week. Mary will need it to follow the services. You will see the book later and will then realize that it is worth the amount paid.

Trusting, etc.

DEAR MADAM:

Thank you very much for your clear explanation. I am not haggling over a few lire, but I wanted to be thoroughly sure of what had occurred.

So long as Maria did not say she was given permission to spend more than had been discussed I am quite content.

Let her pay up to ten lire in two 5 lire payments. Tell her

the rest is being credited from the cioccolatini that would have been sent her.

This is not as punishment, but simply to get it into her head that one cannot be careless about 57 lire UNLESS one is much richer than she is. . . . I am not quite sure that Latin should be learned from German. Wd/ seem simpler to procede from Italian to Latin so far as association of words is concerned. BUT, I don't wish to make this as more than an interrogation, in M's case she may learn better from German, though I doubt it. She might be asked about this. Her own view is worth quite as much as mine on the subject. Etc., etc.

And to me: *"Cara mia* NATURALMENTE *ti perdono."* I was forgiven. As long as I understood two things: when I speak to my mother I must always make myself *clear* and make sure that I have clearly understood her. Then I must not spend money that is not there. This is easy where there is credit, but one must not form the habit.

Education is worth nothing unless one has these two habits. Keep quiet, no useless chatter, don't talk to people you do not know. Or say interesting things, generally interesting, not personal. But *when* you speak to your mother or to trusted friends, *speak* with precision, don't leave things ambiguous. And never spend what you have not *got*. Etc., etc.

For the next three years *"Ora et Labora"* became my motto, myself a model of piety and discipline. The summer I spent at school, to study Italian. I had hoped to go to Gais, but the political unrest in the South Tyrol worked against me. There were only eight of us at the summer place in the Mugello, orphans or girls whose parents were in Africa, in India, in the Philippines. For the feast of our Foundress, we were allowed to wear nuns' habits. Half in jest, half in earnest. The Mothers had great hopes I would apply for novitiate as soon as I was of age. When they caught me making eyes at the young land surveyor — not that one ever had the slightest chance to talk to a man — they wrote to Mamile about the disgraceful tendencies of my nature and Mamile made a big fuss over it for years.

End of September. Babbo, Mamile and I met in Venice as usual. The holiday soon got disrupted by a telegram. Although I was now making real efforts to learn English, I still caught little of the conversations going on between my parents. Babbo must leave for England: an old friend had died. When I told him I was sorry he had lost a friend he realized I thought it was a male friend, but he did not correct me. Mamile was very animated and indignant. Babbo struck his characteristic pose: hands deep in trouser pockets balancing on toes and heels, looking straight ahead of him toward the window, lips tightly closed.

He had arrived in Venice with tennis rackets and had taken a weekly subscription to the tennis courts; he thought it was time for me to learn how to play. But the lessons were cut short, and replaced after he left, by sittings at Mrs. Frost's — an American lady who had rented the Palazzo Contarini on the Canal Grande. She was a painter and had told Babbo she wanted to do a portrait of him. His eyes and smile conveyed that he would rather she did one of me first. He was capable of saying a great deal by just blinking and smiling and shifting his weight from one foot to the other.

To make up for the short stay in Venice he took us to Rome the following Christmas. On arriving in the late afternoon, we saw posters announcing Walt Disney's *Snow White and the Seven Dwarfs*. We must see it. I was delighted. Mamile said she was sure it would run the whole week, but Babbo rushed us to the *pensione* to deposit the luggage. And then to the film before dinner. We had arrived in the middle of one show and naturally had to see the beginning. I was spellbound and hardly realized we had come to the end a second time. The lights went on and Mamile got up, ready to go. Babbo lingered in his seat, we looked at each other, and it was settled. "But *caro!* The child must have something to eat and go to bed." I assured them I was not the least bit hungry or sleepy. Babbo decided: She does not look undernourished, she can sleep tomorrow. I think he enjoyed the film even more than I did. In Venice he had once taken me to see a Tarzan film — it must have been after Uncle George had shown us the animal pictures — and, with Henny, I had been once or twice to see Mickey Mouse or a historical film, but going to the movies was still a great event.

After that first glamorous evening, the flavor of that Roman holiday is mostly of Vapex. Babbo developed a cold. The fuss and the precautions seemed to me excessive; however, he soon got over it. Then Mamile took to bed and remained there most of the time. I was plunked on a chair with a huge anthology of American literature edited by W. R. Benét and N. H. Pearson. "Read out loud." Babbo agreed that the size of the book was unwieldy, but he said it was time I learned some American history and the best way was through the early American writers. But my English was still so limited that I retained absolutely nothing.

The stuffy hotel room and the heavy anthology were alleviated by visits to the zoo and evenings at the Caffè Greco with Italian friends. The caffè: dark, plushy, narrow seats along the walls under huge dim mirrors and shady paintings. Small, heavy marble-topped tables. And the friends: though dressed in black, gay and voluble. Carlo Monotti and his chic French wife stand out most clearly, she with a hat just like the Tower of Babel as reproduced in my German Bible. We also went to tea at the Marinettis. He showed us his Futurist paintings, the portrait of his wife, Benedetta, with vivid circles of color to one side of her head, and he gave me a brochure with a tricolor ribbon stamped on the cover. No, not a catalogue of his paintings but a treatise on how to transform milk into synthetic wool. He seemed more interested in what I knew about sheep than in explaining his art.

And then there was the unforgettable afternoon with Monsignor Pisani. I had been in a convent long enough to appreciate the importance of meeting an Archbishop. Babbo said he stood a fair chance of becoming Pope some day, but for actual usefulness and influence, it was to be hoped that he might remain Sottosegretario. Though in later years, he must have speculated. . . .

And if, say, we had a pope, like Pisani?

Babbo and I were to meet the Monsignor at . . . probably Doney's in Via Veneto, since I remember Babbo being amused that a high prelate of the Church should have picked a place packed with ladies. I remember a small table heaped with pastry, a delicious hot chocolate and an air of precariousness: the two bulky figures talked with such animation that I feared tables and chairs would be knocked over, glasses and cups be upset. Then they struggled over the bill and the Monsignor won; in fact, he took over for the entire afternoon. They kept talking while putting on overcoat and cloak, impatient with the waiter who was trying to be helpful. It was a short walk to the *carrozza:* inside, Monsignor Pisani handed me a gilded box

of Gianduja chocolates. Babbo beamed almost as much as I
did. A cornucopia. I held it in my hands like a calix, it seemed
so precious, and as mysterious as ". . . *prezzo giusto, usura,
Salmasius.*" The conversation, as usual far above my head, was
interrupted now and again to call my attention to some monument as we drove past.

The first visit was to Saint Peter's; Babbo joked: out of
loyalty. And then on to Sant'Anselmo on the Aventino. The
seat of the Cavalieri di Malta: a high garden wall and a door.
The Monsignor told me to look through the keyhole, I was
amazed: the dome of Michelangelo in the pale golden mist of
the setting sun. Something to remember. And:

Apollonius made his peace with the animals,
        so the arcivescovo fumbled round under his
            ample overcloaks as to what might have been
a left-hand back pocket of civil clothing
and produced a cornucopia from 'La Tour'
or as Augustine said, or as the Pope wrote to Augustine
        'easier to convert after you feed 'em'
but this was before St Peter's
    in move toward a carrozza
from the internal horrors (mosaic)
        en route to Santa Sabina

Speculating over coincidences and threads — ". . . *he tied
the end of his wife's 20 sewing cotton to the stem of a large
crimson strawberry and lowered it toward Gargantua. And this
was to teach the infant Gargantua to look about; to look 'up'
and to be ready for the benefits of the gods, whether so
whither they might come upon him . . .*" Thus a mauve
Suchard chocolate roll handed out in an impulse of generosity

and obedience returns in the shape of a cornucopia, tenfold. And — ten years later — when I visited Mr. Eliot in Tennyson Mansions, stooping, "just out of hospital": he took from the mantelpiece, as a priest might from the altar, an identical golden La Tour box and offered it to me with the injunction "This is for your son." Canto XCIII had not yet been written.

In April 1939 I saw Rapallo for the first time. Since I had spent most of the previous summer studying, the school granted me a few days off, to say goodbye to Babbo. He was going to America.

Mamile was at the station to meet me. We drove in a *carrozza* to the bottom of the hill. Then we climbed for almost an hour on a broad cobbled path, on narrow stone steps flanked by gray holding walls, upwards under olives, past eucalyptus and lemon trees. The sea so different from the Venice sea, colors sharp and clear. It was a sunny, scented spring day, the terraces full of daffodils.

Casa 60 was then orange-colored, with Ionic columns painted on the outside walls, a flight of smooth black lavagna steps leading up to the green front door half hidden by Virginia creepers and honeysuckle. *Thk thk thk* GRR: the sound of the olive press on the ground floor. *Ploff, chhu:* the bucket hitting the water in the well.

The ingle of Circe . . . in the timeless air.

The house inside: light. White and empty. Polished red brick-tile floors. A square entrance, and four doors open on rooms with a view to the sea, olives and a blossoming cherry tree. Pale blue and pink vaulted ceilings with painted morning glory convoluting into bouquets and wreaths.

The furniture, unpainted, was all made by Babbo. A long bookcase and a mirror in the entrance; a table in the dining room and four plain straw-bottomed chairs along the walls; a desk, a high broad shelf for music and violin and a narrow bookcase fitted in under the window in Mamile's room. The only spot of color was given by the orange damask couch; the only ease was suggested by two armchairs, a broad one and a normal-size one, twins to the ones in Venice. A Babbo-made desk stood also in "my" room, where the rest of the furniture was an iron bed, a night table with a marble top, and a chair. This was referred to as the Yeats furniture. It came from the flat my grandparents took over from the Yeatses. The only items in the house with a touch of hardness.

There was nothing else in the house. Sheer beauty and scent of — honeysuckle? lemon or orange blossoms? One painting: blue sea, white shell. In the kitchen: an iron funnel over the charcoal and a row of dark-brown clay pots on the broad mantelpiece, No junk, no clutter. Only candlelight.

"Miao" — and the rattle of Babbo's stick on the front door. He was laden with parcels, papers and envelopes sticking out of his pocket. We relieved him of the encumbrances while being kissed and gently buffeted on the cheeks. He went into his room to change and then threw himself on the orange couch. There was nothing in "his" room except two of his stools, a change of clothes and a packing-case dresser ingeniously disguised by chintz.

Mamile in the meantime prepared the tea; I laid out the cakes and was told to carry everything into her room on a low tray-table. Her room was the center of the house. After the tea ritual and some chitchat, Babbo: "She feel up to the Chaconne?"

And I heard Bach's Chaconne, probably for the first time. It registered for good. Mamile had placed the iron music stand in the center of the room and herself in front of the window. In Venice I had heard her practice for hours and had been oppressed by the sounds. I had never watched her. At concerts in other people's houses I would glance at her now and again, but never really saw her. Now a new person stood in front of me. Was I looking at her through Babbo's eyes? Some mix-up, exchange of perception, or fusion of vision? Or was it because she was playing exclusively for Babbo going on a long journey? Love flowing into the groove *dove sta memora*. "The birds answering fiddle and her between me and wisdom and view of the bay" — called to my mind, years later. For the duration of her playing I saw no shade of darkness, no resentment. The violet-blue eyes clear and luminous. Finally I had a glimpse of their true world *nel terzo cielo*. But as soon as the music stopped the vision came to an end. Mamile resumed her authoritarian ways and the switch to their third-person language:

"He take the child for a walk and show her." "Yes ma'am." "You go and talk to Babbo." We obeyed.

In the setting sun we walked along the hill path, to the old Roman road above the new Aurelia by the sea, al Triedro and Castellaro, over to San Pantaleo, past the church to the very edge of the hill from where one looks down on the cliffs of Zoagli. All this Babbo named and pointed out to me as we walked along. We sat for a while on a low wall beneath the church, just gazing at the changing sea. When we got up he put his arm around my shoulder and leant heavily on me — this was the old game: *"il bastone della mia vecchiaia"* — "the prop of my old age." But he was in no joking mood, rather spoke as though something was weighing on his mind. Perhaps he sensed a repressed question. *"Il nonno?"* I knew that outside this rarefied world of the three of us, there were grand-parents in Rapallo. The Herr Grossvater had come to Gais and I had seen him in Venice and in Bozen. At the time Mamme's polite inquiries had been answered by saying that the Grossmutter was in Rapallo, the trip would have been too tiring for her, she was a very old lady.

I was fond of grandfather; he had sent me a big photograph of a painting of himself while I was still in Gais and I treasured it.

As though placing the needle on a record at random — well knowing the beginning and the end — words came to the surface: *Il nonno* wants to see you again. He strained his back when he saw you in Gais the first time, you don't remember, so pleased and eager was he, he picked you up too quickly. The same color of the eyes. But two emotions at once is too much for an old lady. If I can get anyone to listen to me over there, if I can talk some sense into the President, to stop him from allowing the country to be run by crooks, help prevent the ruin of Europe, perhaps in the future America will become a fit place to live in, for all of us. They take me to the boat tomorrow. There is not room for everybody in the car. Your mother will show you Genoa." He talked further about Roosevelt's politics and Uncle George, of which I understood too little, and then came back to points raised, so that in the end I realized that, for some reason or other, I would not see my grandparents and that they would accompany him to the boat instead of Mamile and myself. Also, that he was going to America not for any private gain or motive but because he felt he knew more about Italy than American officials, thought he knew of a remedy against war if the President or a sufficient number of men in power were ready to hear him out. War was not inevitable; Italy and America should not get involved and above all should not be enemies. Mussolini had no evil intention, he had only the benefit of the people in mind. And there was need of a strong Italy to counterbalance the growing power of Germany.

Babbo left Sant' Ambrogio early next morning. Except for repeated bear hugs, it was as though he were merely going across the canal in Venice to his workroom. Mamile was once more distant and impenetrable, but I had had a glimpse of her great beauty and my fear of her changed into a kind of veneration. There was no way or reason to express this change of feelings. Besides, the thought of Babbo going to America was very exciting and kept me busy, especially this new fantasy that we might soon go and live there.

The usual "Hurry up or we won't see the boat pull out." My fascination with the Ligurian landscape, lunch at a restaurant, some place high up from where one could see the harbor; in the afternoon, the exploring of the narrow streets behind the harbor and the shop windows in the center of Genoa; the return to Rapallo and the lit-up coastline — all seemed a prelude to my own great voyage and made me forget the disappointment about not seeing my grandparents.

The walk up to Sant' Ambrogio in the dark had something unfathomable, something fluid, almost eerie. Mamile seemed familiar with each stone, but she flashed a torch for me in spots where the sky and the sea were hidden and fireflies provided the only specks of light. In high open spaces the darkness was attenuated by the reflection from the lights in the bay and the stars above.

We had hidden a pair of old espadrilles at the bottom of the *salita*. — "That's what all the peasant women on the hills do when they go into town. One can't walk on these stones with proper shoes. After concerts I sling the fiddle over my shoulder; I need both hands free to carry my music and the shoes and hold up my evening gown. . . . Tomorrow we'll have tea with some friends, they have a delightful garden, Else is very kind, she usually asks me to dinner before a concert, that gives me a chance to powder my nose . . ." Mamile was in a talking mood. After the last flight of stone stairs, under the church, we sat down for a while on a narrow bench in front of the long gray stone house at the top. — "I always have to sit down here. Gee, I am tired sometimes."

The image clung to me: Mamile, alone on the hill path in the middle of the night, climbing with the violin strapped over her back, carrying high-heeled golden or satin shoes and a music case in one hand and holding up the long evening gown with the other. In an old pair of espadrilles. And "Gee" was all she said, after endless practicing and the walk down and the climb back, alone. — "It's awful when it rains, the violin is so sensitive."

I knew exactly what Babbo meant when, later on, he once told me: The real artist in the family is your mother.

How is it far . . . ?

No longer so very far — neither in time nor in understanding. Did I at fourteen or fifteen start to understand? Or merely store and believe?

'Without character you will
be unable to play on that instrument . . .

"*Constans in proposito.*" There had been concerts in Rapallo since the early thirties, their impact shored, shelved, with a name to come. Things accomplished on sheer willpower, for the love of music and poetry. The struggle to preserve and create culture, the concern with the "laboratory idea," old music and new music, to draw comparisons, to gauge technical progress or regress, to find out what remains to be done for the musician as well as for the poet.

Fanned by his disinterested and unflagging enthusiasm, rare and unforgettable little concerts sprung up, according to the frequency and incidence of musicians. One remembers blocks of music. 'Block,' in this context, was a great word with Ezra at rehearsals. He not only insisted on blocks of light and shade in the execution of old music, he also always demanded integrated and consecutive programs. The season started under the sign of Mozart, all of whose violin sonatas were played at least once by Olga Rudge and Gerhardt Münch. One wonders when the whole series had last, if ever, been heard in its entirety. In the thirties Pound developed an intense interest in the vast, unpublished output of Antonio Vivaldi, much of which, largely thanks to Olga Rudge's research work and to microfilm technique, has since become accessible to the public. Some Vivaldi given at Rapallo was being played for the first time. The Bartok played here by the Hungarian Quartet, though published, was still extremely *avant-garde*. Ezra preferred to depend, whenever possible, on local talent, and yet he was far from excluding good or excellent professionals, on condition that the program was not made up to show off the performers but based on intrinsic musical worth. Nor was any discrimination ever made on grounds of race or nationality. Besides the artists already mentioned, we heard Tibor Serly play Mozart's Sinfonia Concertante, as well as compositions of his own. Renata Borgatti in Bach, Haydn, Mozart and Debussy; Chiara Fino-Savio singing arie antiche and Lonny Mayer singing Hindemith. . . .

Thus an Englishman, the Reverend Father Desmond Chute, summed up those activities after the war. He had been one of the sustaining members of the Amici del Tigullio. Most of them were foreigners. After such names as Marchesa Solferina Spinola, Marchesa Imperiali, Contessa Gabriella Sottocasa, Conte Nicholis di Robilant, etc., etc., Dottoressa Bacigalupo, Mrs. Townley, Mrs. Brooks, Mrs. Watkinson, Miss Natalie Barney and of course Mrs. Pound. Basil Bunting was musical critic. The programs issued and the concerts held "sotto gli auspici dell'Istituto Fascista di Cultura." The same spirit as in the days when All rushed out and built the duomo

And the perfect measure took form

The local authorities lent the Sala del Municipio, the hotels distributed programs and were in return recommended by the Amici del Tigullio. The Comune paid for the heating of the *gran sala municipale* and "Railway reductions of 50% to Rapallo are available from all parts and frontiers of Italy for these concerts; Tickets valid for 30 days." To hear, as said, Olga Rudge, violin, L. Franchetti, piano: Mozart, César Franck, Bach. Olga Rudge, Gerhart Münch, Luigi Sansoni: Francesco da Milano, "Canzone degli Uccelli"; Terzi, Berard, Bach, Mozart, Debussy. And Scarlatti and Scriabin, Boccherini, Purcell, Young, etc., etc. Achieved without state subsidies or grants from foundations, without restrictions — although the performances were considered to conform "to the most recent currents of thought." All their inner urge and need was for peace. To build the city of Dioce whose terraces are the color of stars.

Babbo had faith in the Verbum made perfect, in the *semina motuum*. And was a practical nature, a seer and *do*er in all things, always wanting to go to the root. His ideas were bearing fruit: "enough of one composer to show his scope and

limits; his force and his defects" — the Musical Academy in
Siena was planning to devote a week each year to one composer, or group of related composers, mostly forgotten or neglected. But by no means did he restrict his interests to the arts.
Good art was based on sound economics. Throughout the
Cantos one sees Usura in relation to the harm it does to the
arts . . . the line grows thick
By this time Confucius was his Master. Confucius was concerned not only with the Odes but also with history and good
government.

In 1933 Mussolini had received him. Babbo had presented
him with a copy of the *Thirty Cantos*. He read a passage to
him and

'Ma qvesto,'
said the Boss, 'è divertente.'
catching the point before the aesthetes had got there;

Just as Babbo caught the Romagnol accent. He thought the
Fascist regime might be a good platform for monetary reform.
He spoke to Mussolini about the theories of Douglass and
Gesell. He also had a list of books which needed immediate
translation into Italian for a better understanding between the
two nations: the writings of John and Henry Adams and
Thomas Jefferson. Essays, such as *In the American Grain*, by
W. C. Williams. He had, above all, a great curiosity — want-
ing to see the man, form his own opinion, put his ideas in
order —

'Perchè in ordine?' (vuol metter le sue idee)
said Mussolini.

"for my poem" — "Pel mio poema." There were

                       . . . in short the usual subjects
Of conversation between intelligent men

in a country where culture was alive.

Bottai also phoned Torino
              instanter, to dig out Vivaldi

Bottai being, at the time, the minister of education.

Bellum cano perenne
                 . . . between the usurer and any man who
                 wants to do a good job
                 (perenne)
without regard to production

                                 a charge
for the use of money or credit.
              'Why do you want to
' — perchè si vuol mettere —
              your ideas in order?'

                     . . . .
       If I had known more then,
              cd/ have asked him,
as Varchi — one wanting the facts.

   And now he was on his way to talk to the man who, in his
mind, could have avoided a second world war. Not megalo-
mania, but a sense of responsibility carried to the extreme. At
his own expense he was going to enlighten a man for whom
he felt little sympathy. And as usual, wanted to verify his own
convictions against the most authoritative sources.

"I am not insisting. I am wondering how far this is correct"
— an expression I heard often.

But in New York he was met by a hostile press which announced that his old friends had turned their backs on him because he was a Fascist. A friend of Mussolini. True, as early as 1926, he had declared: "I personally think extremely well of Mussolini. If one compares him to American presidents (the last three) or British premiers, etc., in fact one can NOT without insulting him. If the intelligentsia don't think well of him, it is because they know nothing about 'the state,' and government, and have no particularly large sense of values. Anyhow, WHAT intelligentsia?"

And Roosevelt never received him. He talked to as many senators as he could; George Tinkham had provided him with a batch of introductions. On May 5 he sat in the reserved gallery for the 76th Congress, mainly as grandson of T. C. Pound. The futility of his striving and the difference of quality in the human elements are summed up by Senator Borah's comment:

'am sure I don't know what a man like you
    would find to *do* here'

And so he returned to Italy, where there was plenty to do. In Rapallo he was Il Signor Poeta.

From the boat I received cheerful messages, ribbons, postcards. Although he had paid for cabin class, they had offered him the "state room." Italian courtesy.

The Christmas holidays of 1939 started out in grand style. Mrs. Frost had offered us her guest flat in Palazzo Contarini on the Canal Grande. The polished floors in the entrance and in the great *salone* projected chill, despite the enormous fireplace. Although the bedrooms seemed cozily carpeted and warm, Babbo immediately announced it was too cold.

More than of the place itself, I have a vivid impression of Mamile telling me how elegant and right things were. Her own little house was let at that time of the year. There was some talk about a friend of Babbo's joining us. He was referred to as the Possum. It's an animal, Babbo said, but he did not tell me what kind. Among our acquaintances in Venice there was a Signora Elefante and a Miss Poodle, and my animal name was Leoncina. The Possum never showed up. And after the second night in Palazzo Contarini, Babbo decided he had had enough. He was not going to freeze for the sake of elegance. I don't know how gracefully they managed to extract themselves. By lunchtime we were comfortably installed in the Pensione Seguso on the Zattere, the heating and the food superabundant. Mamile expressed some regrets for my sake; it would have been good training for me to live in the palazzo and acquire high standards. I had not felt the cold, but was pleased to be on the Zattere; the atmosphere was so much more relaxed. And we had a view.

"Not the Canal Grande, but very handsome," Babbo kept repeating. And one morning the view surprised us: San Giorgio, the Giudecca, the barges and gondolas along the Zattere covered in snow, the sea hazy gray and hushed. In the middle of the morning the sun came out, the sky turned very blue, the snow glittered for a few hours and then melted, vanished. Babbo and I walked on the Zattere. Even he had never experienced Venice under snow, though he was proud to have seen the old Campanile before it sank to the ground; he went down in his knees, slowly, to illustrate how it had sunk to the ground.

Mamile was as busy as ever copying music, correcting

proofs of the *Accademia Chigiana Bulletin,* and there were a few concerts in the drawing room of the Somers-Cockses in Palazzo Bonlini. Mr. Somers-Cocks played the cello, Mamile the violin, and a young Italian, Bagnoli, the piano. Having by now had lessons in reading notes, I was asked to turn the pages for him. Sheer agony: I feared I would be, and was, too slow.

Mrs. Somers-Cocks was a minute old lady, completely deaf, but she could lip-read. One of the most indomitable and active British ladies I have ever met. Her drawing room was filled with enormous paintings: her own copies of masterpieces done mostly in the Prado. I think her husband had been consul in Madrid for many years. There were a good number of foreign service people among Mamile's friends, mostly retired, cultured and well-traveled. When Babbo came to these musical afternoons, he sat unobtrusively and quietly in one of the deep armchairs by the window.

One evening we went to see a Ginger Rogers–Fred Astaire film and came home late. All the way home from the cinema Babbo tapped and leapt and encouraged me to do likewise and "get nimble." Mamile laughed and we were very gay. As we started to undress we heard a loud fracas in Babbo's room — now that he had thrown off his coat and jacket he leapt and tap-danced more freely. Mamile had quite a bit of difficulty in putting an end to it: "*Caro!* I refrain from practicing for fear of disturbing the other guests and you bring the house down in the middle of the night." Babbo was mortified and sorry; it was hard for him to keep still before having fully danced out the rhythm he had absorbed.

Just as the tap had stirred his legs, so did George Santayana's presence in Venice stir his mind. I had seldom seen Babbo so eager and yet so contented: "A relief to talk philosophy with someone completely honest — a nice mind." From odd remarks I gathered that the two strayed from philosophy into politics now and again and saw eye to eye on most things. They believed in Mussolini's basic humaneness and peaceful intentions; certain foibles in his character did not diminish the fact that the country had improved greatly under his regime. They had both lived in Italy with open eyes for a long time. This attitude was common to almost all of our acquaintances: Americans and English, mostly elderly couples who had settled down in Italy. They seemed convinced that Italy did not want war. Were all the fortifications along the Brenner not indication enough that Mussolini's heart was in the right place? If the friendliness of the people meant anything at all, Italy would never declare war on England and France.

I was allowed to accompany Babbo only to the entrance of the Hotel Danieli, where Santayana was staying. "No philosophy until you are forty" was the refrain, but on our way I sometimes had the impression that he was using me as a sort of blank wall to shoot his thoughts at, like tennis balls, in an attempt to put his ideas in order, round up his sentences, and hit the bull's-eye. I understood little or nothing of what he said; there were names I had never heard and concepts that resembled religious speculations. Since he still had to speak in Italian when trying to make me understand something, he groped for words as though verifying a coin from both sides. Sometimes he would quicken his step and start humming, completely oblivious of me, yet communicating a strange joy and excitement as I trotted beside him.

Mamile had been offered tickets for a performance of Respighi's *Fiamma* at the Fenice. She and Babbo debated for a while, were inclined to turn down the invitation; the music was below their standards. In the end they decided it was

time the "sprig" saw an opera. They would show me something better as soon as they had a chance.

The promise was kept the following September, when I
was taken to Siena. The flat Mamile had been able to rent that
summer was rather cramped and bourgeois and she kept repeating: I wish you could have come here sooner, you should
have seen the flat at Capoquadri's, the view and the frescoes.
— And to Babbo: "He liked it there, didn't he?" — "Yes
ma'am." And he recorded what he had seen and enjoyed:

Thou shalt not always walk in the sun
        or see weed sprout over cornice

while studying the Leopoldine Reforms and the history of the
Monte dei Paschi and having fun with

                        O —
razio della Rena to be recognized
as illegitimate father of the bastards of Pietro de Medici.

And the Palio:

                four fat oxen
having their arses wiped
and in general being tidied up to serve god under my window

etc.
And in Pisa he remembered:

        whereas the child's face
is at Capoquadri in the fresco square over the doorway

And Mamile's clothes and hair style:

> she did her hair in small ringlets, à la 1880 it might
> have been,
> red, and the dress she wore Drecol or Lanvin
> a great goddess. . . .

Dyed red — Count Chigi teased her — in honor of Il Prete
Rosso. Vivaldi was known to his contemporaries as the Red
Priest because of his flaming hair. "And, given the mores of
the times, the Prete Rosso's blood must be flowing in her
veins, for her devotion and enthusiasm are otherwise inexplicable." Chigi carried his joke to the extreme of introducing her
as Miss Rudge-Vivaldi.

For many years Mamile had been secretary of the Accademia Musicale Chigiana, Count Chigi being the Fondatore
e Presidente, the last perfect Renaissance art patron. He had
restricted his field to music, filled his palazzo with fine instruments, and invited the best musicians in the world. Mamile
had been introduced to him socially by a friend. It turned out
that she personified the ideal public relations secretary for the
Musical Academy the Count was dreaming of. As usual it's
not what you are most passionately interested in and best
equipped for that lands you a job, so that she who was described as "one of the very few violinists before the public who
have a definite gift for the work they undertake . . . em-
phatically a musician." — ". . . *violiniste au jeu sobre, au son
pur, a l'archet souple, à la musicalité toujours compréhensive
et d'une qualité si fine.*" — ". . . *Possiede compiutamente la
technica del violino e rivela doti . . . di schietta musicalità
. . .*" — "Most capable artist, impeccable technique," etc., etc.,
was forced to lay aside her instrument for many months a year.

To earn her living, she had to rely on her charm, her flair for dressing, her *savoir faire,* her fluent French and Italian and of course her talent for organizing and her knowledge of music and musicians.

And the great Vivaldi revival started in Siena — via Venice and Rapallo. "She pulled it off on her own" — just as previously her concerts at the Albert Hall, the private audition for Mussolini and the concerts for d'Annunzio at the Vittoriale. Of the last two occasions she cherished mementoes: a signed picture of Mussolini in civilian clothes, playing with three lion cubs; and a small silver bird, studded with bright stones, which d'Annunzio had pressed into her hand wrapped up in a silk scarf.

The Count had inherited from an uncle the Palazzo in Siena and various country estates with sufficient revenues to keep the places up. He had no heirs, but three great passions: Siena, the Palio and music. He also liked beautiful women. As a young man, the family, trying to make him travel, put him on a train for Paris. At Turin he turned back. He could not bear the idea of leaving Italy. He even went to Florence very rarely, mostly so that he could speak ill of Florence as a true Sienese should. Trains, airplanes, and women in trousers or with red fingernails were taboo. Yet he gladly paid the fares to have artists come to him from all over the world. His drawing room housed the greatest collection of photographs I had ever seen, mostly in heavy silver frames: queens and princes, musicians and dancers and singers. A bric-a-brac of faces crying for attention. Personalities so strong that they clashed with the strong personalities present.

Ever since I had gone to school, Mamile had hinted that she wanted to take me to Siena, but that first I must learn Italian and French, and above all look pretty, well groomed, graceful. "*Salonfähig*," Babbo would joke. Had he behaved nicely? Yes but. It was a constant struggle to get him to meet so and so and to attend parties. Mamile had to spend most of her time at the Palazzo. We would meet at some small restaurant for lunch, usually the Tre Croci. Babbo hummed and banged his typewriter for a few hours, while I studied Greek and Latin. Towards the end of the morning we went out, for food and for culture. First stop was at the Cannon d'Oro for an aperitif of orange juice and *Krapfen*. In the afternoon it was *Apfelstrudel*. This was our great weakness. In Siena, as in Venice, Babbo had discovered the best pastry. But since his trip to the States he had a tendency to be overweight, at least in Mamile's eyes. Her regret at his losing his beautiful figure was almost unbearable — "and to let the child indulge and put on more baby fat, well, that's just silly." So we played a lot of tennis in the afternoon — it kept our weight and her temper down. Babbo taught me the correct basic movements with great perseverance and, when he was tired of sending back the ball, he would take off a shoe, place it at some strategic point, and say: "Hit it; I am an old man." I soon made enough progress to play properly and have some fun, though for him it must have been a bore since he was such a good player.

When it was not tennis, it was history or art. He showed me Siena stone by stone, as he had done Venice. The paintings of Simone Martino, the frescoes,

Riccio on his horse rides still to Montepulciano.

To the floor in the Duomo he devoted special attention — I wish I could have understood all the things he said. The word "gnomon" stuck in my mind since I was studying Greek and was fascinated by Greek roots in Italian words. We spent much time watching the ray of light that would hit the brass disk on the floor precisely at midday. He took me inside the Monte dei Paschi and to the various doors and fountains of the town. His favorite walk was to Fontebranda and then up to San Domenico

where the spirit is clear in the stone. . . .
Narrow alabaster in sunlight, the windows of the crypta —

As usual, he would make me describe in writing what we had seen. I remember his approving: *L'interno di S. Domenico è a forma di T.* "Yes, yes, T-shaped, tells the reader something." Or out into the country, towards the convent of the Osservanza that stood out intact and serene above the olives — evoked with regret after the war:

and the Osservanza is broken
and the best de la Robbia busted to flinders

The opera that year was Alessandro Scarlatti's *Il Trionfo dell'Onore* with a delightful Zareska in the role of Rosina. The Count was enraptured. The audience scintillating, effervescent under the spell of the Scarlatti high-quality champagne. Bruno Barilli was there as musical critic. He and Babbo were the two outstanding figures at the gala opening in the Teatro dei Rozzi; and Count Chigi, the *grand seigneur* from top to toe, tall and lean, slender long hands and feet, and well-sculptured aristocratic features, nonchalantly conscious of his role, always making fun of Americans and their accents, stressing his Sienese *h* and cadences. Presidente e Fondatore della — at the time still Regia — Accademia Chigiana. Babbo liked him, but never had much to say to or about him. Whereas Barilli, good writer and composer, he recalled with nostalgia when thinking back on Siena

and down there they have been having their Palio
'Torre! Torre! Civetta!
    and I trust they have not destroyed the
old theatre
             by restaurations, and by late renaissance giribizzi,
                dove è Barilli?

Barilli: a flint. His rather horsy face haloed by a bristling gray mane, erect, waving long hands, wrapped in a long scarf.

All the people had left the theater, after a loud ovation, Babbo had tapped his cane and Barilli had shouted bravo, and now the two were still standing, talking softly to each other, alone, falling into silence, listening to echoes, until the hush was broken by the ushers wanting to close the doors.

The composers Ildebrando Pizzetti — sharp and small — and Alfredo Casella — round and heavy — were there too. Old friends. There were pleasant afternoon teas in the garden of the Ravizza where Mamile and Babbo seemed to enjoy themselves, whereas I was being plagued by Casella's butterfly-hunting daughter Fulvia — a pretty little redhead of seven or eight equipped with all sorts of nets, chasing anything with wings and wanting me to help her. But at fourteen I was self-conscious; I wanted to sit silently with the grown-ups and, moreover, was shocked by the cruelty of Fulvia's game.

I forget whether it was at the beginning or at the end of our stay in Siena that Babbo took me with him to Rome for a few days, and whether the purpose of the trip was to equip me with an identity card or whether we had to get one because the hotel demanded it. We stayed at the Albergo Italia in Via 4 Fontane. Babbo seemed harassed, as though something was out of control; perhaps he was merely distressed at the waste of time. He explained to me that it was necessary to have an identification document that was valid in Italy, but that my legal status and citizenship would be set right as soon as we were able to get to America. When it would be possible for the two of us to satisfy the legal residence requirements was hard to foresee. I had no clear idea what was wrong with my status, nor did I care. I enjoyed seeing Rome and meeting people. And we met a great many. Babbo spun like a top and it may well have been on this occasion that he made his first records, addressing America via the Italian radio in a final attempt to accomplish what he had failed in during his visit to the United States. "A responsible citizen must do everything in his power to prevent his country from entering an unjust war." And he spoke of ignorance: *"Il nemico è l'ignoranza"* — the enemy is ignorance. I heard the slogan for the first time.

We went to the Stampa Estera offices a couple of times to see Reynolds Packard, whose candid reports about China had interested Babbo; he credited him with political insight and informative capacities: "Tell the American public, tell the American people . . ." But Packard was just a newspaperman, without aspirations to messiahship. The conversations with the Italian economist Odon Por seemed to give Babbo greater satisfaction; with him he was not as restless as he was with Packard. We also went to see a *femme de lettres* — someone very important, it seems, but I have forgotten her name, out of cussedness, perhaps, since I did not like her wiggly coyness.

October 1940 was our last holiday in Venice. Babbo did not stay for very long — it was too cold to do much swimming. We went to the Lido a couple of times to play tennis. There were no concerts. The sparkle had gone out of Venice. An air of gloom and austerity impending, in sharp contrast to the previous year. Mamile's main concern was finding new tenants for the house. She had always leased to foreigners; now they had all gone. A plump elderly lady came to look at the house. She paced up and down and took measurements and counted on her fingertips — in the end she sighed and gave up: no, too small, too expensive. When she left, Mamile said: "Poor thing, all these Jews not knowing where to go and with so little money left. But we are no better off either." I sensed the great shortage of money and that my school fees were a burden. I said to Babbo: Would it not be easier for you if I went back to Gais; couldn't I come to Rapallo and help Mamile instead of returning to the Quiete? "Yes yes, my noble ch-i-aild, but it ain't that simple."

And so I went back to Florence. After my first three months of despair and then the levity of looking, probably smiling, at a young man in the country, my record over the past three years had been excellent. I prayed and studied and climbed the ladder of honors: *"beniamina, angelo, aspirante figlia di Maria, figlia di Maria, assistente"* and on December 8, 1939, I was elected President of the Daughters of Mary. Unprecedented: no one so young ever had made it, no one so fast — and no one so quick to fall. In fact a president was president for the duration. In my case — given my strong, and at the time real, spurts of mysticism, with hours and hours of prayers and meditation in the room of our Venerabile Madre Eleonora Ramirez di Montalvo, whose coffin I pulled out from under her bed and kissed before leaving the room (she having died in sixteen something-or-other and still queuing to be made a saint) — it was expected I would stay on and become a nun.

Whereas, on December 8, 1940, my name was removed from the board of honor in the chapel. I had declared myself a heretic, and, after reading Florence Nightingale's memoirs, I decided my calling was not for the convent but for the battle-fields. I would become a nurse, perhaps study medicine. Dreams of heroism were in the air. Even in convent schools it had become obligatory to listen to the news bulletins. We were to knit socks and mittens for the soldiers. From Gais I received news of boys being called up.

But my change of mood, my rebellion, was mainly intellec-tual. The dogma of the Holy Trinity bothered me; I tried to work out a system by which Heart, Soul and Mind could re-place the Three Persons and thus have God within me. We were studying the French Revolution, and the idea of Reason as Supreme Being fascinated me. Napoleon became my pinup. I read Papini and Cronin, de Kruif and who wrote *Vol de Nuit?* — Saint-Exupéry. The days were not long enough. I read in bed, with a flashlight under the blankets, and was nat-urally discovered and punished — *"Eh, signorina, he ci ha l'angelo hustode nel letto?"* — a jolly Florentine *conversa,* a lay sister serving as maid, asked whether I had my custodian angel in bed with me. I had Dumas, and Dumas was on the Index!

Babbo had started sending me his articles in an Italian pa-per called *Meridiano di Roma:* "Something you can now un-derstand, or time you learnt." The nuns were disturbed; it was not permitted to receive newspapers, and yet "it was a special case" and they could detect nothing immoral in the paper. I had an argument with my Italian teacher over the *"putrido ottocento"* — bad language, she insisted, and besides it was false, the *Ottocento* had been a glorious era, and who was this Ezra Pound anyway to fan such opinions. No one in Italy had ever heard of him. "*È il mio babbo,* he is a poet."

Und überhaupt stamm ich aus . . . Pourquoi nier son père?

Consternation. "It is a *nom de plume.*" I had no better answer on the spur of the moment. The name was as elusive to me as it was to the teacher probably, nor could I lay claim to having read his poems, except "The Gipsy," which I found in the *Albatross Book of Verse.* Babbo had given me the book for Christmas, with the injunction I stick to the early period. My English was still very poor, but I had started to appreciate poetry. French was the required foreign language; I wrote imaginary letters in French, imaginary letters in Italian and sometimes poems. But on the whole I did not waste much time and translated more of Ovid's *Metamorphoses* than was required by the teacher because Babbo had spoken well of Ovid. His opinion on any subject became dogma to me and no one was to question his opinion. He sent me *Ta Hio* — The Great Learning — and I studied it carefully. In the *Meridiano* articles Confucian ethics were mentioned, most seriously. The nuns and teachers fought me for a while but finally decided to leave me alone, with the final remark: "You behave as though you were carrying the weight of the world on your shoulders." I stooped, pretending I had a geographical globe on my back. The impudence was punished by three days' segregation in a small, unused music room. It must have been towards the end of school, because gardenias were in bloom. I was happy with that scent and wished the segregation would last three weeks instead of three days.

Underneath all my theological dilemmas and dreams of heroism, I listened most attentively to the summons: learn how to write. I was a slow thinker. THINK — it baffled me. How does one go about "thinking" — thinking as different from describing, remembering, inventing. The question seemed too complicated. Babbo had written:

17 Nov.

CIAO CARA

To learn to write, as when you learn tennis. Can't always play a game, must practice strokes. Think; how was it different to go to the Lido to play tennis? I mean different from when one went to play in Siena?? Write that. Not to make a story but to make it clear.

It will be very LONG. When one starts to write it is hard to fill a page. When one is older there is always so MUCH to write.

THINK: the house in Venice is not like ANY OTHER house. Venice like no other city. Suppose Kit Kat or even an American needed to be told HOW to find the Venice house? How to recognize you and me going out of the door to go to the Lido. He gets off train, how does he find 252 Calle Q.?

Describe us or describe Luigino ariving at ferrovia? has he money, have we, how do we go?

A novelist could make a whole chapter getting protagonista from train to front door. Good writing would make it possible and even certain that Kit Kat could use the chapter to find the house.

ciao.

THINK about this quite a good deal before you try to write it out.

On the whole, despite its anachronisms, the Quiete was a good school; above all, a beautiful place. I formed no lasting friendships, but retained respect and affection for a few of the nuns. Madre Francesca Chiara lived up to her name. As a young American painter she had gone to Assisi to copy Giotto. La dolce Umbria had conquered her, converted her. She was baptized and became a nun. She seemed to live in a trance, in contrast to the lively and bustling Italian nuns, and yet she had retained the American urge to *do* things and founded a nursing school nearby, all on her own. She was supposed to teach me English. My reading sent her to sleep. By that time she was an old lady.

I have never revisited.

5. Back to Gais for the summer. Freedom, joyfulness and common sense after a lot of restrictions, mannerisms and artificialities. Working in the fields once more was fun. People treated 's Sâma Moidile like a young lady who knew best. Mamme and Tatte, instead of giving, sought advice: they had been forced to choose between Germany and Italy as a result of the agreements reached by Hitler and Mussolini over the disputed frontier. This had left them in a state of confusion and insecurity. Old values and beliefs were being uprooted, their homestead and fields and animals computed into numbers, counted, changed into hypothetical money, of which

they would receive the equivalent in some country conquered for them by the Führer. Precariousness in place of stability. The only reality was war. Having opted for Germany, the young men were being called up. Songs like "Wir fahren gegen Engeland," had swept the country in place of the old "Heimatlieder." No longer "Tirol isch lai oans," but "Deutschland über Alles," "Heil Hitler." If old songs were sung at all, they received a new twist: a *"Sieg Heil"* at the end.

The alliance with Italy did not interest them in the least, just a political move one had to forgive. What mattered was that now everyone was free to sing German songs, wear not only traditional costumes, but German uniforms. The word ideology was not heard. Margit had grown into a handsome girl; she had lots of admirers. She played the zither and sang beautifully. Young people flocked to our house and there was much singing and music and I loved dancing with the young men in their Tyrolean costumes or *Alpenjäger*, on leave after their training, before the *Einsatz* on the front.

From bucolic freedom and frolicking back to Siena. My pace and aesthetic values had to be readjusted once again.

Mamile had rented a small flat overlooking the market. Babbo joined us for the Music Week.

Then came the great evening of Vivaldi's opera *Giuditta Triumphans*. I think it was the first time it had been performed in this century. At the door, Babbo offered an arm to Mamile and to me and took us for a stroll. At the bottom of the steps leading from Via di Città to the Piazza del Campo we stood for a long while. Was there a moon? Probably. I remember a clear sky and stars. We stood in silence, until Mamile said: "Say 'O!' — I can never get either of you to say 'O!' " Babbo inhaled laughter for a while and I smiled and we moved on without saying "O!"

It was the last Music Festival in Siena that we attended. It was uncertain whether Mamile's job as secretary of the Academy could continue. She was an American. The Count was distressed; his world was being dispersed. Mamile and I were very frequently invited to lunch or dinner. Chigi still had supplies of wine, oil, wheat and vegetables from his *tenute*. On our leaving the palazzo the butler would hand us a neatly wrapped parcel: a loaf of homemade bread — *pane casereccio*.

While with us, Babbo banged the typewriter most of the day. Our outings were now only to the post office, and an occasional visit to the Conca d'Oro for whatever sweets one could get. A threatening feeling of hunger seemed to be hanging over us. Then he suddenly left for Rome.

The war had spread into Russia. He had still hopes that the crime of a war between America and Italy could be avoided. At the time, I think he even feared that America might be the loser. Germany's *Blitzkrieg* had cast a sort of iron cap over people's heads. But Babbo kept saying that it would be sheer idiocy for America to come to the aid of England; and an alliance with Russia was a monstrous prospect, throwing the American people at the mercy of Communism: only international financiers and warmongers without scruples could conceive of such a thing. Still, he was in great conflict. Emotionally he had no leanings towards Germany. The same Boches who had killed some of his best friends during the First World War were lurking in the background. And culturally? The *Götterdämmerung* and a Valhalla at the end of it was far removed from his aesthetic imagery. But there was a certain kind of discipline and honesty that seemed to appeal to him, especially in their economic system. And there had been that attempt in Wörgl to introduce money based on work — the kind of solution that might "save the world" — *Arbeitswert. Schwundgeld.* International Jewry, whether the bankers and cannon merchants were Jews or Gentiles, were the true enemy. If the British Government and the American President befriended them and played their game, it was a sign of evil and corruption. Their own people would get more and more indebted to anonymous powers and no peace could ever be achieved. Every responsible person must transcend his own predicament and inclination and help strive for a lasting peace, not just a respite, long enough to rearm and grow stronger and start in some other part of the world.

And as for the purity of race — what's wrong in wanting to preserve that, as long as the issue isn't distorted and blown up artificially? Race distinction, not prejudice. John Adams's sense of the natural *aristoi*.

To me these things seemed to make sense, to be very important. But when he felt that he was being misunderstood or contradicted intentionally or out of feather-headedness he became exasperated and fell prey to language exceeding his intentions. He kept hammering on one thought: people must know where their money comes from, who issues it, upon what values it is based. Self-sufficiency — *autarchia* — order. Order. A strong Italy to counterbalance Germany, to preserve civilization. And he hoped America would not side up against Italy. Groping for facts. But few Italians were eager to enlighten him. In Siena they were mostly artists not interested in politics, or aristocrats interested mainly in keeping old privileges, tossing off generalities or wit. They could not understand why an American should feel so strongly about saving Europe. Or why a poet should bother about economics:

Infantilism increasing till our time,
     attention to outlet, no attention to source,
        That is: the problem of issue.
Who issues it? How?

I have retained a general impression of his arguments, which nonetheless seem to tally with what he wrote then and twenty years later. He had not yet defined usury as concisely as he did after the war: "A charge for the use of purchasing power, levied without regard to production, often without regard to the possibilities of production." — But the process of clarifying, defining, was going on.

On his way back from Rome to Rapallo, Babbo stopped in Siena for another couple of days: to say goodbye. He was going back to America.

Mamile shortly after left for Venice, "to see about things" and to make arrangements about the house in case we too should be leaving Italy. Her house in Venice was her only source of income, aside from the job in Siena. I was put into a boardinghouse for students and was, for the time being, to study on my own. I had fears that my parents might go to America without me, and instead of studying fretted away my time. However after two weeks or so, Mamile wrote that I should come to Rapallo, and first go to say goodbye to the Count. An embarrassed, clumsy teenager in pigtails crossed the deserted courtyard of the Palazzo and up the broad stairway to the left. The butler ushered me into the big drawing room and told me to wait, he would call Il Signor Conte. The place, empty and silent, had assumed a different dimension; the faces in the silver frames were asleep. The Count entered and could well have been only his shadow: "*Povera mimmina.*" He pitied me, loudly, in Sienese, I didn't know why. I pitied him in silence. He seemed suddenly so alone, and gray.

Were we not going to America? Not even Babbo? No. Not for the moment. Impossible. Things were too complicated. The officials at the American Consulate had been very nasty. Grandfather had a broken hip and was too ill to be moved. It would be cruel to leave the old people behind.

"I will have to pass you off as my cousin. One never knows what might happen to foreigners. Permits, reports to the police. We might be deprived of our ration cards. It will be easier for you to get along on the Italian identity card." Thus Mamile.

It irked me. I was young and objected to scheming and pretending. I winced when the peasants or the shopkeepers talked to me about the *signorina:* I sensed malice in their tone. However, I never put questions to Mamile, and fell into the pattern of our new existence with a resignation that soon turned into contentment.

Mamile worked out a strict schedule for both of us. She set the alarm clock for six A.M., got up and did exercises in front of the looking glass in the hall, then called me. Exercises. Wash and throw a basin of cold water over my chest and shoulders and get dressed. *Quick!* I loathed it, not so much because of the cold, but because in the looking glass, instead of my real self, I saw a pathetically naked girl, trying to cheat herself out of the ten genuflections, palms to the ground, stiff knees, prescribed by *Vogue,* and at the end of it the shock of the cold shower. Why did I do it? What did I care how I looked with a war going on and my never seeing a soul? When Mamile felt especially energetic she would watch me and correct me and throw the cold water over me herself to make sure no drop was wasted — undoubtedly with laudable intentions, despite, or unaware of, the humiliation I felt. The truth is that I was plain lazy: I had to fetch the water from the well, a very deep one. I hated pulling up that endless rope with the bucket jerking against the walls and spilling — and then that nonsensical fear that I might be confronted by a severed head because of the picture in the *Ingoldsby Legends* — the head in the bucket a young girl was pulling up — which had frightened me as a child in Venice.

But soon I came to see the logic and the beauty of my new life: strict discipline and routine left more freedom for one's thoughts. I was glad for Mamile's rigorous perseverance.

Mamile practiced the violin all morning. I worked by the little iron stove which was installed in her room to take the chill off the house. We burnt pine cones and boiled dried chestnuts and potatoes on it. In a sense our life too had become a work of art: nothing superfluous, nothing wasted, nothing sloppy. The only "ugliness" we had to put up with was electricity in place of candlelight. Candles were no longer on the market.

I still had some bad half-hours, before lunch. *Languore per fame* perhaps. Mamile would tell me to go and get a breath of air: run, skip. I'd walk to the *punta* beyond San Pantaleo and there sit on a rock from which it seemed possible to jump right down into the sea several hundred meters below. I played a game with the sea's suicidal attraction; nothing seemed sweeter than to let myself glide down and disappear under the waves, live there with lost heroes: every day one heard of ships being sunk, of airplanes crashing into the sea. I composed morbid verses, influenced perhaps by de la Motte Fouqué's *Undine,* which Father Chute had given me to read and which I loved. Moments of loneliness. I felt homesick for Gais, for people.

The only person I saw between 1941 and 1943 was Father Chute. I went to him twice a week. He had offered to give me lessons in French and Latin. He would deserve a book, or at least a chapter to himself. But I could not do him justice: too many aesthetic nuances. He was an English abbé who had settled down in a lovely little villa in Rapallo, in the early thirties I think. He had been a pupil of Eric Gill and did beautiful lettering. In fact, he did everything to perfection: he was a musician, and sometimes after my lesson Mamile brought her fiddle and he accompanied her on the piano. He painted — and has done some good drawings of W. B. Yeats, Pound, Hauptmann, etc. He wrote, and found time to do "good work" and to hear confessions. A good mind and a noble spirit handicapped by a languid appearance.

Thin and very tall, a long, pale face, with lots of hair and a beard (dyed red), melodramatically stretched out on couches with layers of capes and blankets and three kinds of curtains at the windows which had to be drawn according to the slightest change of light outside, a series of eyeglasses and eyeshades and reading lamps. His health was poor, his eyesight very delicate. But his discipline must have been adamant, for he could not otherwise have been such an accomplished and honest dilettante. He did everything with extreme *diletto* and care, never pretending to be a great artist. Giving me lessons — because of his sympathy with Mamile's difficulties — fell into the realm of his "good work." He was extremely reserved; the closest he would come to private communication would be a sigh or a weary smile if his Italian housekeeper brought him a hot water bottle or tisane that was not quite hot enough, or if I drew the wrong curtain. We never exchanged a word, other than greetings, that did not strictly pertain to the subject of the lesson, and since I never saw his eyes he remained for me somewhat of a mystery man.

Because of his poor health and because he was a priest who had lived in Rapallo for such a long time, he remained there, although he was an English citizen. He was an excellent teacher, though Babbo made fun of his choice of texts. His favorite reading was Bossuet's *Oraisons Funèbres,* and I had to learn long passages by heart. Father Chute recited them, gently, with no emphasis, it seemed, but with such inner participation that the stream of words flowed like a clear river — nothing funereal about them. Racine and Corneille he also declaimed. He came from a family with long theatrical traditions, and it showed. I forget what we did in Latin — Virgil, I suppose, and Horace.

Babbo spent every second afternoon in Sant' Ambrogio with us; sometimes he came for lunch, sometimes he stayed for dinner, which meant that I had from two to three hours' instruction every day. Evenings Mamile continued her coaching in English, sometimes also a few hours after lunch, so that in those two years of seclusion we read through all Jane Austen, Thackeray, Stevenson, Hardy and about a dozen volumes of Henry James; and Alice James's diary.

With Father Chute and with Mamile it was learning and reading in an orderly manner, but Babbo provided action, work, in streams and in flashes. He brought me Hardy's *Under the Greenwood Tree* to translate into Italian. I felt flattered and challenged — at being admitted into his workshop. The job of translating was much tougher than I had foreseen, but with the passing of time I listened more and more eagerly for his cane on the cobblestones of the *salita* and then the rattle on the door, for he brought with him a dimension of — no, not stillness, but magnitude, momentum. He made me feel that work, learning, was worthwhile, exciting.

Our life centered around Babbo's visits and the pattern was much the same as on that afternoon in April 1939, the day before he left for America. Except that now he no longer arrived laden with parcels. Yet never emptyhanded: a few roast chestnuts or peanuts, a slice of *farinata* or *castagnaccio*, pancakes made with chestnut or chickpea flour, for our tea; and in an old envelope the cat's food, scraps from his lunch.

[149]

In place of the bunch of letters he read us his radio speeches. We were his first audience and, in the light of what we read in the papers and heard over the Italian radio, they seemed to me clear and justified.

"Damn it all, if you had a single-minded objection to violence you could have prevented this war." — "Freud is not the answer to violence."

After reading to us what he had written, it was my turn: I had to recite five lines from the *Odyssey* and translate. He then read five new lines as my next assignment. And it seemed as though he possessed two voices: one angry, sardonic, sometimes shrill and violent for the radio speeches; one calm, harmonious, heroic for Homer, as though he were taking a deep, refreshing plunge into the wine-colored sea after a scorching battle.

Then I had to read my translation from Hardy, usually one or two pages. The following year it was Cantos. Both tasks were really beyond my capacities, but he never lost his patience, just corrected and recorrected: "Take the thing and rewrite it in Italian. If a poem is good in the original you must make a good poem in translation, and it applies to prose too." But discussions were reserved usually for the *salita*.

It was time for tea: *camomilla* or mint was all one could get. But the tisane was still followed by music: Mozart, Bach, Vivaldi, Beethoven.

Time is not, Time is the evil, beloved
Beloved the hours βροδοδάκτυλος
    as against the half-light of the window
     with the sea beyond making horizon
le contre-jour the line of the cameo
profile 'to carve Achaia'
     a dream passing over the face in the half-light

Venere, Cytherea 'aut Rhodon'
vento ligure, veni
'beauty is difficult'

And here achieved. And later: "The birds answering fiddle and her between me and wisdom and view of the bay."

Nulla per me io desidero
che la vita continui così . . .

was the refrain of a poem I wrote then. For me nothing, stillness — stillness outlasting all wars — Mamile playing. Babbo and I walking down the path to Rapallo. A crystallized image set amongst green-gray olives by the changing sea. Yet there was a war going on; Germany and England were destroying each other's towns and people and Babbo wrote speeches in anger and disgust. The artist-antenna sensitive to the fury of the madness pervading the world. At times I felt the urge to *do* something — but what? "What the world will need most when the war is over is someone with an education" — and he tried to expand it as much as he could, dipping back into his own school years: "Now let me see, when I was your age . . ." And up came tidbits of geology, arithmetic, geometry.

And there were dramatic moments and periods of great tension following the news of Pearl Harbor. Babbo went to Rome. When America officially declared war he stopped broadcasting over the Italian radio. Impressive envelopes arrived summoning all American citizens to return to the States, to get in touch with the Swiss legations. Mamile seemed at a loss. And what about me? What, who, was I?

Babbo came back from Rome, indignant and discouraged. They would not allow him on the last clipper out of Rome. It was reserved for American diplomats and press envoys. If he and his family wanted to leave Europe it would have to be by slow boat. Months on a route full of mines and torpedoes. "Is that the way they want to get rid of me?" — I think a way out was suggested by train to Portugal. I do not remember details. The words that stick in my mind are: clipper, the last clipper, frozen assets, frozen bank account. Grandfather's U.S. government pension withheld, the old man in the hospital with a broken hip. Mamile's house in Venice sequestered as alien property.

Checkmate?

Babbo resumed his broadcasting. More violent. But what I remember most clearly — and the document obviously exists — is a long letter he wrote to? — perhaps the Attorney General — via the Swiss legation, in which he explained the reasons for his broadcasting. American officials had made his return to the States impossible. The Italian Government had offered him the freedom of the microphone, assuring him that he would not be asked to say anything contrary to his conscience as an American citizen. And as an American citizen he felt it was his duty to avail himself of the only means open to him to protest against the politics of a President who was exceeding his rights, endangering the Constitution, who had promised American mothers that their sons would not be sacrificed, while actively preparing for war.

The result was indictment for treason. And Babbo's answer: Treason is being committed in the White House and not in Rapallo.

Also:

that free speech without free radio speech is as zero

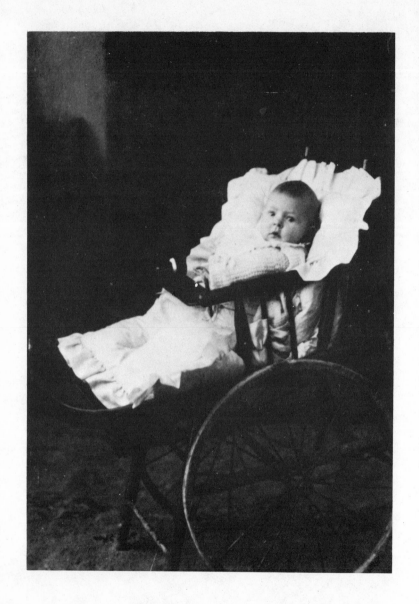

Moidile, November 1925

Der Herr – Tattile – is pleased. Gais 1927

Moidile is given a violin, 192

With Mamme and Margit on the road.
Gais 1928

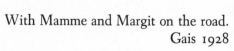

Tattile and Moidile in the picture;
Mamile, as always, behind the camera.
Gais 1928

Olga Rudge:

cameo and fiddle. 1928

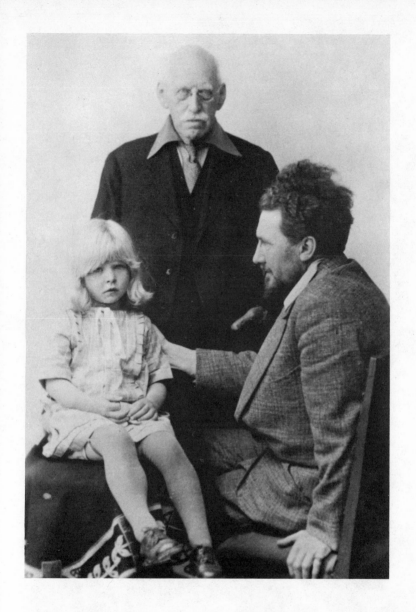

Three generations: Homer and Ezra Pound. 1929

Johanna and Jakob Marcher —
Mamme and Tatte

The Kirchtamichl

Famile and Frau Langenham.
Meran 1935

The Sama Family:
Tatte, Mamme, Loisl, Margherita 1936

Mamile

Venice 1935

Tattile

Shepherdess 1936

La Quiete, Florence 1937

Casa 60, Sant' Ambrogio

At Sant' Ambrogio 1941

Neuhaus, Gais

Brunnenburg

A

At Brunnenburg with the family, 1959. Ezra Pound with:
A) Patrizia de Rachewiltz; B) Mary, Patrizia and Boris de
Rachewiltz; C) Mary, Patrizia and Walter de Rachewiltz

B

C

Tattile and Tatte
on a visit to Gais, 1960

Gais 1960: Loisl, Walter, Tattile and Tatte

Ezra Pound with his grandson in front of the
magnolia at Martinsbrunn, 1961

On Christmas eve I was approached by an old woman on the *salita:* "Signorina, I have three eggs, do you want them?" It seemed like a miracle: "Yes! how much do they cost?" I did not have quite enough pocket money, but she let me have them for what I had and I was overjoyed; it would be a splendid contribution to our Christmas dinner. But at home, though Mamile was pleased with the gift, she said we must be careful, as foreigners we must not do anything illegal. And Babbo disapproved because Italy was fighting a war and no one must indulge in black market. My rashness had brought to light my parents' insecurity. I was on good terms with the butcher and the baker, always gave them my most radiant smile, and they were generous in their weighing of our scanty rations. Still, living exclusively on our ration cards was tough.

End of February 1942: Babbo stood at the door with red eyes. He hugged me and said: "Il tuo nonno è morto." — Grandfather was dead.

Mamile led Babbo into her room. I knew they needed to be alone. He left early and I walked down the *salita* with him. He was silent and I did not dare break the silence.

"The old lady has been admirable, for weeks she has nursed him all on her own. His death has come as a relief; he was in great pain." It was the first time Mamile mentioned my grandmother. After a few days we took some flowers to the grave. It was only a marked spot with a number in the Protestant section of the Rapallo cemetery. The tombstone had to wait until after the war and it was Father Chute who saw to it. Babbo had followed certain Confucian rites and had placed some jade on his father's body.

For a few visits Babbo just threw himself on the couch and wanted to be left in peace and listen to music. Then he went to Rome again.

When Babbo was away Mamile and I sometimes went into the hills for long walks, to gather pine cones for our fire; in spring to pick ferns to hang up and keep flies and mosquitoes out of the house. Sometimes we bought from the peasants dried figs or chestnuts, which were not rationed but were hard to come by, and the only thing that we could afford. We enjoyed them immensely. We also now and again went into Rapallo together and on the *salita* Mamile would reminisce about Paris, how beautiful her flat had been, ". . . and what will have happened to my piano?" . . . She described the city, Place de la Concorde, St. Germain, the Seine, concerts, parties, balls. How she and Babbo had been to a bal masqué — in black domino and red kimono? — And how Ford Madox Ford had asked her: "And where do you come from?" — "Youngstown, Ohio" — "I did not know such beautiful flowers blossomed in that desert." And Mamile was pleased with the compliment from the great novelist. He was, despite his bulk and drooping chin, a great favorite with the ladies. But they had a second dance and again he asked: "And where do you come from?" She was astonished: "Ohio." — "I did not know such beautiful flowers blossomed, etc., etc." If the war ever ended, if any of her friends were still alive, we would certainly go to Paris.

The trick to chase melancholia was to have me recite all the French poems I had learnt at school. It was a good game; we also learnt a number of La Fontaine's fables by heart — in them somehow some person or animal was always going somewhere or climbing a hill; the hare and the tortoise; the horse and the fly; the girl with the milk pot. Even on my own I would recite these poems when my mind was too dull to think, and it always made the climb much easier.

By the end of 1942 I was already steeped in the translation of the Cantos. Their sound, the way Babbo had so often read them in Venice, without my having understood a word, was somehow embedded in me, something very harmonious and beautiful. But reading them myself came as a shock. I was like a hungry person with a basket of exotic food in front of me, not knowing where to start, the flavors being totally new. Perhaps if I had read the first Canto first, things might have fallen into place earlier, but a consecutive reading was discouraged, mainly because of my ignorance and limited English.

One day Babbo arrived in high spirits with an Italian literary magazine called *Prospetti,* of which Curzio Malaparte was the editor. It contained Luigi Berti's translation of the second Canto. Babbo was pleased, not so much with the translation, I think, but with the event. He liked the daring format and color of the magazine, a feeble reminder of *Blast.* I eagerly started to read the Canto in Italian, but Babbo took the magazine away from me and said: "Suppose you try and see if you can do any better." And so my task began. It had been bad enough to translate Hardy and the result was more or less that of a school exercise; however, perseveringly, I had almost reached the end of the novel and Babbo was seriously thinking of finding a publisher for it.

But now: who were Lir, Schoeney, Picasso? Questions of this sort I had to reserve for the *salita,* and then: "It doesn't matter. The sire of some bloomin' nymph. Picasso had a good period, the so-called Blue Period, when he used to put a lot of blue in his paintings. Picabia is really much more talented and intelligent, but he is lazy. I was choosing paintings for an exhibition, and Picabia: 'No, not that one, it's one I've done in the country, no good.' And I: 'Well, at any rate, not this one.'

And he: 'No, that's a Picasso.' Picasso started out with serious intentions, but then the dealers set such high prices on his work which for obvious reasons they had to keep up — that he got so disgusted with the stupidity of the public and did whatever thing he liked." Very seldom a straight answer at first, but eventually he would return to my questions and say clearly: "Eyes of Picasso means that Picasso has eyes like a seal. So-shu is a Chinese mythological figure. Lir: probably Shakespeare's Lear is derived from him. Schoeney is to be found in Ovid, old spelling."

Unless I had reached some insurmountable impasse, I was not to show him my translation before having a full typed page. Invariably he set out to tear it to pieces. Gradually I realized that this was a way for him to reconstruct his own Cantos in Italian, a trying-out of his principles on translation with his own poetry. "How would the author express himself were he writing at this time in Italian?" In this particular case the author was of the opinion that Italian poetry had steadily gone downhill since Cavalcanti and Dante — with the exception of Leopardi — so he would tend to use their voice and modes rather than the contemporary language. If I ventured: *"Non si dice,"* he would say: "Time they did." Or, in a whining voice, teasing me: " *'Non si dice, non si dice'*: it's your job to put it into Italian." And then I'd go and ruin his rhythm.

Having taught myself to type with two fingers on one of Babbo's discarded old portable Corona typewriters, I cherished the childish notion that once a page looked neat one should not touch it again, but Babbo always would change around a word, scribble in an alternative: try it out. My slow, careful typing all messed up again. Eventually I developed a kind of fatalism: this is not the final version. It never was. And now I know that none of my translations are "finished." And how often have I heard Babbo quote Brancusi: *"Mais finir!"*

After several weeks I was told to try Canto 13; this was a
much easier one. Kung had become a beloved, familiar, figure.
The imagery in the Canto was clear, the thought of Confucius
— the way Babbo rendered it — was comprehensible and in
accord with the rules of daily life: order, discipline, sincerity
— it was in the air. I wonder if Babbo had made that air on
the hill of Sant' Ambrogio. Like Frobenius:

Der im Baluba das Gewitter gemacht hat . . .

in a different context but with the same magic?

Babbo was translating his English version of the *Great
Digest* into Italian and wrote: "The greatest gift I can give to
you, is the thought of Confucius."

— "The men of old wanting to clarify and diffuse throughout
the empire that light which comes from looking straight into
the heart and then acting, first set up good government in
their own states; wanting good government in their states,
they first established order in their own families; wanting order in the home, they first disciplined themselves; desiring
self-discipline, they rectified their own hearts; and wanting to
rectify their hearts, they sought precise verbal definitions of
their inarticulate thoughts [the tones given off by the heart];
wishing to attain precise verbal definitions, they set to extend
their knowledge to the utmost. This completion of knowledge
is rooted in sorting things into organic categories.

When things had been classified in organic categories,
knowledge moved toward fulfillment; given the extreme
knowable points, the inarticulate thoughts were defined with
precision [the sun's lance coming to rest in the precise spot
verbally]. Having attained this precise verbal definition [*aliter*,
this sincerity], they then stabilized their hearts, they disciplined themselves; having attained self-discipline, they set
their own houses in order; having order in their own homes,
they brought good government to their own states; and when

their states were well governed, the empire was brought into equilibrium.

From the Emperor, Son of Heaven, down to the common man, singly and all together, this self discipline is the root.

If the root be in confusion, nothing will be well governed. —

It was perhaps an unconscious dialogue and an attempt to educate and save the man who had asked him: Why do you want to put your ideas in order?

From Confucius back to the intricacies of the modern world and its revolutions. I was started in the middle of Canto 27.

Let the five last build the wall;

refers to the warriors in the Cadmus legend, the five who survived of those who had sprouted from the teeth Cadmus had scattered over the ground — the teeth of a monster he had killed with a stone.

And *tovarisch* is the Russian *compagno*. In Russia there is no civilization because there is no stone and they had a revolution without arriving at anything. Tovarisch is like the corn, unconscious; like the corn, being sowed in the earth and then baked and eaten —

And that tovarisch cursed and blessed without aim.

When the second half got into the flowing stage, I could start at the beginning of the Canto: 'Observed that the paint was — "refers to one of Kipling's naval reports." And they elected a Monsieur Brisset — "A damn country boor, intended to be a poet and they got him to Paris, all sorts of attentions and honors and I was passing through Paris at the time . . ." And then in more general terms he would explain: "You know how a fugue of Bach is composed, one instrument comes in and the others repeat the theme. The Cantos start with Homer, the descent into hell. Then a theme of Ovid — Dafne, my own myth, not changed into a laurel but into coral. And then Dante — Dante has said everything there is to be said, so I start with Malatesta . . ." I would jot down these notes as soon as I returned home after having walked down the hill with him. We switched to the Malatesta Cantos and Babbo turned up with books and documents; Yriarte's *History of Rimini* and his own notes. And I asked for Browning's *Sordello* and found it more difficult than the Cantos. Three volumes on the life and work of the troubadours became light reading. The more I got absorbed in the Cantos the more eager I became for further knowledge.

The pattern of our life, in its precariousness, had become set. By the beginning of 1943 the hope that England would, like France, surrender and America make peace with the Axis had almost vanished. It looked as though the war would go on forever.

The Germans started to retreat in Africa and in Russia; Voronezh, Tripolitania, abandoned. Stalingrad could not be taken. Feldmarschall Paulus decorated and then made a prisoner. A note of desperate optimism had crept into the news bulletins.

For Babbo, however the front shifted, the enemy was always in the same place, rooted. "The last American to live the tragedy of Europe" expresses it; and more and more "the lone ant" struggling to preserve his own ideas and visions — listening to a different drum.

A wave of horror swept over us when we heard about the Katyn massacres. The Italian papers showed gruesome pictures: thousands of Polish officers shot by the Russians and thrown into ditches, some while still alive. Of Auschwitz and Buchenwald we did not hear until after the war. Katyn was the first real horror report. Russian cruelty was easier to understand than England's connivance.

Babbo applied for a permit to join the International Investigation Commission as a neutral observer. The Polish Government in exile in London had requested such an investigation by the International Red Cross, I think. Babbo's motives for wanting to join it may have been, as usual, the man wanting the facts, wanting to see things with his own eyes; and possibly the hope: if he could tell the American people that this was not a propaganda stunt, his country would understand that the alliance with Russia was not a good bet.

He was preparing for a risky trip. He thought in case he was not allowed on the International Commission, he might be able to go on his own. For a few weeks we waited for an answer. Finally his request was turned down. I think Babbo had the vague suspicion that Italy did not trust him out of the country. Later the papers announced that Russia had refused to allow an investigation. By then the Germans had also given up Smolensk and were in full retreat.

or did they fall because of their loose taste in music
    'Here! none of that mathematical music!'
Said the Kommandant when Münch offered Bach to the
                    regiment

Gerhart Münch, with Mamile one of the regular performers at the Rapallo concerts, had been called up, as entertainer for the troops. He and his wife came for two days to Rapallo — from a world out of the past it seemed — on a short leave,

Gerhart
    art thou come forth out of Phlegethon?
with Buxtehude and Klages in your satchel, with the
Ständebuch of Sachs in yr/ luggage

a refreshing visit, but also one that stirred up perplexities.

A nation afraid of beauty and too rigid. Babbo could not refrain from telling a German officer who was lunching at the
Albergo Italia that they'd lose the war if they didn't learn to
bend their necks.

Rapallo had become a resort for the German army; one saw
quite a few uniforms around town and Babbo watched them
carefully and shook his head: they walk as though they had
swallowed a broomstick. You should see their necks at table,
stiff, stiff.

One day as we passed by the Capella di San Rocco on our
way to Rapallo, we saw a man on the other side of the street,
stretched out as though dead. Babbo rushed over to him and
the man started to shiver violently, upon which Babbo ran to
the nearest house, and banged on the door, and rang the bell
furiously. A woman came to the door. "Quick, some water, a
man is sick. Do you have a telephone?" The woman merely
looked up the street and said: "*Ah, quello lì fa apposta* — he
does it on purpose." But Babbo was firm: a glass of water,
please. He rushed back to the man and lifted his head and
made him drink. The man stopped shivering and stretched
out his hand to beg. Babbo gave him some lire and I took the
glass back to the house. The woman had not moved. "Only a
foreigner would be fooled," she exclaimed. Babbo merely said:
"Scusate, grazie." He seemed puzzled. So was I. It was the
only time I ever witnessed an Italian being nasty to Babbo. As
for being fooled by a tramp — we never mentioned the inci-

dent. It seemed to me as though Babbo attached some ill omen to it.

For Christmas 1942, together with *The Complete Works of Alfred Tennyson,* which had belonged to his grandmother, Mary Weston, Babbo had given me a thousand lire. This seemed to me, and in fact was, a handsome sum of money. "And what will you do with it?" was his question when I thanked him most enthusiastically. Money must be spent, money must circulate. — This gave me courage to venture: "I would like to go to Rome with you." It really was the only thing I wanted — to be with him and go around, as on previous occasions, to see his friends. I think Babbo was pleased with my request.

I felt that he had given me the money to encourage me in my work. I had by now three items which he thought were good enough for publication in the *Meridiano di Roma,* all done at his suggestion: a translation from Frobenius's *Erlebte Erdteile* on farming in Africa; the translation of a chapter from W. J. Gruffydd's David ap Gwilym in a Welsh and English edition. And an article of my own on folk customs in Gais — the Kirchtamichl, whom Babbo associated with John Barleycorn and with bacchic rites. He always suggested work that had a direct bearing on my own life and Gais background and at the same time that might be news to the Italian reader. When I first saw my name in print I was beyond myself with excitement; it was as though my life was made: *"traduzione di M. R."*

The piece on the *"Usanze in Alto Adige"* had been rejected, on grounds that it was not cultural enough. I did not mind; translating, I felt, was much more important, and Babbo agreed that this might be a way to earn my living and be useful. The two things went together: to be useful and to be self-sufficient. He probably had realized that I was a bit discouraged at not getting paid, though I had hardly dared hope I would ever get printed. He drove home to me that to be paid was fair only when the work was good enough.

In order to go to Rome, I had to overcome a series of difficulties. "The child has nothing to wear." We set to unpicking and dyeing the gray school uniforms; the material was good and a little seamstress on the *salita* turned them into wearable clothes. "You don't know what to do with your hair." — And I started practicing different coiffures. But above all: I was too plump according to measures set by *Vogue;* not graceful enough, my face had too much baby fat and too little expression. I did not know how to smile; one must learn how to move the muscles in one's face. — So the fencing and face-exercise period started. As soon as Babbo arrived, hop, with a broomstick: one two, keep your back straight, knees apart, down down. He pranced around and I was supposed to do likewise, but there seemed to be absolutely *no* space in the hall when he stretched out legs and arms. I had to practice in front of the looking glass. As soon as we would sit down for tea, again: "Loose, loose, knife in hand, the movement from the elbow, the movement from the shoulder." Babbo was extremely deft in these movements, whereas it seemed the more I was made to practice the stiffer my arm became. The worst of all was moving the face muscles: I felt embarrassed, but Babbo seemed ready to push his face into the most extraordinary grimaces to show me how the muscles worked. When on top of all this I was made to learn "The Hippopotamus" by heart in order to always bear in mind that

> *Flesh and blood is weak and frail,*
> *Susceptible to nervous shock*

I was almost ready to renounce my trip to Rome. — "If you want to go around with Babbo you *must* look pretty and well-groomed." By April it finally seemed that I had fulfilled Mamile's requisites and she gave me a lovely emerald ring to wear on my little finger.

In Rome I was to stay with her friend Nora Naldi. The train arrived four hours late because of air raids, in pouring rain and complete blackout. I did not look for Babbo outside the station as agreed and went straight to Nora's house, dashing for the last tram. Babbo had been waiting. Over the phone he said: *Oca* — goose — and hung up.

This was a bad start for my much-longed-for trip to Rome. I dreaded facing Babbo next day. Nora had invited him to lunch. She was a wonderful cook and prepared meals out of practically nothing; also she was cheerful and pretty, a petite English girl, married to a nice, but dull, Italian who worked in some government office. When Babbo arrived I saw he was still annoyed, but all he said was: "You missed a good dinner." However, by the end of the meal he was quite cheerful and told Nora he would bring me back in the evening. I would be eating out and there was someone he wanted me to meet in the afternoon. So things turned out the way I had hoped. We went to see Princess Troubetzkoi, a white Russian working at the Italian radio. Her special kind of propaganda consisted in making up optimistic sketches of life in Italy which she transmitted to Russia and to England; she was equally fluent in both languages. Babbo seemed a bit uncertain about her, but it was plain that she had a great liking for him and was eager to take me under her wing. She told me young people in Italy were wonderful, intelligent, serious, that all this talk about Fascist education being bad was nonsense. She would introduce me to some young friends of hers.

I spent my mornings in Rome walking around with a Baedeker. There was so much I wanted to see and find out. Babbo spent his mornings and most of his afternoons at the

Radio making records of his speeches, but we always met for lunch and dinner, his pockets bulging with manuscripts and a bundle of papers under his arm. Someone or other always gave him something or other to read, and I felt the pressure on him: his time was precious and short. I was relieved that after the first evening he gave up trying to "entertain" me and allowed me just to join him at meals whether he entertained someone at a restaurant or was asked out. The second day we had lunch at the San Carlo with Signora Agresti Rossetti. There was deep friendship between them, and she was one of the people he was most at ease with. She had a solid literary background, but at the same time was well informed about politics, economics and agriculture. She had been on lecture tours in America and in Russia, and with Henry Lubin she had set up the International Institute for Agriculture, which later became the F.A.O. There was great serenity and tolerance in her, except when she spoke of Roosevelt.

Two days later, on a Sunday afternoon, we went to her house for tea. There was quite a group of people — all men — in her drawing room. I seem to remember Camillo Pellizzi and Luigi Villari, officials of the Ministry of Culture. In their conversation, from historical topics to literature ancient and modern, they seemed equally at home in English, French, Latin. Pellizzi struck me as extremely witty and sarcastic, chewing on his pipe for a while before throwing out a remark. Villari spoke Italian with a British accent — his mother had been English — and he lowered his voice respectfully when mentioning some *gerarca*: Sua Eccellenza so and so. He was the only one to attempt mild jokes about prominent Jews. But Signora Agresti immediately silenced him. She strongly believed in cultural rather than racial values and above all in Italy's basic good sense. Her admiration for Mussolini was boundless. She had attentively studied the man and his politics —

'Will' said the Signora Agresti, 'break his political
but not economic system'

was the opinion she ventured.

After dinner we went to quite a different gathering, in the
house of Felice Chilanti in Via Frattina. The steps leading to
the flat and the room where we sat seemed dark and cramped
compared to the harmony and luminosity of Signora Agresti's
drawing room. We met a group of young people, enraged,
tense, opposed not so much to Mussolini and to Fascist ideology as to *"quel branco d'assassini intorno a Mussolini"* — the
assassins surrounding Mussolini, primarily Farinacci and
Ciano. They had a paper, *Origini*, on which they invited
Babbo to collaborate. He was tempted, for they advocated
freedom of speech, frank exchange of ideas between Fascists,
anti-Fascists and Marxists. But the situation was tricky. There
was an air of conspiracy. I heard the word *Resistenza* for the
first time. A new political movement?

"Sono svegli," Babbo said as we left. — Wide-awake, these
boys. But too violent for his taste. Chilanti's twelve-year-old
daughter had suggested Ciano should be poisoned:

'I would do it' (finish off Ciano) 'with a pinch of
    insecticide.'

But, crime is stupid, not the right way out. That Mussolini
did not have enough good men about him, there was no
doubt,

    . . . poor old Benito
            one had a safety-pin

one had a bit of string, one had a button
    all of them so far beneath him
half-baked and amateur
        or mere scoundrels

He witnessed discontent not only in these young people.

'If he wd/ *only* get rid of Ciano' groaned the admiral

— his good friend Ubaldo degli Uberti, also remembered for
his likeness with the ancestor mentioned by Dante:

. . . Farinata, kneeling in the cortile,
        built like Ubaldo, that's race . . .

Too bad that straight men — *galantuomini* — like the admiral
never got close enough to Mussolini.

'Ten men,' said Ubaldo, 'who will charge a nest of machine
                                                    guns
    for one who will put his name on chit'

was one of the troubles in those days.

After the secluded life in Rapallo, Rome and its political
unrest made me feel wide-awake. Babbo had many friends and
they all seemed eager to entertain and feed him; he always appreciated a good meal. One day we had lunch at Ranieri's
with the San Faustinos, cheerfully arriving on bicycles since
no more gasoline was being distributed for private cars. Rice
with spring peas — *enough* rice — and Babbo insisted that the
cook be called out and then complimented him for such a perfect risotto. We were asked to dinner by his old friends the
Monottis. Signora Monotti was charming and gay. There were

other guests, some newspapermen, one Hungarian. They showed great admiration for Babbo. He complimented the hostess for such an excellent meal in wartime, but when for dessert a bottle of champagne was brought in, in his honor, he clammed up, refused to drink and said none for me either. Protests and coaxing to no avail, he became quite angry and we left as soon as we got up from table. I felt sorry and embarrassed, the company seemed mortified and perplexed by his behavior. As we walked out of the house he said: *"Non è tempo per frivolezze"* — this is no time for frivolities.

Babbo went back to Rapallo before my week was up. Princess Troubetzkoi was to be my chaperone — she had arranged a picnic for me. It was to be a party of four: I was to meet some of her young friends: an Italian boy and a Czechoslovakian girl. They were engaged, she warned me. But at six o'clock in the morning, in front of the church where we had agreed to meet, only the boy showed up. His *fidanzata* had sprained her ankle. We took a train for Cori, an ancient town at an hour's distance from Rome with cyclopic walls and a temple to Juno. All my walks through the archaeological zones of Rome with my guidebook had given me but a slight feeling of atmosphere compared to what I experienced at Cori. The cobbled, steep, narrow streets, the enormous stones of the holding walls, the majestic perfection of the columns in Juno's temple filled me with awe; but above all the air, the sky and the hills. And I thought of Goethe's Roman sonnets. Looking for the landscape of familiar poems, comparing lines with what I saw, had become a habit — or following some Roman itinerary as described by Henry James — just like translating, comparing sounds in English and Italian, even when I was not completely alone. Fortunately the Princess's young friend turned out to be an attentive listener, full of imagination, mythology and ancient history, and, as soon as I gave him a chance, he was also an enticing and brilliant talker. While we sat in a field by the round wall of an old well eating our picnic lunch, a Cociaro joined us, out of nowhere it seemed. No, not a faun or a god in disguise, though nothing would have seemed more natural to us, but the owner of the field, friendly, eager to talk. "If only one could give Italian and Russian peasants a chance to talk to each other!" Princess Troubetzkoi remarked. "Above all to young people." She was already mentally composing a new sketch for her broadcasts, and described it to the Cociaro: the temple of Juno, the peaceful, clear spring day, an Italian farmer, Giovanni, and her young friends: a boy, Boris, with an Italian father and a Russian mother, a girl, Mary, with American parents, brought up in Italy, all understanding and liking each other. Why wars?

Always back on the same question: Why wars? And Babbo's answers seemed the only ones to make any sense: an economic system by which a group of financiers lusting for power manipulated wars according to their interests. The peasant thought this might well be the answer. He too was of the opinion that Mussolini would have preferred to let his people work in peace conducting only *la battaglia del grano* — fighting hunger. He then asked us to his house, in a narrow street in town, up steep steps. Yes, it could well be of Roman construction, the vaulted kitchen. His wife was friendly too, deplored the war, offered homemade bread with a few drops of olive oil and slices of onions; and it tasted so wonderful I have never forgotten it. She would not accept money, but then sold us some cottage cheese.

After such a sunny, idyllic day in a landscape softer, more luminous and tolerant than the hills of Liguria, it seemed incongruous to hear the sirens as soon as we got back to town. That night the Allies flew over Rome and dropped propaganda leaflets: Africa was in their hands, Italy should surrender. According to the Italian papers and to talk in the streets, they also dropped fountain pens and similar objects that exploded as soon as one picked them up.

Back in Rapallo I returned to my studies and work with greater eagerness. On and off Mamile and I would go for a swim early in the morning, to the Pozzetto or to the little bay halfway between Rapallo and Zoagli. We never lingered on the beach, for there were soldiers stationed along the railroad close by, and on the beach itself high cement walls had been set up. All the coast was heavily guarded. In Africa the Germans kept retreating and Allied air raids had started over Genoa.

Babbo brought me more and more books to read: *La Sibylle* by Zielinski; *The Enormous Room; The White Mule;* Yeats's *Plays* and the *Noh Plays*. Of his own work: *Gaudier-Brzeska,* and *The Chinese Written Character*. The latter shed light for me in many ways on the Cantos and also on his conversation. I must have told him so — he suggested I translate *The Chinese Written Character* into Italian. And of *Cathay:* Try "The Lament of the Frontier Guard," suitable for our times. I worked on the poem for a few weeks and he was pleased with the result and thought he might be able to get it published. He brought me also three letters that Thomas Hardy had written to him, to read and to copy for myself. He treasured them greatly:

> so that leaving America I brought with me $80
>   and England a letter of Thomas Hardy's
>   and Italy one eucalyptus pip
> from the salita that goes up from Rapallo . . .

Mamile continued to play the violin for him and had now started translating too — a pamphlet by Arthur Kitson. She was reading through all sorts of books, mostly history, looking for facts that supported Babbo's ideas, supplying new items for his speeches. Speeches and articles had to be written regularly; we now all depended on them for our subsistence.

In July, Mamile thought I should go back to Gais for a month or so: a change of air would do me good; I would get more to eat there, and at the same time could leave my ration card behind and it would mean a little extra for Babbo. He was not getting enough to eat and he was overworking. Translating Confucius into Italian, writing pamphlets on the causes of war; writing the radio speeches and articles for the *Meridiano di Roma,* translating Enrico Pea's *Moscardino* into English —

"Trying to save the world." And one felt that the pressure — inside, outside? — and the seriousness of purpose and dedication were such as to turn the hyperbole into an understatement.

I would have preferred to stay on in Sant' Ambrogio, not to interrupt my own struggle to grasp, to catch glimmers of his thoughts. I had come to hope that someday, if I followed him closely, I might understand everything he said and wrote, all the references and shades of meaning. The sincerity of his expressions and intentions conferred such dignity upon him that I felt sure he was enunciating eternal truths. The beauty of it was that he believed it too. It never occurred to me at the time that the Axis might not win. But "victory" had become something so abstract that it seemed not to matter which side won. *Il nemico è l'ignoranza* — ignorance was the enemy. And usury the cause of all wars.

Again and again he told me that, as soon as he had turned his thoughts to monetary problems, to the causes of wars, the British and American publishers had turned their backs on him. They were ready to reprint his "*pipi*" — that is how he referred to his early work — but nothing serious, nothing that might rouse people into thinking about economic matters. What is money for, where does it come from, who issues it? The terminology about money and credit was so damn obscure, no one understood anything about it. And it was not his job but the job of economists to attend to the details. Italy and Germany at least had some honest economists; he thought people in the government, like Rossoni and Delcroix, had understood the mechanism of money-scrip — *"moneta prescrittibile, Schwundgeld."*

Rossoni: 'così lo stato . . .' etcetera
   Delcroix: 'che magnifica!'
       (prescrittibile)

 If money were based on work done, the gold standard abolished, and money itself taxed . . . Sometimes it seemed as though he had it all clearly worked out, could submit it in a simple sentence to the Duce, who would have it enacted. And all mankind would benefit from it. If he succeeded in putting the mosaic of his economic theories into a clear pattern, the working people would no longer be cheated by financiers, the general public would have insight and therefore control over their money and credit.

     Hath benefit of interest on all
the moneys which it, the bank, creates out of nothing.

      "Very few people
"will understand this. Those who do will be occupied
"getting profits. The general public will probably not
"see it's against their interest."

In our land of utopia I had followed him thus far. His aim was precise:

> Bellum cano perenne . . .
> > . . . between usura and the man who
> wants to do a good job

For this battle he availed himself of the Italian microphone and of the Italian newspapers, with total disregard of his own welfare. He thought only downright corruption and malice — and stupidity, of course — prevented people from seeing, and therefore fighting, the true causes of war.

But there was an inner, metaphysical war going on at the same time, over which he had no power. The usury of time itself was at work inside him.

Time is the evil. Evil.
. . . Geryon twin with usura

He was losing ground, I now see, losing grip on what most specifically he should have been able to control, his own *words*.

lord of his work and master of utterance

— he was that no longer. And perhaps he sensed it and the more strongly clung to the utterances of Confucius, because his own tongue was tricking him, running away with him, leading him into excess, away from his pivot, into blind spots. I know no other explanation for some of his violent expressions — perhaps he felt the exasperation at not being able to

[173]

get his real meaning across. The long hostility of his country must have weighed heavily upon him, but he remained free from self-pity. I think Babbo was as little eager for me to go back to Gais as I was. On the other hand, Gais still stood for security, the only place where food and a welcome were assured. Besides, underlying his teaching was the belief that one should never be separated from the soil for too long; to grow things should be one's primary concern, especially in times when food was scarce.

And so in July 1943 I went — "for a month or two" — but in a sense it was for good.

6. After working for about a month in the fields I felt a strong desire for complete relaxation in an *Alm*. An *Alm* is a pasture dairy, a small hut in the high mountains where the big farmers take their cattle for the summer. As a rule these huts are quite isolated, but just beyond the Italian border is a little hamlet composed exclusively of such dairies and therefore inhabited only during the summer months. After the First World War, when the new international boundaries were fixed, no account was taken of this pasture, and the Pustertal farmers were separated from their property by the frontier; later, arrangements were made and the shepherds

and cattle drivers were given passports, but everything was strictly controlled, especially on account of smugglers of saccharine and tobacco and political offenders. Nevertheless there were several small paths which expert mountaineers secretly used, unknown to the Italian guards.

This hamlet, called Jagdhaus — Hunting House — was always spoken of as something like an earthly paradise. Mamme had been there as *Sennerin* — dairymaid — when she was a girl, and her eldest brother still owned a hut, and he had often invited me. Mamme had succeeded in getting a passport for herself; the doctor had prescribed high mountain air. I made up my mind to follow her on the first Sunday in August, no matter how.

Luise, Herr Bacher's niece, had a permit to go over for a fortnight, during the haymaking in the mountain-meadows. She was my special friend and knew a girl in Uttenheim with a similar permit who was ready to lend it to me — it was a bit out of date and the girl in question only fourteen, but her picture bore a vague resemblance to me if I put on a very stiff peasant dress and did my hair in two braids wrapped tightly around my head. We set out on a Sunday, long before sunrise — a camera, forbidden in wartime, hidden in the rucksack. Everybody had made fun of us when we told them our plans; they said we would never dare do such a thing.

At seven we were in Rain. We attended Mass, had our breakfast and resumed our march. Now we would have to reckon with a frontier guard any minute and it was still a six-hour walk to the pass. After two hours, at a sudden turn in the path, we found ourselves close to three customs officials going in the same direction. They walked very slowly and the only thing to do was to double our pace and pass them boldly, as if we had as much right as they to be on that road. I was afraid of never reaching the frontier if I ever had to show my passport. We overtook them and they saluted very cordially. We passed on, pushing them aside. They made some remark about our impetuosity, but did not call us back.

When we had reached the Knutten, a group of four huts half an hour from the frontier, we sat down and fortified ourselves for the last push with *Speck* — the good Tyrolean smoked ham — eggs and bread. As we were packing our rucksacks again, a guard suddenly stood before us — I never understood where he came from — and asked where we were going. "Jagdhaus" — and Luise burst into a sort of nervous laughter at which the man asked for the passports. I started blowing my nose and stuck my head as deep into the rucksack as possible, feeling his eyes fixed on my back and my cheeks burning. He remarked that I looked very old for my age, that the photograph didn't do me credit at all. Without turning I asked if that was meant as a compliment, if so, he was very kind. Luise started to giggle again and the man must have thought he or I was being witty and returned the passport, rather distracted. Now I turned bold and asked how far it was, and whether there were any shortcuts, etc. He was very polite, taken in, I believe, by my good Italian accent. Still, when we separated, he said, "I am not quite convinced that that passport is yours." I reassured him with a smile and moved on as quickly as possible.

A shallow green lake at the foot of a horseshoe gap marks the end of the country. Klamml, it is called, and a dull gray tollhouse spoils this perfectly beautiful spot, together with the usual flag one finds wherever three Italians get together.

At the opening of the adjoining valley stands a little shrine and there Mamme had assembled all the shepherds, for it was Sunday, a good day for a procession. A group of *Alpini* watched our approach and when they moved towards us the shepherds started yodeling; so did I, jumping over the boundary stone and dancing around with Mamme. The *Alpini* checked the passports which Luise held out to them triumphantly once I was near the shrine. They were rather puzzled at my enthusiasm and looked at us with envy.

On the way back to the hamlet the procession had naturally turned into a merry walk and the little boy who had the privilege of carrying the leading cross found it rather an awkward object, as he had still to hold it in a dignified manner. In the evening no allowance was made for our weariness and after a strengthening *Melchamuis,* the traditional food of an *Alm* made with butter, flour, milk and more butter, the cowherds came to fetch us to another hut, where the entrance-kitchen-dining room had a wooden floor and one could dance. It was a great event having two girls among them, so they shaved, washed their ears and necks, and put on clean shirts and the leather breeches, well smeared with butter.

We finally and literally hit the hay after midnight, its smell of sunshine dissipating all weariness. In the morning when I awoke I saw the sun burst through the clefts of the brown boards like gold dust. To my left, three imprints of human bodies in the hay: a long one, Heinrich the herdsman's; a short one, Nikl's (the little shepherd who had carried the cross); and close at hand, a roundish one, Mamme's. In the distance one heard cattle bells of different tones, mixed with the bubbling of the nearby rivulet. The hamlet was deserted during the day.

When the sun went down and the mountaintops put on a hood of very delicate mist, the cows and calves streamed in from every direction, mixing their мuuu*hh's* with the *"Kuis, Kuis"* of their drivers, to an accompaniment of bells. Those still far away yodeled, thus signifying that they were all right and would come soon.

Luise and I didn't do much mowing, we spent most of our

time plucking edelweiss, rambling around the bulky mountains, too high for any trees to grow; only bushes of rhododendron could stand that keen air. Once we pushed along in the Deferegger Valley till we reached St. Peters, the first Austrian village; only a few miles separated us from Lienz, but as the German guards were much stricter we didn't dare go any farther: we had already been stopped once but had the excuse that our papers were left at the hut.

One of our greatest pleasures was churning the butter — heaps of fragile snow changing slowly into white clay, wherein one could plunge one's hands and make little puppets with it, finally molding the whole into an enormous plump egg, passing a wooden roller over it, crosswise, with imprints of edelweiss, cows, and roses.

The following Sunday the priest from Rain came for his monthly visit. We wondered what he would say on finding two girls, but he proved to be a right sensible man and started his sermon by quoting an old Tyrolese folksong, *"Auf dr' Alm gibs koa Sünd"* — there is no sinning in an alpine dairy — which must be true, for he showed a perfectly satisfied face, after having heard twenty male and three female confessions.

I had almost forgotten that there was a war going on, but that evening, as we sat all gaily together, the priest among us, beating his foot to our dancing, two frontier guards came in and said that a German airplane had crashed in the vicinity. Apparently it hit against a high mountain and caught fire. The priest and the men lit their lanterns and rushed out of the hut, while we were told to remain with the old man.

Two days later seven coffins arrived from Lienz with a squadron of aviators. On their way out, the procession stopped for a short rest outside the hamlet chapel singing *"Ich hatt' einen Kameraden."*

The end of our holiday was drawing near. Indeed, I had no

great desire to stay on much longer after this calamity. The day before our departure we went far into the pastures to pick edelweiss, for we wanted to bring home a conspicuous trophy. Thomas went with us because the really beautiful white velvet stars grow in the most dangerous places and one must know the spots. He was a young farmer on long leave, having lost his left arm in Poland. With his help we filled a whole basket with edelweiss, rhododendrons, gentians and several other kinds of mountain flowers and healing herbs — giving out a most intoxicating, honey-like scent. We put them in the cheese room, on the windowsill, and in the afternoon two severe German frontier guards entered the hut and asked for explanations . . . They had looked through the window to see Heinrich's cheeses — three boards stacked with wheels of different colors and sizes are a beautiful sight. But the scene was hidden by our flowers. After long and rather flirtatious entreaties we were, however, allowed to keep our flowers and brought them home safely. By law one was not allowed to pluck more than twelve edelweiss: they were becoming very rare.

Next morning early the cows were driven southward, for that was our direction, and most of the young men accompanied us halfway to the little shrine. In Taufers we caught the last train; we were glad enough to save two more hours' walk; here the air seemed heavy and the scenery flat.

Margit was waiting for me at the station. Strange. And Mamme? She was staying on for another week or so. Margit burst into loud lament and said if that was so, she was afraid to go home. What was the matter? "Yesterday afternoon Töite had to cover him with a veil." Cover whom? "Tatte, he looked dead." I was full of sun and fatigue, for a while I did not grasp. Then things unraveled as we walked towards our house. A few days after I left, Tatte got a *Hexenschuss* — he had strained his back. Common enough; it happened so often that a bottle of larch oil was kept on the shelf. But it was Mamme who had always rubbed his back with the oil and she was not there. Margit did not do it right. Next day Tatte went around all twisted with terrible pains; then he took to bed. Margit called the Töite. She massaged him and gave him schnapps and probably a good dose of verbal venom about his wife — what business had she to leave him alone and go and have a good time in the *Alm?*

That there was no love lost between Mamme and her sister-in-law was an old story, but it was not until Mamme had turned her back that Töite could stab her. And Tatte fell a victim — to jealousy. He stopped eating. He could not sleep. Very early one morning, he had crawled toward the river. Luckily Margit had heard him and dragged him back into bed. He had yelled at her that he wanted to drown himself, and she had been frightened ever since. This morning, though, he had seemed better; he had got up and shaved and put on his Sunday clothes and had sat all day on the bench in front of the house, waiting for Mamme. She had again been so scared when she saw him with the razor in his hands. She had then hidden it, also the kitchen knife.

A silhouette, Tatte's shade, got up from the bench: *"Wou isch die Mamme?"* "She sends greetings. She will come next week. The weather was so lovely. I persuaded her to stay on. To recover once and for all . . ." He fled into the house shouting: "Where is a rope, quick, give me a rope. I'll put an end to this." I grabbed him, he was so thin and frail — and yet so strong. We coaxed him into bed, I sat by him for a while, I said I was going back straightaway, that Mamme would come tomorrow, we had no idea he was ill. Finally he seemed asleep. How was such a thing possible? Barely two weeks, and he seemed to have lost all flesh and all color. His eyes were sunken in and his nose yellow and pointed, as sharp as a sickle. To my few questions Margit had no answer. It all started with a *Hexenschuss* and ended in an insane jealousy. Margit used different words for it: *"Vodruss, doloadit."* I was too tired and worried and sad to think or undress. I just threw off my walking shoes and lay down on the couch in the living room, in half sleep, waiting to get up for the early train to Taufers.

I had not thought things through. All I knew was that I must hurry. I was a different girl from the gay carefree creature of yesterday, walking through that endless silent wood. I felt so driven I hardly noticed the passing of time. And I no longer felt weary; on flat stretches I ran. On the border the police recognized me. No fooling this time. They did not even try to stop me, they must have read on my face that I was on an urgent, legitimate errand. I was back in Jagdhaus before lunch. And Mamme at first did not believe that I had been home. Then she realized there was no time to lose. She changed her shoes and instructed Heinrich to send her things after her. And we were in Taufers in time to catch the last train, having prayed a few rosaries on the way, but mostly hurrying and Mamme lamenting: "And just as I was feeling better, *a sella Molleh* — such a *malheur.*"

Tatte was again sitting on the bench. He moved towards us. *"Iz pische wo dechto a mo kemm!"* *"Jo, a sella Limml, hosche gimoant i kimm nimma?"* In plain words: "Finally!" "You silly." I had heard it often enough, but I had never seen Mamme and Tatte fall on each other's necks, and Mamme sobbing against him . . . Two different human beings sat down in front of the house and held each other's hand and talked in low soft voices. I went into the kitchen with Margit; she had dinner waiting on the stove. "Even now no one comes to eat!" I tried a few spoonfuls. We were too embarrassed to talk; sitting on the chicken coop I just stared into the dying

[182]

embers. Margit went outdoors: "Don't you want something to eat?" "Yes, yes, we'll come presently." Margit came back with a look of relief on her face: *"Iz rachta wo widdo!"* The crisis was over. Tatte had lit his pipe. Such peace; I had earned my rest. My muscles hurt for a few days, otherwise life continued as though nothing had happened. Tatte ate and was cheerful and followed Mamme around the house as much as he could — she had made him feel a bit guilty. Such a fuss! but it was more in jest and to keep her countenance that she said it.

I thought I might be going back to Rapallo any day and was waiting for a letter. We had no radio; the news had to go through many distortions before truth could be inferred. But gradually it became clear that Italy had surrendered, that Italy had gone over to the other side, that the Germans had taken over. I wondered how all this would affect Babbo. But there was nothing to do except to continue working in the fields. The great excitement in Gais was getting rid of the carabinieri.

One midmorning Mamme joined us with milk and bread for our snack, and when we were all seated on the edge of the field around the big wooden bowl she said that a German truck was stationed in front of the carabinieri's house with six German soldiers standing guard. Tatte's eyes burned with curiosity; he went back to his hoe and rushed along the furrow as though digging for news instead of beets. Finally lunchtime came and we hurried toward the village. Ân irregular crowd of onlookers had gathered in front of the police station. Presently Herr Bacher came down the outside wooden staircase of the building, a gun on his shoulder, followed by four carabinieri, Moar and a German sergeant. The brigadier was missing. They went to look for him at his mistress's house. She had hidden him. Tatte thought it was wiser to leave. "You never can tell, the carabinieri might come back. And if they do, I would not like to be in Bacher's or Moar's place." The Germans threw the carabinieri's guns and pistols in the back of the truck and departed. Herr Bacher escorted the disarmed men on foot to the German Command in Bruneck. Their luggage was taken after them in Moar's horse cart.

Even internal correspondence was censored, so one did not spend much time writing letters. Thus I do not know how the news of Mussolini's fall — shortly after I left Rapallo — had affected Babbo. He never had a high opinion of Badoglio, that I know, and of the Savoia:

'tranne nella casa del re'
B. Mussolini

A breach of hospitality in the house of the King, a trap laid for the man from whom the title of Emperor had been accepted and at whose side some members of the family had fought, who had brought order into a demoralized and disoriented country — Babbo registered and probably shared the Duce's shock. Mussolini was prepared for treachery, but not on the King's doorstep.

Babbo had returned to Rome after the regime fell and the events of September caught him unprepared.

September 3: Allied troops land in Italy
September 8: Italy surrenders
September 10: The Germans take over Rome.

The afternoon following the arrest of the Italian police, I had been to Uttenheim on my bicycle to return my borrowed pass. A carefree and lovely September day. But my heart sank when, from a distance, I saw Mamme standing at the corner of the house as though on the lookout for me, her hands curiously wrapped up in her apron, which I knew to mean she was upset and trembling. I feared something might have happened to Tatte. Although he had been cheerful ever since Mamme's return, I was still apprehensive. As I halted my bicycle: *"Iz isch 's Tattile kemm!"* She saw I did not grasp, I had Tatte on my mind. — *"Do Hearr!"* — *" 's Tattile?"*

'Grüss Gott', 'Der Herr!' 'Tatile ist gekommen!'

"Yes, he walked into the kitchen and I did not recognize him, I said to myself: what new beggar is this? Then he said: Grüss Gott, and I recognized his voice: Der Herr! He said: *Wo ist Moidile?* and I said you had gone to Uitnom and would be back any moment. I gave him water to wash with; he was all covered in dust, like a beggar. Like a beggar, but he wouldn't eat anything. He said: *Müde.* He is lying down on your bed."

I ran upstairs. A long silent embrace. Finally I managed to speak: How did you get here, where from? And he pointed to his feet, red, full of blisters, his ankles swollen.

"I walked out of Rome." And slowly he told me of the confusion at the Radio offices as soon as it became known that the Allies had landed. All the high officials moving out of Rome, some to the south, some to the north. No one thought of him. He returned to the Albergo Italia to pay his bill and leave the small leather case and the black cane and his wide-brimmed Borsalino hat with the clerk at the desk. Then he went to the degli Ubertis'. They lent him a pair of walking boots — which did not fit him as he thought at first, hence the blisters — a narrow-brimmed, unobtrusive hat and a knapsack. He stopped to say goodbye at Nora Naldi's; he wanted to let Mamile's friend know his whereabouts. He told them he was going to see his daughter in Gais. They tried to dissuade him, offered to put him up until one knew what was going to happen. The war might be over in a few days, things might return to normal. No. He accepted two eggs which Nora prepared for him and walked out of Rome.

He said I should study the map which he pulled out of his knapsack. A very detailed map which the degli Ubertis had given him, full of his own markings and comments written on the margin and on the back. "And only in Verona it dawned upon me that this was a military map and if they caught me with it they might have taken me for a spy." The predicament he was in was almost grotesque, even to his own eyes. During the following days we went over that map very carefully; once his weariness had been conquered he seemed proud of his feat. He had not walked all the way, naturally. Bologna had been the last precarious place. He had slept in an air raid shelter. From Bologna to Verona it was all one stretch by train, in Verona he spent a day trying to come to a decision as to what he should do — keep going north or take a train to Milan; a few trains were running, perhaps as far as Rapallo. The situation seemed under control, under German control. He decided he would stick to his original plan and come and see me first; he had something important to tell me.

And after I had brought him supper and Mamme and Tatte had come in to wish him goodnight, failing utterly to hide their perplexity and curiosity as to what had happened, what would happen, but repressing all questions, so that he should have a good rest — he started to talk. "Sit down and put out the light." His eyes were smarting.

"I don't know how much of this you already suspect, the doors at Sant' Ambrogio are not exactly soundproof." No, those doors did not close very well, but I had never overheard any conversation between him and Mamile. I felt he almost wished I had, it might have made things simpler for him. Not only did I show no curiosity, but I was completely unsuspecting about what was on his mind. He tossed about for a beginning. Where? When? And it was almost three o'clock in the morning when he finally thought he had said everything, "*Mi par d'aver detto ogni cosa*" — though the following days he returned to the subject several times. Now I learned that in Rapallo there was also a wife. His wife, with a son in England. The news was not imparted as a secret, simply as facts that I was only now old enough to understand. Things would be set right — "If this war ever ends . . ." All plain and simple. I felt no resentment, only a vague sense of pity.

Buona notte. Buon riposo. I tiptoed into Margit's room. She groaned and moved over in her bed.

THE GOAT SONG

All plain and simple. But that was not the way it worked out. I had heard the goat song. I had a glimpse of the madness and the vision: Zeus-Hera-Dione. Whose madness? Whose vision?

"And Agatha spoke like the goat, *bhê bhê,* and the goat sang *Goas Goas.*" Gais, a new northern Dodona where we listen to the swish of the river under elms, to the rustling of an old oak tree.

The deed comes before the word. Each country pays in its own coin: a piglet for new year's luck, a lamb for spring resurrection, a goat for the song.

[187]

The scapegoat gnaws and gnaws late into the autumn. With wind-ruffled feathers the black dove coos in the willow. Though the temple is destroyed, the Oracle still mutters by the pool. Outis, Outis on a short visit. By no means imaginary.

One disloyalty provokes another. One cannot transfer affection. The old people's pain is one's curse and one's character the doom. One cannot transfer affection. To Euripides and Hermione a clap of thunder out of a clear sky. And sorrows. Why continue the deception for so long?

Les larmes que j'ai créés m'inondent

There is no rogue in this play.

Only sorrow, until the tragedy turns to farce. Catharsis. Catharsis: the voice: "Don't lose your sense of humor!" And I: "Don't make use of the dead!"

Years later, in London, at the Etoile, in front of a dainty dish of seagull's eggs in cream-sauce, Mr. Eliot posed questions about mountain goats: Are they black or white? Do they have horns?

There is no such play for a goat. Nor evidence in archives. Who will write it down? Who will write it?

'The Africans have more sense than the greeks.' More sense than the white men? Perhaps they will unravel the record.

❧

Somewhere between Mamme and Tatte's world on earth and God in Heaven there was an island of demigods not ruled by human laws. Here the range of imagination was wider, feelings more passionate and ruthless. Long before I had been fascinated by oracles, doom, hubris; before I had been made aware of and warned against Freudian trends and the dangers of oversimplification, I had felt uneasy with Mamile. "The impossibility of winning the mother's affection" was a fact now named. She had wanted a son. A torchbearer. Babbo's candor sustained me and his vision:

A little light, like a rushlight
            to lead back to splendour.

Splendour, it all coheres. The dark echoes of the threat ". . . Thy truth then be thy dower!" did not reach me in Lear's voice.

Every myth I came to know I believed in, and lived through, giving it new twists. This did not interfere with the plane of daily life, nor with my Catholicism. Moreover, during the past two years in Sant' Ambrogio I had come to enjoy and be eager to participate in Babbo's work through translation, to understand some of his ideas and theories through study. This meant more to me than being legitimate or illegitimate. Records would have to be set straight, eventually, simply because it was in keeping with the norm. Falsification of history, falsification of records tied up with:

'And if a man have not order within him
'His family will not act with due order. . . .

What carried weight in my life then was Babbo's inner order; everything would forever depend on that. Later remembering:

What thou lovest well is thy true heritage

Many shades of emotion will remain hidden, embedded in the Cantos as mythology, since poetry is the true medium for truth. Prose fits facts, but facts carry little weight, they can simply be recorded as part of "the tale of the tribe."

And the trip out of Rome we find best described in the Cantos:

> the man out of Naxos past Fara Sabina
> 'if you will stay for the night'
> 'it is true there is only one room for the lot of us'
> 'money is nothing'
> 'no, there is nothing to pay for that bread'
> 'nor for the minestra'
> 'Nothing left here but women'
> 'Have lugged it this far, will keep it' (il zaino)
> No, they will do nothing to you.
> 'Who *says* he is an American'
> a still form on the branda, Bologna
> 'Grüss Gott', 'Der Herr!' 'Tatile ist gekommen!'

After a few days, word must have gotten around and reached the *Ortskommandantur* about the foreigner in our house. The commissioner from Bruneck, Herr Bernardi the butcher, and Herr Bacher came to our house. They were old friends, but Mamme and Tatte looked frightened when they entered with rifles over their shoulders. In times like these *"woass man nio"* — one never knows.

"Who is this man out of Italy who says he is an American? What business can anyone like that have in Gais?" The beginning was thus peremptory. *"Inso* Moidile's Tatte, you know the Herr, you must have seen him, he came often before the war. *A gscheido,* the intelligent tall blond Herr, he has aged a lot, you might not recognize him. Moidile, go and fetch him." It was Mamme dealing with them. Babbo came down-stairs smiling, ready to show his documents. But his *Ausweis* made as little sense as his being "our" daughter's father. The only damaging thing in the eyes of Tyroleans was that he came out of Italy and showed an Italian Radio and Press mem-bership card which allowed him to travel at reduced rates, in short, that he was connected with Italy. Although the news of Mussolini's liberation by a German helicopter, the resurrection of the Fascist regime and its renewed pledge of alliance to Ger-many had become official news, for Tyroleans the enemy num-ber one was always Italy: they still felt revengeful and arro-gant.

But what to make of a man who was clearly not Italian, not a spy, not a Fascist, not a Jew? Too bad he had spoken over Radio Rome. That was because he believed in the Axis. But Tyroleans did not. Actually, even if they now thought of themselves as Nazis, they admired Americans; they could not even pretend otherwise, especially Herr Bacher, since he had a brother in America and was proud of it.

The investigation was soon over. They started to discuss politics in general. Tatte was an expert in leading any con-versation on to politics; he was genuinely curious and Bacher knew it. And der Herr was equally expert in leading the con-versation from politics to economics. The Wörgl experiment, which no one in the South Tyrol had heard of, seemed very interesting: a Bürgermeister's horse sense could be trusted. Very interesting, very, but what connection has this with the war, this is not war propaganda, what did you say in your broadcasts to America? That America should either keep out of European affairs or else help the Axis win the war against Russia. The discussion went on and on

So that after two hours entered der Schwiegersohn,
    considered the family's low in intelligence:
        'Was sagt er?'
Herr Marcher: Der Jud will Geld.

Herr Marcher — Tatte — summed it all up: the Jew wants
money, to his brother-in-law (not *Schwiegersohn*), whose single dangling Thaler on the watch-chain shifted interest from
paper money and stamp-scrip to the

Thalers from Maria Theresa . . .
        and they forged those Thalers, in our time,
                                    quest'oggi
Brits did, nacherly Brits did.

All the while Herr Bacher was studying Babbo's head. The
artist was triumphing over the improvised patriot and Nazi
official. Had he been a Gaudier he might have started carving
his rifle butt with a penknife. "What a head!" — *an interes-
santer Kopf* — applied to both shape and content. He invited
the Herr to his studio, and it was strange going there with
Babbo the following afternoon. Although I had been as a
child with Tatte to listen to the radio, in the *Stübile,* and to
see Bacher's nieces, in the kitchen or their *Stube,* I had never
set foot in the big hall where Bacher kept his father's carvings
and his own and his brother's.

But Herr Bacher's father made madonnas still in the
                                    tradition
carved wood as you might have found in any cathedral
        and another Bacher still cut intaglios
            such as Salustio's in the time of Ixotta,
where the masks come from, in the Tirol,

And that a Madonna novecento

cd/ be as a Madonna quattrocento
This I learned in the Tirol

And Babbo speculated: would Herr Bacher take him on
as an apprentice? It might be interesting to see what he could
do with his hands, he had tried marble once — in Brancusi's
studio, or while Gaudier was chiseling away at his marble
head; I forget. — Or perhaps, under the circumstances, he
might be more suited for the sawmill, physical labor might be
better. And so we walked to the sawmill at the foot of the
mountain. I could not visualize Babbo lifting tree trunks and
boards in the roaring noise and velocity of that mill and said
so, venturing advice. He told me of his grandfather's lumber
business; of how he had watched the trunks float down the
river . . . But had he ever tried handling trunks? No. To
the owner of the mill he looked strong enough; they were in
need of help, the sons were in the war, one already killed in
Russia. He would rest another couple of days, and in case he
should stay on, we would call again.

In the meantime Babbo could not conceive of remaining
idle. He looked around the house for things to mend and got
to work on the staircase, to Mamme's great delight and Tatte's
fun. "See! the Herr has been in the house for a few days and
has already done what I told you to do twenty years ago and
ever since!" To Tatte's embarrassment, Babbo insisted on eating at table with us and he fully participated in the family's
life and conversation, absorbing, to some extent, the Tyrolean
point of view:

hence the valise set by the alpino's statue in
Brunick

> and the long lazy float of the banners
> and similar things occurred in Dalmatia
> > lacking that treasure of honesty
> which is the treasure of states
> > for the dog-damn wop is not, save by exception,
> honest in administration any more than the briton is truthful

The monument to the *Alpini* in the Piazza in Bruneck has always been one of the Tyrolean targets for anti-Italian manifestations. In September 1943 they placed beside it an empty valise, to remind Italians it was time to pack up and leave.

The morning after Babbo had arrived I went to Bruneck to send a wire to Mamile, giving news and requesting Papier Faillard bandages for Babbo's feet. I had no great hope that the telegram would reach its destination, but it did, and after a few days we received a letter with the Papier Faillard. Ever since their French walking tour they swore by this onionskin and kept a supply, probably more for keepsake than actual use. Mamile wrote that things were calm in Rapallo, and Babbo's vague plans to settle down in Gais to manual labor were promptly dismissed. We had been to the *Ortskomandantur* in Bruneck — the old Hotel Post — for an *Aufenthaltsbewilligung*. Herr Bernardi introduced us to his brother who was the Ortskomandant: and why not go to Berlin? That was the place for such a brain, the German Rundfunk! Babbo merely blinked in friendly fashion. Mamme's levelheaded brothers kept repeating: A man like this should go to Switzerland, he was wasting his time in Italy; besides, the Tyrol was not a safe place for him with all the confusion and political wobbling. They would show him how to get to Switzerland.

No, he would return to Rapallo. And we went to Bruneck again, this time for a permit to leave. They were reluctant, could not allow him to go outside the Provinz Bozen. We

might try the Gauleiter. And could I return to Rapallo with
him? "No, better wait and see, you are better off with the
Marchers." But I accompanied him to Bozen. The city looked
desolate.

'Das heis' Walterplatz'
heard in Bozen (Bolzano)

no longer Piazza della Vittoria. Nor did we go for lunch to
the Greif, occupied by German commandos and officers.
Babbo was depressed and bewildered by the arrogant mili-
taristic atmosphere. I did the talking. "Look here — this man
has to catch a train!" Catching a train seemed to carry some
prestige in a place where no one, stolidly, knew what he was
heading for. By early afternoon Babbo had his permit to leave
the province. Though I am sure, had he been less scrupulous
and law-abiding, he could have left without permit. The train
he boarded seemed of ill omen. Only one carriage with
wooden benches was for passengers, the rest a long row of
open freight cars, loaded with cannons. "Always preceded by
something," was Babbo's wry remark. "I moved out of Idaho
in 1897 behind the first rotary snowplow." And I stood around
the station for a while, heavy-hearted, waiting for a late train
back to Bruneck.

By September 23 Mussolini had formed a new government:
La Repubblica di Salò. Hitler had accused the Italians of treason. The idealists, especially the very young, were eager to
wash the shameful blot in blood — *lavare la macchia col
sangue* — while Churchill, Roosevelt and Stalin coolly pur-
sued victory and Italy's unconditional surrender. In November
the big Fascist Congress in Verona took place. *La Carta del
Lavoro* was published: work as basis of money. No right *of*

property but *to* property. Work no longer the object but the subject of economy — *"Quello della casa non è soltanto un diritto di proprietà, è un diritto alla proprietà — e fare del lavoro il soggetto dell' economia e la base infrangibile dello Stato."*

Jactancy, vanity, peculation to the ruin of 20 years' labour

seemed to be over. Mussolini had drawn up a new program, clear and strict. It must have fascinated Babbo, and it became a Leitmotif:

'alla' non 'della' in il Programma di Verona
the old hand as stylist still holding its cunning

Foresteria, Salò, Gardone
        to dream the Republic. . . .

But the dream of the ideal republic had materialized too late and under bad auspices. Some of the *gerarchi* whom he had thought honest men had been shot, along with Ciano. Bottai had gone into hiding. All the while the Germans' watchfulness, mistrust, danger and pressure increased.

(bein' aliens in prohibited area) — in the spring of 1944 Babbo was requested to move out of his flat on the waterfront and to go into the hills. So he went to Sant' Ambrogio. His wife went with him — to Casa 60.

    The accumulation of twenty years of books and papers, letters, manuscripts, drawings, was all slowly carried uphill. Old Baccin gave a hand now and again, but most of it was carried by Babbo and Mamile in briefcases and knapsacks.

    Bombs fell, but not quite on Sant' Ambrogio

Heavy bombings over Genoa and all along the coast to destroy the bridges and the Aurelia road. In Rapallo only the church and the schoolhouse were hit.

Despite all this Babbo relentlessly kept working, like a lonely ant, fighting his own battle. He wrote articles for *Il Popolo d'Alessandria,* a paper of the new republic; a copy now and again reached me in Cortina. By the end of the year he had written Cantos 72 and 73 in Italian. He sent them to me as a gift for the Befana of 1945. Full of vigor and images, exalting his old friends F. T. Marinetti, the founder of the Futurist movement, who, true to himself and his "interventism," had gone to fight in Russia. And Admiral Ubaldo degli Uberti, whose phrase *chi muore oggi fa un affare* — untranslatable: dying today is a good bet — sums up the state of mind of the loyal Italians as defeat inevitably approached. Idealism and heroism were by no means all on the side of the partisans. Babbo was infected by a desperate fighting spirit and faith. It is hard these days to define that faith or that spirit; it no longer seems a component of the air one breathes.

While the British and the Americans systematically, so it seemed, and senselessly bombed Italy's beautiful cities — and Sigismundo's Temple in Rimini — Babbo, equally systematically, and senselessly perhaps, kept up his translations from Mencius and Confucius. The printing press of the orphans printed colored poster-strips for him which he pasted on the walls of Rapallo: *"Il Tesoro di una Nazione è la sua onestà."* Fascist propaganda? Honesty is the treasure of states.

"Vivere così chei tuoi discendenti ti ringrazino" — live in such a way that your descendants will be grateful. What could this mean to the men hiding in the hills and to the sly ones, in town, waiting to slip over to the winning side?

Perhaps because he wanted me a bit more within reach, but mainly because culturally life might have been more interesting, Babbo looked around for an interpreting job for me at Salò. But somehow I could work up no enthusiasm for this plan and did not budge. I shared his faith in the Republic — primarily as a luminous *idea* — though basically I had the Tyrolean mistrust of Italians. And my instinct for self-preservation has always been strong. All I did was, now and again, to send food parcels through the German couriers as far as Gardone. From there they were forwarded.

After having seen Babbo off in Bozen, escorted by tanks and cannon, I went back to digging potatoes for a little while and, in an almost comical fashion — abulia or destiny? — landed myself in a set groove.

The main excitement in the Tyrol at that time was the witch-hunt for Italians, and indirectly I was affected by some of its consequences. By the third of October they had got rid of the magistrate and his two girl-secretaries and the annual Thanksgiving was celebrated for the first time without the presence of Italian authorities. However, I couldn't help thinking that something was wrong with the Kirchta. There was a lack of spontaneity and the exuberant shouts had none of that genuine joy that used to be felt everywhere when I was a little girl; the best men were missing and nothing could make one forget the war.

That very evening Mr. Bacher came to our house, on business. Such a thing was really a violation of the rules because on Kirchta in normal times nobody thought of anything but eating and drinking and making merry. He asked with great solemnity:

"You know how to type?" I nodded. "You know how to write in German and Italian?" I nodded, rather curious to know what he was driving at. "Moar has been elected Bürger-meister" — at this communication, Tatte and Mamme showed their surprise by a faint OOHH. "He needs a secretary and we have chosen you, as a post of honor, though there are some irregularities in your position."

When he was through with this little speech, he resumed his natural air and told me quite frankly how matters stood — there was nobody in the village who knew anything about office work (not that I did, for that matter); the younger people did not even know how to write German properly, for at school they were taught only Italian and that they had refused to learn.

My first day at the municipal job I spent listening to gossip from Mr. Bacher. With great glee he described how a crowd of youngsters had demolished the monument to the Italian *Alpini* in Bruneck. It was a horrid pile of cheap cement and stone stuck up in front of the baroque Capuchin church, depriving the little piazza of all its character. They had pulled its head off with a rope — it broke quite easily — and then with pikes smashed the rest to pieces. "You ought to see the long faces of the Italians; they go around now, tails between their legs, and smile at you like dirty Jews. An Italian green-grocer is supposed to have carried that head off when the children had finished spitting on it."

After the first day Mr. Bacher never came into the office again; he wanted to make it quite understood that he was no employee.

The second day I came into contact with my "chief." It was rather awkward for both of us to meet in an office when previously we had often worked together in the fields. That very summer I had helped his family bring in their corn, stayed for meals at their house, and for the rosary after dinner. I was very fond of his mother and always found some pretext to call upon her, not only because I was sure of getting some of her extremely good cakes, but also because there reigned such dignity in her wooden *Stube* full of tradition. The paneling was very old, painted in reddish-brown, and in the corner, over the table, stood an antique carved statue: the Almighty (looking very much like Jupiter) with a round ball in his left hand and a scepter in his right hand. On the ball sat Jesus, in the act of kicking his heels against the world, quite amused and graciously holding out the first three fingers of his right hand. The Holy Ghost was perched on God the Father's head, the wings spread wide and the claws a vivid red. The rest of the group was unpainted — or perhaps the color had vanished with centuries of Easter-scrubbings, from which in a respectable farmhouse not even God could escape. In the same room hung an enormous crucifix between the two deep-set windows. The size was rather awe-inspiring, but the stripped figure was so lithe and alive with love that one felt almost a desire to embrace it. Attached to the rusty nail fastening the feet was a rosary of wooden beads bigger than walnuts which Moar every evening dragged through his strong hands, as had his fathers before him. . . .

In those surroundings I used to call him simply Franz, but in a room with skeleton-like white walls, a typewriter, a writing desk blotted with ink and the enormous line of drawers which kept the public from coming in contact with any papers, he appeared quite a different man — tremendously conceited and stupid, looking down on me with suspicion. In these circumstances I couldn't call him by his Christian name; on the other hand Herr Bürgermeister was too much, so I decided to use the name of the house, which, though respectful, would always remind him that he was a peasant.

Well, there he stood, near the desk, handling a few letters, arrogant but helpless, and in that moment I was fully aware that I had been cornered into a position which would require heaps of patience.

At last he decided that he must give me the letters to translate, as they were written in Italian. I asked if I had to make a written translation. "No, that's not necessary, we won't bother much with Italian letters." But a great difficulty arose. One letter contained an appeal to the farmers to bring more milk and butter to the *"ammassi,"* and it came from the Italian Prefect in Bozen, since dismissed. What was one to do with a thing like this; one couldn't possibly post it now that Italy had lost all claims over the country, and must be regarded as an enemy.

I asked if all this pooling business had to go on. "Of course, but better arranged, as in Germany."

Finally it was decided that I should make a written translation. I sweated over it all morning, then a few things were changed, so as to bring it up to date, and when I had typed it for the third time, Moar put his own well-rehearsed signature to it and hung it on the blackboard, quite pleased; so pleased in fact, with his *"Kundmachung"* that in the afternoon he told me to make some more copies to send to the heads of the four hamlets attached to our parish.

People thought that as soon as they got rid of the magistrate they would not have to bother with papers any longer, as before 1918, but they soon saw their mistake. Food was still rationed. The new cards did not arrive until the tenth of October. There was I, with hundreds and hundreds of cards to be distributed. There were of course the filed lists as background and the people came in quite orderly, but nearly everybody had some changes to make and many complaints were uttered.

"The Italians have put down two cows and nine persons, that's not right; now that we have become German, at last, we must put things in order, we are eleven and one cow is going to have a calf at Christmas, therefore we have only one cow to milk at present, so we must get oil cards for at least four persons."

They were right, I thought, so I gave them the oil cards, and to another the bread cards, and so forth. When Moar discovered this, he was furious, saying that I had favored all the small farmers, at which I pointed out several big farmers who ought not to get any cards at all. He was annoyed at my picking at him, but soon got over it and tried to win me over with "the best apples from that tree in the south corner, you know the ones I mean, and here are some cakes which mother sends you."

After a week the distribution of the food cards was over and the statistics turned out better than I had thought. So for one day I looked out of the window, wondering what would turn up next. This was the first occasion I had had of reflecting upon wild chestnut trees, watching the yellow leaves fall with a weight of doom in the ditch along the road. The sun did not come out that day, so I was deprived of shuffling sounds of feet among dried leaves.

One morning a young man was already waiting for me at the office door. It was Heinrich, herdsman of the Jagdhaus dairy, and when he recognized me he turned purple and a desperate desire to run away pierced his eyes. I, on the contrary, was very glad to see him and couldn't make out his embarrassment, so I asked in a playful tone if he wanted his marriage papers. He simply exclaimed: "What, you in this office?" — "Yes, it's not so amusing as plucking edelweiss and making cheese, but, here I am — and what's the news?" Seeing there was no way out of it, he confessed the crime: his sister had had a baby, born at 3 A.M.

I knew already that she was going to have an illegitimate child, because a scandal of this sort is already an outworn topic of gossip by the time the brat arrives, even if, as in this case, the girl lived in a hamlet four miles off. I consoled him as well as I could, and then started wondering what to do, looking with awe at the enormous census registers; but my wits failed me for the moment. I asked the young man to inform Moar. "Oh no, I won't go and tell *him* about this baby," he said, "but as I must go to Bruneck shopping I'll tell him when I pass his house that he is wanted in the office; I'll come in again on my way back."

When he was gone, I looked up the latest register and to my great relief found a scrap of paper with the following instructions:

Illegitimate: mother must come personally — otherwise the Segretario Communale must go to the house — two witnesses — certificate from midwife — cards for clothing, soap, rubber nipple, etc.

Fortunately that was not the first illegitimate child in the parish, so I started to translate the long and complicated formula, for I was sure now the register must be continued in German. When Moar arrived I showed him the translation; he pondered over it for a while and finally approved. But I fear that that birth certificate was worded in a very strange idiom.

Then the idea came to me that I might do a bit of research into my own papers. As far back as 1925, wherever I found traces of Maria Rudge figlia di Arturo, I changed the "*di*" into "*fu*": "of" to "was" — the late. That much was settled, I thought — my legal father was dead. Always had been.

After having muddled through tax forms, birth certificates, ration cards, a new census of domestic animals and people for a month and a half, I was all of a sudden commanded to go and work in the town hall in Bruneck. A competent secretary, trained in Innsbruck, presided over the municipality of Gais.

And on the following Monday I took the early morning trolley and at eight o'clock presented myself in the antechamber of the Burgomaster. A thin, goitered, middle-aged dark woman received me with a rather distressed air; she did not know what to do with me; I would have to wait for the Burgomaster himself. When he arrived I found that he was a very pleasant man, rather distinguished, about thirty-five. As Burgomaster he received no salary; therefore he appeared very seldom, having to earn his living by his profession. He was said to be one of the best dentists in town. He treated me very courteously and I soon found out that it was not at all his doing that I had been shifted; he had never known of my existence till Moar had pointed it out. However he made me feel as if I had come into better luck; my salary was to be 1000 lire a month (I received 500 lire for one and a half months in Gais) and my work — well, for the moment just little odd jobs. This was the only time he ever spoke to me, until my last interview.

The first job happened to be a catalogue of the town art collection. It was very interesting to find out that so many old pictures and carvings still existed; apparently all this stuff had been stored away *chez* Mr. M. during the last twenty years, and now that the Italians had gone the new town council wanted to open a museum and thus give one more proof of their Germanness by works of art. The scheme was still rather a secret, very few people knowing of these treasures, and I think the reason they gave me the catalogue to copy was because they knew I had no acquaintances in town and thought I was too dumb to find out what it was about. Later, when Mr. M. once came to see how the work was getting on, he was very startled to see that I knew Latin. Only after the war did I learn about the Germans pilfering art works in Italy.

On the first of December I was shifted to the third floor, together with a very fat blonde. Being newly married and thus having a household of her own, she looked down upon me as a very contemptible being. Our chief was Mr. von Grebner, owner of the Hotel Post and the farmers' head man in the municipality.

His voice and manners were more like those of a bear than a human being and thank heavens he came very seldom — he too was not paid for his work, as it was an honorary post, but he had the benefit of getting more artificial manure and salt, etc., for his farm as he was entrusted with the allotment of these articles. Here again I had to witness how big farmers always came off better in everything. My special job was to control the milk and butter pool, to distribute petrol cards to those who had no electric light, to keep the horse census; those fine animals had indeed more papers than a man: precise (or not) description of each, name, sex, age, if seen by the vet, if fit for the army.

And then the season of the pig-killing started — that required lots of work, as precise accounts had to be made of the quantity of meat and number of persons, and if a farmer was not good enough in his mathematics (i.e., admitting a pig weighed more than the ration for so and so many persons), the thing was still more complicated and more forms had to be filled in for the pool.

During all my stay in the Town Hall I came in contact only with farmers, and alas, sometimes with farmers' wives. It was in a way more amusing here than in Gais where everybody knew me; I had more occasions to make reflections on queer characters. My companion tried to be mellifluous only with the well-to-do class, and thought my talking to the small farmers in dialect very degrading, showing off her patronizing manners towards me in public — she having risen from country-inn waitress to shopkeeper in a Bozen pastry shop and later employee in the electric works at Salzburg. Still, considering the pettinesses and quarrels that were continually agitating the other employees, I may say I was very fortunate, as we were able to keep always on good terms, and with the others I had nothing to do. For Christmas Day all the German employees, from the Town Hall concierge to the head of the German Commission, were invited to a party by the Burgomaster. At 7 P.M. we assembled in the Jugendheim — formerly the Casa del Fascio, the building for Fascist reunions — where an enormous Christmas tree was lighted. Our places were marked and everybody found a book, and I had the luck to be seated near Dr. Waldner, who, I observed, was the most charming man of the party, and though we then met for the first time we carried on a very interesting conversation on art mixed with a bit of gossip about our common friend Mr. Bacher. The Burgomaster made a speech; "Stille Nacht" and "O Tannenbaum" were sung; sausages and wine were served and "Deutschland über Alles" closed the party.

That evening for the first time I heard rumors that the younger girls were going to be called up for the army — several girls in town had already left, but voluntarily. At the end of March two girls from the telephone office were called up and I started to be seriously alarmed, for since I was not a member of any Nazi group and had no influential friends, the German Commission would probably not hesitate to give me over to the army, in which case my only alternative was a munitions factory in Germany. Of concentration camps I luckily knew nothing. I had made the acquaintance of a few O.T. (Organisation Todt) men who had their quarters in the castle of St. Georgen and they probably could have taken me over instead, but I thought they were a rather ambiguous lot and preferred to do without their help.

Weeks later my companion told me that the German hospitals were looking around for typists. This gave me an idea. On the fifteenth of April, 1944, I made an excursion to Cortina and on that occasion collected as much information as possible. Having heard that a secretary was needed at Pocol, I went to see the doctor of that department. I told him how matters stood and that I was afraid of being called up. He was extremely nice and said: "Take care not to slide between two chairs." It was arranged that he would let me know whether I was going to get the job or not within three days, then he asked me to go into the office and type a few lines so that he might send a sample to the doctor in charge of staffing.

My heart sank when a group of soldiers gathered around me and one started to dictate; however, my abilities must have been considered sufficient because three days later I was called to the telephone and told to start work on the first of May. No questions about my nationality were asked — I suppose they took it for granted that I was a real Tyrolean coming from the Town Hall.

I hadn't spoken to anyone about my plans yet when I went to the Burgomaster asking for dismissal. He said that was not possible; it was wartime and we were considered as good as mobilized. The only shifts possible were into the army; hospitals did not count, especially if one went there as a civilian worker. However, with the intervention of Dr. Waldner, who happened to be Burgomaster of Cortina and had somehow the responsibility to provide workers for the hospitals there, I was able to free myself by the evening of the thirtieth of April.

On the following morning I took the train for the most charming place in the Dolomites.

7. Why I should have been given work in the conva-
lescent home of Pocol, I could not understand. There was no
work. Perhaps the young lieutenant in charge of the place or
the old gentlemanly doctor had just liked me. They had nothing to do, either. There were eighty soldiers in all, no longer
in need of medical treatment, but not quite fit to go back to
their regiments. They lounged around and played records on
the phonograph. Only at mealtimes it came upon me that I
was not just having a holiday in a very comfortable hotel on
top of a mountain, for we ate all together in the big dining
room. I sat with the doctor and an elderly nurse and the lieu-

[208]

tenant at a small table near the entrance; along the walls and in the center were long refectory tables with the soldiers.

The nurse, whose name was Clementia, was kind to me but made me understand that I had nothing to do with her — I must do what "the men" told me. She acted as though they were respectively her husband and son. After every meal she went for a rest which lasted until the next meal.

The men only asked me to have drinks with them and play cards, but I did not like drinking and did not know how to play cards, so we went for walks towards the Falzarego Pass, never to Cortina. Sometimes I just sat near the brand-new typewriter in the office musing on how queer all this was.

But after a week the lieutenant got orders to leave for the front. The doctor accompanied him down to Cortina and when he returned he was very sad. Not only had they taken the lieutenant, but I was to go and work at the Bellevue hospital next morning. I was not surprised, I knew that one can't get 1300 lire a month with an excellent room and good food for nothing.

At the real hospital, everything was different: the work serious, the war somehow nearer.

I was given a bed in the hotel-turned-into-hospital, in a beautiful apartment in fact. Two rooms and a bathroom for four nurses and myself. They were so-called "little nurses" — girls in their twenties, without superior medical exams. The three full nurses, that is to say, the head nurse, the cook and the one on night duty occupied another apartment on the first floor. No doctors slept in the house; only two medical corporals were stuck in a low room under the roof.

It took me some time to get acclimatized. Three nurses were Austrians, the other from North Germany, heavily built with a clear-cut face, bronze-colored and with a hard green look. Her bearing was frank, rather bold, and she was the first to shake hands with me. During her two years of service in Russia she had learned to like the people there; she hated Italians. As soon as she found out that I was not Italian she made room for my things in her cupboard and told me that I had to clean the bath and make my bed first thing in the morning, and that if I wanted anything, to tell her. "I am Schwester Irmengard." We became good friends.

The nurses started service at seven o'clock, I at eight, and we really never met much. There were two hundred and ten patients in our house; two smaller hotels were attached to us, with one hundred patients each.

As I entered for the first time the doctor's office (Room No. 16), I was saluted, but by no means welcomed, by the "Professor." I felt sure this was the professor to whom I had to present myself. A mingy man with excessively thin legs, flat-footed, spectacled, a broad forehead with sparse hair parted in the middle, and, to show his character, a mouse-shaped mouth with four big and irregular teeth sticking out under the thin and pale lips.

He got up from his chair and I told him that the doctor-major had ordered me to come and work with him.

"Do you know how to type?"

"Yes."

"How quick at stenography?"

"I don't know stenography."

"That's all right then, I'll do my work alone. You better go downstairs and wait for Oberarzt P. Heil Hitler."

Without another look he resumed his place at the desk and I, extremely mortified, left the room with a "Heil Hitler."

I went to the ground-floor office. There were three soldiers, two of them looking extremely worn-out and old, the third, a sergeant, wore a brighter look and, though gray-haired, had a supple figure. Here nobody saluted with "Heil Hitler." They spoke Viennese. I was informed that the Professor was in an awful mood because they had taken away his secretary.

"But P. is a good fellow," said the sergeant. I felt this must be true, otherwise nobody would have dared mention the name without specifying his rank. I felt at ease when I saw him. A very ugly face with kind blue eyes, low and wrinkled forehead with heaps of brown hair scattered around.

"Oh, that's the new girl? Come along, awful amount of work!"

That afternoon I came for the first time in contact with patients. About four in every room. We stopped at the new ones and the doctor dictated to me their "status" and case history, in an undertone and using as many Latin words as possible. Before the patients I was too shy to ask if I did not understand, and when I had to type the things out I spent most of the evening wondering what certain words meant. After having dictated to me, he turned to Schwester Lydia, the head nurse. With her a few words were enough: the therapeutics.

Most of the men had malaria, jaundice or gastritis. Haggard faces and white hands. I don't know if it was the effect of the white sheets and shirts, or just the fact that they were in bed that made such an impression of shivering feebleness. After all, they were fighting men and I could see no resemblance to the superb soldiers one used to see marching through the streets. A few were over fifty, with rare melancholy teeth, bald or gray-haired. But they did not complain of their illness; there were still hopes of victory; nobody tried to tell lies yet.

If they mentioned pains in their legs the doctor made them get out of bed and walk — some, especially the younger ones, appeared very annoyed at having to stand in their shirts before a girl, and I myself felt rather uncomfortable. It was a depressing sight, thin and yellow legs sticking out under the shirts. I felt an immense distance between myself and all these men but got over it after I saw the first dead. The rooms were extremely well kept. On entering one saw cigarettes fly out of the windows, which made the doctor shout threateningly at the men, but after two minutes he would pat their shoulders.

That night coming back from dinner I felt very disgusted at hearing music going on in a café. I could not associate war and sick soldiers with music, but later on I did.

The Professor fell ill with appendicitis and was sent for special treatment to Vienna where he stayed for three months. By the time he came back I had learned a lot and he seemed in a better mood, so I had the honor of working with him too. There was so much to do that I used to take down the case history by myself and have it ready by the time the doctor made his visit to the new ones. It was not always an easy task, especially as I knew so little about medicine, and some men were so very dumb, some even impertinent. The first question was about the family, inherited diseases, T.B., insanity. Brothers? Married? How many children? Wife healthy?

(2) What illnesses had he had in childhood? Many would remember none, others at least half a dozen.

(3) Illnesses or accidents before entering the army.

(4) Illnesses or wounds during active service. Malaria patients had five extra questions. Was it the first time? If not, how often had he had it already? Malaria tropica or tertiana? Where contracted? How many per cent of his regiment were affected by it? Had he had antimalaria treatment? (That was to say: did he swallow those yellow bitter pills or throw them away, or make a collection of them and leave them in the gas mask?)

(5) Present illness. When did it start, what symptoms? If feverish ague was the main complaint, I felt relieved, but if

they started mentioning their stomachs, or even worse, their lungs and heart, I was worried. A stomach history — *Magenanamnese* — is something rather complicated for a medically untrained person. The four last questions — Do you smoke? — Yes — How much? The patient would look perplexed and then say: "Normally." I insisted: What do you call normally? "As much as we can get." This certainly was the truth, but I had not the faintest idea how much he contrived to get. The regular allowance was only four cigarettes a day. Alcohol? — "If I can get hold of some." Sport? Many would start recalling all the prizes they had won, the mountains they had climbed, etc., till I had to stop them with a question they did not like from me and which I hated to put. Venereal diseases? In our house we had very few cases.

Room No. 20 was small, with a single bed. It was called the dying room; very seldom did anybody get out of it alive. The most hopeless cases were put in there. I felt sorry when Schwester Lydia told me there was a new one. Before entering I read the cover of his booklet, already filled in because he came from another hospital. Aviator Peter Schulz — 170 cm — 20 years old — student, etc. He looked like a child of fourteen — big, helpless gray eyes, blond curls around his pale wet forehead. His face was so thin that one could almost perceive his teeth through the skin. Extremely long and thin arms.

On seeing me he twisted his mouth with a great effort, displaying a perfect row of teeth. I think he wanted to smile as he said:

"What a funny little doctor."

I went near him and told him I was no doctor.

"I know, I know, the doctor has already seen me, you are just a funny doctor."

"No, Peter, I am no doctor."

He stared for a long time into my face, then shook his head slowly.

"Why don't you wear a cap, then?"

"I am not a nurse, either. I am the secretary."

He tried again to smile and motioned for me to sit down. I did so, for the first time since I had entered the hospital.

"I have a sister in Nüremberg. She too is going to be a doctor." And he started telling me all about his family. Then he wanted me to look at his pictures and Silver Medal. He was proud of both and I displayed them on the night table so that everybody could see them. I paid him a compliment about his good looks — in the photograph a healthy, lively boy in lederhosen — conscious, however, of the futility of such a compliment now that he was reduced almost to a skeleton. When I made ready to leave the room he would not hear of it, looking so much more dead than alive that I was quite scared.

"I want *you* to look after me," he said.

This was such an impossible request that I could not agree to it, so I tried to make angelic descriptions of the nurses.

"I hate them all, they always call me Baby."

I assured him this would not happen again and left the room before he could get on to another subject. For the whole morning I was not able to get him out of my mind. I spoke to Schwester Lydia about him.

"He is at a very critical stage," she said, "but if he goes on living for another week or so he might even recover."

This made me very happy and I told her all about our conversation, but she seemed annoyed. I had already noticed that the nurses were extremely jealous of their patients, but had not expected to find this fault in Schwester Lydia too.

When I went into Peter's room in the afternoon there she was, trying with the utmost patience to get him to drink something. This time he took no notice of me, so I retreated and

[214]

went up to my room. Here Schwester Hilde was playing the phonograph and enjoying some real coffee (at least the smell was of real coffee). I was an intruder.

It may be just as well that nurses are jealous of their patients, because Schwester Lydia watched over "Baby Peter" like a mother, and I think it was she who saved him. Peter remained in our hospital for several months and when he left he looked much the same as the boy I had admired in the photograph. I think he had quite forgotten what he had said to me the first day, for he never cared to speak to me later on.

He was the only boy who ever came out alive from Room No. 20.

In November work grew less and less; the number of doctors and nurses increased considerably. They were clearing central Italy. Our Professor had in the meantime assumed the title of NSFO (it was supposed to mean something like "leading Nazi officer"), and as such got back his former secretary, who in the interval had become a nurse-assistant. And of course she had to lodge with the nurses. I had to make room for her towards the end of the month. It did not displease me too much because I rather longed for a room of my own. I found one that suited me very well, halfway between the hospital and the Hotel Post, with a stove in it. By this time I had made some friends in the hospital, and they arranged with the administration to send me a weekly supply of coal. And I settled down quietly in my new home and felt perfectly contented. But one morning on entering the office I heard "Jawohl, Jawohl . . ."

P. leaned against the desk with the telephone in his hand. "Jawohl, Herr Oberarzt, jawohl." I was very puzzled at this speech consisting only of "yes." At last he put down the receiver and said, "I am transferred to Verona," and left the room. This was bad news and I phoned it down to the other office. The section sergeant declared that he would go with him.

"Are you crazy?" I asked.

"No, I have worked with this man for over two years; he is an Austrian; I don't want to have anything to do with the Pifki." There was not one single person who did not regret this sudden change. Only the Professor, who no doubt was very fond of P., bore it with great stoicism and did not complain. All these sorrows would be rewarded by victory, and he went on with his work as usual, while I tried to console the sergeant who had been refused his request of following P.

It was said we would get a "father of five children" as a substitute. The following afternoon the new doctor arrived. I was looking for the Professor and on entering a room found a stranger, half lying over a patient while examining him. I asked for the Professor and he followed me out of the room. He introduced himself as Stabsarzt G. I told him my name and asked him if he was the substitute for Oberarzt P.

"I really don't know, nobody seems to acknowledge me here. I arrived last night from the front and today at lunch was told to come to the Bellevue. I can't find the Professor to get further instructions and the head nurse seems to be a dragon . . ."

I felt sorry for him, everybody was prejudiced against him, but it certainly was not his fault if P. was sent to Verona. As I looked at him I could not help smiling. He cursed and said he wanted to go back to the front immediately.

"This is no life for me, this stagnant smelly pool with swollen frogs in it. Who the devil do you think you are back here?"

He looked like a real fighting man. Not very tall but very broad-shouldered, his short legs stuck in too-tight boots, a leather patch on the seat of his breeches. His jacket was worn out and the silver on his shoulders very shabby. But on his breast were three medals; the Iron Cross, which I had never seen on a doctor, the Silver Medal, which meant that he had been wounded three times, and the War Merit Cross. He carried his big head very high. There were gray threads in his brown hair, his nose straight, a thin mouth under flabby cheeks.

"How many patients are there, anyhow, and what's this famous Professor like?"

"Well, he is a very good doctor . . ." It was not easy for me to tell a stranger what the Professor was like. I risked: "A bit bad-tempered sometimes."

"Aha, and what is there to do here?" Then he looked at me and added, "I suppose it's the wrong person I am questioning. One never knows in these war hospitals; they are so far from the front that everybody is different."

I told him that very probably I would be his secretary, that there was not much work at present — only one hundred sixty patients, as the other houses had a doctor of their own now.

Stabsarzt G., who in a moment of enthusiasm about the front said that he used to cure horses as well as men, was nicknamed "the Vet." He shocked all the nurses by carelessness about sterilizing, had a terrific quarrel with the kitchen nurse because he had entered her sacred realm and helped himself to white bread and butter, but was very much liked by the soldiers. He treated them very rudely and swore all the time (he had a very rich vocabulary). He threatened to throw them out of the hospital if they did not follow his instructions and then started long conversations with them about their homes and regiments and officers. He seemed acquainted with the whole army in Russia and Italy. His stories about Russia were exciting; apparently he had done more fighting than doctoring.

He sat on clean, newly made beds and called Schwester Lydia a dragon before the patients. The little nurses liked him in the beginning because he was always ready to make love to them, and they soon found out that he was not the "father of five children" but a bachelor, a rarity in that hospital. But he was terribly unfaithful and soon complained that there was not a nice girl in the house. He was an unserious doctor, very good at curing little sores and odd diseases but at a loss before a serious case, and if one of his patients died he was upset for a whole week. Then he would lift his head again and tell of his miracles as a ship's doctor. He had been in America, China and Africa and God knows where else, and his stories certainly had charm. The things he most hated were responsibility and papers. "This damned *Papierkrieg!*" — paper-war. He did not know how to dictate, always inverted the order of the human body, preferably starting by inspecting and describing the stomach and showing great sympathy for venereal diseases.

In short, no more quiet, serious, methodical work. This man brought the first signs of confusion and doubt of victory. He sneered at the Professor's title and was proud of his own, Verteidigungsoffizier — leading officer for the defense (against partisans). He drilled the medical corps.

About this time a captain came for an examination of his lungs. He did not look strong and said he was ashamed of not being able to work along with the others, that his major always complained of his laziness, but that he simply had not the strength to do more. Nobody took him seriously. We thought him one of those officers who wanted a rest and then a fortnight in Pocol. But when the Professor examined him he shook his head and sent him to bed immediately. Once in bed he made a pitiable impression. His jacket must have been well-padded. In the beginning he was always cheerful. At the radiology Dr. B. pointed out to me a sort of whitish rind over his lungs, with various black spots: suspicion of carcinoma of the lungs. Everybody knew that the man would die.

He was a man of forty-three, with the most juvenile plans for his future, a bit crazy sometimes. He had been a school-teacher in Sudetengau. He somehow took to me and I often went to see him. He had been attached to Headquarters and knew Kesselring very well, but did not approve of him because he had made him ride 120 kilometers to fetch some fish for him. The captain had taken this as an insult and asked for dismissal from HQ.

His conversation gradually grew dull, after a month decidedly boring, but he insisted more and more on my going to see him. He became avaricious and though he did not smoke asked for his cigarettes every day, counting them over and over together with his money, of which he had a great deal. Then he would not shave nor eat and one cheek slowly drew back towards his ear so that when he tried to smile one could see the mouth only on the left side. He wanted to read Dickens, which was nowhere to be had. As a substitute he grudgingly took Karl May. He said I must read aloud to him. He closed his eyes, his hands crossed on his breast. When I thought he had fallen asleep I tried to slip out of the room, but there was no deceiving him; he shook his finger and said: "Don't run away from me. I have been fighting all this time with the devils, nine on my left and three on my right; if they see you in the room they don't dare to torment me so much, but once you are gone they are cruel, especially on my left side, they prick me with their horns and play me all sorts of tricks."

When I insisted that I must go to work he looked very

ferocious and did not utter a word more. He would not eat liver "because it is not from a healthy animal, and I don't want to contaminate my liver." At the end he stopped eating altogether, and I felt almost relieved when the doctor did not allow me to visit him any longer. The reason for this was that I had fainted while the doctor was dictating to me in the ward next door and he thought it was because of the captain's groanings and curses. All the patients had jumped out of their beds and stood around me perplexed just after the doctor had told them not to get out of bed for any reason. The truth was that I had been so anxious to get off skiing that I had skipped my lunch.

After a week I was told the captain had died. I went to see him, but regretted it. The face consisted only of bones covered by two inches of beard, a hole in the region of the left cheek — there was no way of shutting it. The ears stuck out ferociously from his hair as if they too wanted to fight and curse. Two extremely large feet seemed to be all that was left of his body.

We wrote the usual letter to his wife and a long summary of his illness, made a bundle of all his property. To no purpose; his wife and two children were in Russian-occupied territory. So it all went to the "archives" in Berlin.

As I was going one day to the eye clinic I met a patient in the corridor whom I was sure of having seen somewhere before. As I looked at him closer I remembered having danced with him at a village festival, three years back. I inquired about him and the nurse told me that, yes, he was from the Pustertal, blind and no chance of being cured. She took me in to him and I waited until with great effort he had reached his bed again. I was at a loss to explain who I was, but he seemed so pleased when I spoke to him in Tyrolean dialect that he made it quite easy. He did not remember me, but there were many girls we both knew and we had a long talk: "Do you remember this one, do you know that one?" A week later I went to see him again. He had been home in the meantime; his father had come to fetch him, and he got three days' leave. The only complaint I heard was: "If those Tommies had only aimed somewhere else instead of right into my eyes."

He was a farmer's son, twenty-three years old and extremely handsome and healthy. He told me all about the cows they had in their stable at home and did not approve of his father buying a new horse which he had not seen and letting the old cows get so thin that he could count their ribs with his fingers.

He was sent home before the war was over and somebody told me he had cried out loud when he heard the Germans had lost. Later on every time I passed his village on the way to Brixen I saw him on the high road, walking very carefully with his stick; once a little girl pulled him by the hand and they seemed to be in a great hurry. Somebody in the bus asked me if I knew what the yellow band round that man's arm meant. Yes, I knew.

> 'both eyes, (the loss of) and to find someone
> who talked his own dialect. We
> talked of every boy and girl in the valley
> but when he came. back from leave
> he was sad because he had been able to feel
> all the ribs of his cow . . . .'

I evidently had written Babbo about my encounter, and in Pisa he remembered.

In the first days of April, I became a patient myself. It was only angina, but enough to keep me in bed for a fortnight.

When I went to hospital there were lots of rooms free. Ten days later Dr. B. told me I must hurry and get better because there was no room — "and I don't suppose you would like to have a few soldiers on mattresses put next to your bed!" As usual he was joking, but I had visitors enough to keep me informed about what was happening.

The attack foretold for Christmas had not taken place. The German army was in retreat. The hospitals of Verona and Riva were packed up and sent us all their patients. The field hospitals without warning sent hundreds of wounded, and in the Cadore the Italian partisans were beginning to become more than a nuisance. When I left the hospital the first person I met was Oberarzt P. He had brought the patients from his field hospital and worked at the Bellevue again. Many new houses were opened, all for wounded soldiers, and I had to work in the surgery section as well.

The Japanese envoy had fled to Switzerland; their legation had been turned into a hospital. Two hundred patients sent from God knows where, not very serious cases, but all fresh wounds. Men that had escaped from the disaster at the Po river. Most of them had to lie on straw in their dirty clothes and shoes. They had no papers nor luggage; they were all fighting men, defeated soldiers.

Everybody saw the absurdity of starting fresh booklets for them and making regular case histories, but nobody had the initiative or the power to give new orders.

The doctor inspected the wounds and dictated to me and bandaged and gave orders to the nurses, all at the same time. There was everywhere a great silence. The men showed their wounds as a child would show you a cat. Many had not even received a tetanus-serum injection, many had never changed their bandages, and there was pus and dirt and blood and lice everywhere, mixed with the asphyxiating odor of medicaments.

Plaster casts no longer fitted; and on cutting them, swollen and inflamed limbs burst out. The patient would only say: "They put it on in a hurry, just to let me get back."

Everything was done in a hurry. Doctors and nurses got in one another's way. Since things were going so badly with the Germans, the Italian servants relaxed in their work, and many left. At night I helped with the washing of wounded, carrying food, and fetching new patients from the hospital trains. Then for a week nothing happened; only stray soldiers from the vicinity came in. We seemed to be cut off. We brought some order to the new houses; all the patients had mattresses (collected from the cellars of the hotels) and passbooks. Then all of a sudden whole troop units passed through the town. The last days of April. Snowstorms and rain. No more doubt that the war was lost. We received orders not to leave the hospital except for very urgent reasons. There was no room in the streets; troops were standing all around, cars passing through day and night. Soldiers burst into the hospitals for something to eat, for a dry corner to rest. We had to lock the doors. Pale faces gazed in from every window.

In the Hotel Post a captain backed up by a group of hungry soldiers fired into the ground in front of the doctor-major; they wanted to be fed. The major said it was impossible for the hospitals to feed the troops. Later on when calm was somehow reestablished this proved quite untrue. There was plenty in the storehouses, especially brandy and cigarettes.

On the morning of May 1, as I pushed my way through lines of trucks packed with wondering horses, I saw some extremely ragged and wild-looking men with red handkerchiefs around their necks encircle three German soldiers and seize their pistols. They looked fiercely at me, as I wore a Red Cross armband, but let me pass. In the Bellevue I heard the news. The partisans had entered the town in the early morning. No fighting: the Germans had orders not to shoot. All civilians must put on tricolored ribbons to show their sympathy for the patriots and thus be unmolested. I did not.

Patients crowded to the windows and doors to look for their regiments passing. Many whom we thought very ill, when they saw their regiment, threw away their white shirts and insisted that Fritz, a Pole who looked after their clothes, should bring them their uniforms and guns. Then they came into Room No. 16: "My regiment is passing. I am joining it again."

The Professor was so out of his wits that he did not react to such indiscipline; on the contrary, he sometimes shook hands with them and finished their passbooks in a hurry, saying: "It may be of some use to you later." But in those days very few gave any importance to a written paper and signature.

Work went on confusedly. Worn-out soldiers could not be stopped from bursting into the hospital and lying down on the first free mattress or on the floor. Often when I went into a room or looked into a corridor to find someone whose case history (by this time abbreviated) was still to be taken down, I found all new faces. The others had simply left.

"And what's the matter with you?" They did not quite know. Some were simply frightened and thought the hospital the securest refuge. Others were worn out. Many officers had insisted on being admitted a few days earlier, then they changed their minds and preferred to cross the Austrian border while there was still time.

"HITLER DIED FIGHTING" — the Professor announced. Many nurses cried, the Professor was inscrutable, ten years older. Every doctor announced Hitler's death to his patients in a very military manner. They did not comment on the news. Among the medical corps soldiers, all older men, the news was received with suppressed joy: they believed in the story of his heroic death as little as they had believed in Dietrich's saving Vienna.

One patient said: "I wish I had not lived so long." Two hours later he died.

On the second of May the partisans officially took possession of the town. Most of the troops had cleared out. They wanted to force a German policeman to carry the Italian flag on the top of the church tower; he refused and was shot before the Hotel Post. He was the only man killed.

Partisan women sang in the streets: Victory!

I was writing in the radiology station. Stabsarzt B., looking out of the window, saw a woman take away a pistol from a soldier heavily laden with his pack. B. rushed out into the street with such a fierce cry that the woman handed him back the pistol without protest. Then he went up to the soldier: "Don't disgrace us any more by letting a whore disarm you!" He flung the pistol in the man's face. The soldier took the pistol and saluted, bringing his hand to his forehead, not lifting the arm as he had been ordered after the attempt to kill Hitler. To me the Stabsarzt said: "That fellow seems to have something else on his mind."

Italian flags were hung on the balconies, and the doctors were so infuriated by it that we were no longer allowed to look out of a window.

On the third of May the Americans arrived, so silently that nobody noticed it. Somebody said he had seen an. "Ami" in front of a shop window, with a helmet but no gun. At lunchtime we saw about twenty Americans pass before our house, hands in their pockets, smoking and apparently without arms. They certainly were a puzzle for the Germans and a disappointment for the Italians, who had expected them to fall on their necks and slay all Germans, or at least drive them all away.

One could not help smiling at seeing the German doctors, officers and men, stiffer than ever, pace the streets with their pistols, saluting each other as if on a constant parade, just as if they had won the war. The partisans who had been robbing passing soldiers at the corner of our house, disappeared. The last German convoy passed by undisturbed; a few gorgeous cars: officers with their secretary-friends. Then a dozen horsemen followed, the only beautiful horses I had ever seen in the German army, and a gig with two soldiers and a dog, looking as tranquil as if they were riding to market. The section sergeant was so amused that he stopped them and asked how far they intended to go. "Home," was the reply. "We are only forty miles from the frontier." They seemed not to realize that the war was lost on the other side of the border too.

In the afternoon the Italian flags were, for some mysterious reason, taken away by the hotelkeepers. We expected to have the American flags put up — "They certainly have them already prepared and are as willing to put those up as any others . . ." But the Americans did not seem to care for that kind of demonstration. They hoisted their flag themselves in the piazza.

All the doctors and men were waiting to be disarmed and made prisoners, but no orders came until May 7. The Professor was scared out of his wits, not so much of the Allies as of the Germans. He had been the leading officer for Nazi propaganda, but worse than that, he had replaced the Jewish head of a clinic in Vienna. He was a well-known man and certainly could never go back to Vienna. Nevertheless, when the sergeant had collected all the soldiers' weapons (nothing was said about officers), the Professor ordered a roll call. All the patients able to get up were marched to the dining room and there presented to the Professor. He returned the salute and read a new order:

"The whole German army has capitulated, all arms must be consigned to the American command, all swastikas removed from uniforms, the salute 'Heil Hitler' is abolished, the former military salute reinstated, etc."

After having read the order he made a speech:

"Though we are defeated, let's keep our pride as Germans and our reputation for discipline. Destiny has been hard on our country. Now every man must fight alone for his future. Ranks are not abolished, and you must follow your officers, we will stick with you . . ."

The patients were marched back to their rooms and orderlies and nurses took up their work again. In the office the speech was criticized: "It's too late now, they ought to have stuck with the soldiers before, now it's too late. They are scared. I did not see any high officers march back with their troops in the rain and snow. You may be sure they were in the best cars. But they'll get what's coming to them. . . ."

The discussion finished in a roar of laughter when the sergeant stuck the picture of a beautiful baby on the nail where Hitler's picture had been hanging. "This child couldn't have made a greater mess of things." Everybody agreed.

In Room No. 16 the doctors were puzzled what to do with the convalescents. Beds were needed badly for those lying on the floor. That afternoon the SS Hospital of St. Ulrich was moved over to us — patients, nurses and orderlies, but no doctors. I never was able to find out what had become of them. A new house was opened in the "Kindergarten," which had a pleasant outlook into a little park, quiet and neat, with a sunny office room. The patients, SS men, were usually lying around in the garden or sitting in the entrance, but promptly stood up when someone cried "Attention." They came to the office for their medical treatment and there was never much to write about them. I was just an onlooker. After having seen nothing but sick, worn-out, toothless and bald soldiers for a whole year I felt a sort of wonder at seeing these men. Most of them were cripples now, but the beauty of their bodies was not altogether lost. It was an irony that I should discover the "super race" only after the war was over. There were many Latvians among them and they certainly were the best looking, all students, volunteers (at least their papers said so). They formed a group quite to themselves; only a few spoke German fluently. I did not experience any arrogance from them, nor did they seem frightened; they looked grave, but soon a certain sense of humor came back and somehow pervaded all the hospitals.

Nobody spoke of politics. The fighting days were never mentioned, they were over.

Two rooms on the first floor had to be cleared for six American medics. The Germans would have liked to talk to them, but nobody dared to break the ice. I felt embarrassed and shy in front of the Americans. They seemed very reserved. I told the Germans I knew a little English, so one day the section sergeant suggested I should tell the G.I.'s to take their meals sitting comfortably in the patients' dining room, instead of crouching on the ground outside the front door. Then Schwester Clara told me to let them know that they could wash their canteens in the kitchen, and I soon found out that the "old kitchen dragon" had made friends with them, in fact was thoroughly charmed, though she had been one of the most fanatical Nazis I had ever met.

Everybody was thankful to have Americans in the house instead of Italians and in Room No. 16 the official language almost became English. Oberarzt P. was the only one who had no knowledge of this language and persisted in not learning it, making as much fun of it as possible. They spoke of the Americans in a friendly manner; nothing had yet happened to create bad feeling, though everybody was expecting a thunderbolt.

About this time one of our patients had to have a blood transfusion and I offered to give my blood.

As I was lying on a bed next to the patient's, the poor boy seemed very much depressed, but he attempted a faint smile while the other patients in the room looked puzzled. They had not yet seen a girl lying in a hospital ward with soldiers and seemed rather distressed. Three hundred cubic centimeters of blood was drawn out of me, but I felt nothing except the tightness of the rubber band around my arm. The patient thanked me shyly. He soon recovered.

One afternoon as I was going to work the sergeant met me in the street looking very excited, but he could not explain, for soldiers were not allowed to talk to civilians in the street. As soon as I was in the entrance I saw what was up. Half the floor was covered with liqueur and wine bottles and wireless sets, an M.P. watching over them, the first stiff American I had seen.

In the office everybody was laughing. I saw that several had drunk too much. They had tried to absorb as much brandy as possible before giving it up. The Professor had poured his Stock cognac into the wash basin.

Schwester Inge said: "I have still a bottle in my boots. They did not find it, but they threw all my underclothes on the floor and took my camera."

"I knew something would happen soon," said the Professor, "let's not forget that we are prisoners."

I went back to the entrance and tried to speak with the M.P. He seemed very glad to break the rules of non-fraternization. I asked if a few radios could not be spared for the patients. He shrugged his shoulders. "It's an order we have to carry out." But one German military set was left for the dining room.

Room No. 73 was occupied by a staff officer and his lieutenant. They had been there for several weeks and I knew that they were very popular. The afternoon after the wireless had been taken away, the sergeant told me to come to Room No. 73, an invitation for tea! This was exceptional, but the strict rules had been dropped by now, the work halved as everybody admitted it was useless to write long accounts in the passbooks. Formerly these were sent to the War Archives in Berlin, but there certainly was no such thing left in Berlin now.

As I entered the room I hardly could believe my eyes. Two American medics sitting at a well-set table with the lieutenant and a major and Dr. G.; everybody speaking English, three bottles of cognac on the table. "You could have hidden much more," the American sergeant said. Then Schwester Clara came in with an enormous dish of cakes and real coffee and tinned milk.

"Now we can permit ourselves such luxuries; the war is lost, no use saving for Victory." Then she told the latest: "Yesterday the Pole, Fritz, went to the laboratory with a bottle of urine. An M.P. stopped him and took it. Fritz tried to explain in Polish what it was, but owing to his tipsy appearance the M.P. did not believe him and went off with it."

"Well, after a certain hour last night we wouldn't have noticed *what* we were drinking," the medics observed.

From that day German and American medics met regularly

and we had great fun playing table tennis together, but then, having fraternized, they were soon transferred.

The new guard was much stricter, and everybody entering the house had to have a special permit. The patients going to other stations had a card hung around their necks saying: "This patient is going to another hospital for medical treatment." They looked rather like beggars' dogs. Soon a mutual understanding was reached once more and the table tennis resumed. Even the Professor tried his skill! The doctors started to play cards in the office and read Karl May, an author that German boys read when they are about twelve. All the books in the library that had any connection with war or Nazism were burnt — one of the first orders that the German liaison officer issued.

Then one day the section sergeant told me that I could go to Lake Misurina with him; some medical instruments had been left in the hotels there. Such a treat I never had while the Germans were in power. The American guard who signed the paper for the car did not even ask what I was doing, only "Hello, honey!"

I could not help thinking how strange it was to have such a pleasure trip in an ambulance in which previously I had often sat late at night, coming back from the railway station with patients from the hospital train, still dirty and tired and many with only half their limbs, or afflicted with dangerous diseases. I said this to the sergeant. He was in high spirits because of some rumors that Schuschnigg would come into power again in Vienna and felt sure of having been right when he used to say to his comrades: "Wait till the Amis come, you'll see what nice people they are. They won't do any harm to Austrians. If the war were only lost soon enough so that we could take our revenge over the Pifki, etc." Presently he said: "Really, when I think that in a few weeks I'll be a civilian, no more wounded and sick people around me, no more uniforms, no more nurses and smell of hospitals . . . well, I somehow think I'll miss it."

"War certainly has its glamour," said the driver. "Sometimes we had a hard time carrying wounded, but later we had some fun too; I don't care what you think, but you know I am no Austrian and nothing good is waiting for me. God knows what has happened to my family, they were in Breslau. I really wish this life could go on for another couple of years."

He was not the only one who would have liked the war to go on. Many had a real terror, not so much of the prison camps, but of going home as defeated soldiers, poor and ragged, to a perhaps still poorer family. Many had become like children; they were so used to getting food and clothes from the army that they had stopped thinking that there was such a thing as making a living.

"RED CROSS SOLDIERS will be interned like all others." — Official news.

At the beginning of July there were only twenty-three patients left in our house. Two of them were expected to die soon and the others were all very dubious if they'd ever get well. They certainly were not strong enough to be moved.

On the morning of the seventh, as I was nearing the hospital, I saw a row of American ambulances before our house, the drivers scattered around the street and the German orderlies carrying patients out of the house. The American guard told me that all Cortina was going to be evacuated. Presently I saw them carry out one of the dying. I went up to him. He was very excited, in a sort of delirium, and thanked everybody. He thanked even the American driver who shut the ambulance door upon him.

Great disorder and discouragement reigned in the houses;

doctors, nurses and orderlies standing around in the corridors with sad faces, wondering where the patients would be taken to and guessing whether this one or that one would die or get better.

In the middle of the morning the doctor-major came and told Oberarzt P. that all the medical instruments must be packed and the house cleaned and put in order. This was not easy, as most of the servants had left when the partisans arrived.

Two days later all the nurses and women medical assistants left for Meran. They had orders to be ready for eight o'clock, but the cars did not arrive till midday. Schwester Clara had foreseen this and went on making cakes for Dr. P. and the sergeant all morning. While we had our last coffee together the hotelkeeper got the lift running. Many attempts had been made during the last two years to repair that lift, but it had apparently never been possible. The patients had had to climb to the top floor and the weariness of the nurses had never been taken into consideration. This little incident brought tears to the eyes of Schwester Lydia, whom I had never seen cry before. That evening a peculiar sadness prevailed in the house. Most of the doctors and medical students had moved to the Bellevue as their houses were already closed. The only place where life seemed to continue was the big kitchen.

The most elaborate dishes were prepared; everybody wanted to take advantage of the situation, eating being the only pleasure left. Eating, and packing and repacking their rucksacks and talking of what they would do in the concentration camp. After a week of this life, orders came for the whole unit to move out.

In the morning I went to the Hotel Post to say goodbye to the doctor-major and his court. There were about thirty doctors, a dozen medical students and eighty orderlies. A crowd of onlookers had gathered around the cars. I found that Oberarzt P. was missing. Nobody knew where he was. "Seems to be in no hurry to go to Gedi. . . ."

I went to the Bellevue for the last time, empty and silent. I looked into P.'s room. He was snoring in a bundle of blankets, boots and clothes scattered around the room. I shook him, and when he finally realized what I had come for and saw his packed kit, he said: "I have never slept so well in all my life."

I went to the kitchen to make some coffee for him, but there was nothing left except a piece of dry bread and a bit of sugar forgotten in an old tin. When we came back to the Hotel Post all the doctors were already gravely seated in the bus. The medical students tried to smile and the orderlies made a terrible noise, shouting and singing. Somebody had given them wine.

I went back to Gais in a jeep. The American guards of the hospital had arranged everything for me with the courier. Before Bruneck we overtook the column and the driver stopped, and the guards had no objection to my saying goodbye to the prisoners once more. All shouted that I must go to see them when they got home. Finally I waved to them and we went off, the doctor-major's secretary keeping close behind our jeep, for he was on the old motorcycle, at the head of the column, with an American guard on the pillion.

Mamme's home was full of Hawaiians. They had been there for ten days to clear German barracks and felt quite at home. Mamme had of course already told them all about me and that sooner or later I would arrive and that they could then tell her all they wanted because I too knew "American." They were the most polite soldiers I ever met.

One day they took me to Meran in their jeep. I wanted to see who was still there and how they were getting on. On that afternoon the "German Entertainers' Group" held a concert in the Duomo, a fine Gothic building. The American guards all stayed outside the church. I went up to the choir because I knew some of the performers. I was the only civilian. The church was crowded with soldiers, nurses and officers; patients who could not walk were brought in on stretchers and lined up in the aisle. I recognized many doctors and nurses, the Professor and Schwester Lydia.

The musical performance lasted almost two hours. Bach and Mozart. I had not heard such good music for years.

And that was the last I saw of the German army hospital.

$8.$ The letters I had received from Babbo until early 1945 had been calm and enthusiastically concerned about his work. He was proud of my work in the war hospitals and pleased that I was not a cause of worry to them.

I could of course — perhaps should — have left the German military hospital as soon as the Americans arrived in Cortina. The disgust I felt at the civilians who did this made me resolve to stay on until there was work to do, or until I was officially dismissed or interned. It was understood that in time of war civilian workers should remain at their places. However, as soon as things had calmed down I started to cast about for a way to get to Rapallo. I had been without news for two months. I looked in vain at all the available papers. Nothing gave me a clue as to what might have happened to my parents. The gory pictures of Mussolini and Claretta Petacci with their entourage, hanging by the heels —

Thus Ben and la Clara *a Milano*
   by the heels at Milano

— filled me with horror and forebodings. Potentially I saw myself in those shaven Women Auxiliaries jeered at by the partisans. I felt the humiliation and the defeat, especially of those very young Italians — fifteen- and seventeen-year-olds — acutely.

The staff officer, by everyone referred to as Dr. E., to whose party I had been invited, was no ordinary patient. I never quite grasped his story completely, not being really interested at the time, and too ignorant and one-track-minded. But now it is clear to me, patching things together — the friendliness between himself and the Americans and his connections in Milan — that he had in effect been negotiating and probably helping partisans and Americans before the war was over. The slight wound on his hand had either been a mistake or a safety measure. Cortina was a pleasant place in which to wait for things to calm down. When I told the sergeant in the office that I wanted a few days' leave because I must get to Rapallo to see some relatives, he advised me to ask Dr. E. how to go about it. And it turned out that Dr. E. was very eager to have a batch of letters delivered to friends in Milan and was delighted to hear that someone was willing to go that far. He assured me that his friends in Milan would put me up and help me get to Rapallo. He actually wanted me to go on to Rome, too, and take some letters to a friend of his in the Vatican. To make things even stranger, he gave me a heavy gold cigarette case and told me it was not only precious but very dear to him. His friends knew it; I should show it to "Willi" and he would immediately be convinced that I was authorized to carry those letters, and when I got to Rome I should leave it with his friend at the Vatican, Dr. _____. Strange how some of those names have escaped me, but they meant nothing to me. I was merely concerned about not losing or being robbed of that lump of gold.

"What kind of papers do you have?" "An expired Italian identity card, saying nothing more than that I was born in Bressanone." "We'll tell the Americans you must go to Milan to see about your studies. They are very sympathetic to whoever wants to go to school. Say you want to enroll in the University and they will give you a ride." I suppose he spoke to the liaison officer. When I went to the American headquarters I was given a permit to ride on military jeeps. The Cortina courier went only as far as Belluno, but surely from there on I could catch one to Verona, etc. The jeep picked me up at 6 A.M. in front of the Hotel Post. Two rather sullen G.I.'s. I must have been very tense. For the first time I heard the word *relax*. I did not quite know what was meant by it, and they must have been surprised at my inquiring look, since my English was after all pretty good. "Sit back, baby. Have a cigarette." I did not smoke, but had my first taste of chewing gum. In Belluno, as foreseen, after a couple of hours, I was allowed on another courier jeep to Verona. There things looked hectic, hopeless. No American vehicle going to Milan until next day. Stand on the road and hope for the best. I walked away from the town and from the groups of people everywhere trying for transportation. There seemed to be only army vehicles on the road. Raising my arm to every vehicle that passed required willpower. It was a form of begging. The wave of enthusiasm for the Liberators had not touched me. But I must get to Rapallo. A long hot walk towards Lake Garda on a road that felt like pus under my feet. The asphalt, for some inexplicable reason, had blistered, as though the atrocities and bloodshed committed on that strip of land had swollen the ground. Finally one in a long column of trucks picked me up. It was British. The army bakers, the soldier said, going from Trieste to Milan. And immediately he started telling me of cases in which women who had asked for a lift had been driven up some side road and at every off-leading road he said: "Like this, as if I turned now." He appeared utterly crazy and repulsive, a middle-aged skinny reddish hairy creature speaking almost incomprehensible English. I had trouble understanding American slang and Cockney and other British dialects.

In Brescia the column stopped. It was about 2 P.M. I now saw that the truck I was in was the last of the file. The side roads scared me in retrospect. But I did not dare to leave my seat. The Britishers lit a fire in the middle of the road and made tea. The driver came over and handed me his half-empty canteen. I hated drinking from it, was sure the man had all sorts of nasty diseases, but could not refuse and was, moreover, very thirsty. It revived me and made me see things differently. Perhaps it was not such a crazy thing making a fire in the sun and drinking hot tea by the roadside. I felt lucky. Whatever the repressed intentions of that baker, he had been kind to give me a lift and now to offer me some of his tea. He probably sensed my gratitude, for after Brescia he stopped talking. A truck in front broke down and there was a long wait. Around sunset we reached the outskirts of Milan. To my surprise trams were running. I found my way to the address Dr. E. had given me. A charming middle-aged lady opened the door. *Oh, da parte del Dr. E.* In a rolling accent: Come in! Very warmly: "I am Ludmilla's mother." A White

Russian. Her daughter was not at home. Two handsome South African officers were sprawled out in the sitting room, smoking. "Two friends," my hostess said a bit confused, "waiting to take Ludmilla out to dinner." She arrived, strikingly beautiful and smart. She spoke perfect English, cordial and gay and in a hurry. "How darling of E. to send us news. Mama, take care of her." And I was offered borscht for dinner and told how one makes it and how a true Russian will always long for it. It would be unwise for me to go out in the dark and to try to find Willi. My hostess offered me the spare bed in her room and when I woke up next morning I found her bending and stretching her legs in all directions. The previous evening she had looked like a shrunken little lady, almost stiff. I admired her. She was a dancer, practicing, planning to reopen her school of ballet very soon. How plucky, I thought, as I walked through Milan that morning. The city gave the impression of a big mouth with its teeth knocked out. Willi's house was filled with women: the wife, her three sisters and a mother-in-law. He would come home for lunch and I was pressed to stay. They seemed jolly, so relieved it was all over and that they had been wise enough not to take advantage of the war to buy a villa on Lake Como as they so easily could have in their position. Their position was not clear to me, but the lunch was excellent and Willi radiant and waited upon by the crowd of females like a young Teutonic god. He told me there was no need for me to go to Rome, to leave the gold cigarette case and the letters with him. Everything was fine. I should stop on the way back from Rapallo and he would give me a letter for E. I was relieved to be rid of the gold.

On the following morning I was able to board a train for Genoa. The worst was getting from Genoa to Rapallo, but I had learned to follow the crowd, blindly pushing, and got onto a motorboat from Pegli to Santa Margherita after having been rolled out of Genoa on one of those flat trailers railroad workers used around the station. It must have held about two dozen people, all clinging to each other so as not to fall off. It seemed an unending series of tunnels and I had to fight against fumbling hands by hissing: *"La smetta; per favore la smetta"* — Stop it! with rage and shame. At Santa Margherita it did not seem worthwhile waiting around for transport. I set out on foot and after about two hours I was in Sant' Ambrogio, almost incredulous. I had met no one on the *salita*. Mamile opened the door, very pale and tense. "And Babbo?" "My dear, I don't know." We embraced and cried for a while.

Gradually it sank in, draining me of all power of reasoning and feeling, as calamities always do.

Two partisans, two common ex-Fascist convicts, had heard there was a ransom of half a million lire on the head of the Poeta Americano. One of them — mad for a little slave money — was later accused of manslaughter and got killed; the other was imprisoned for theft. The peasants on the hills of Sant' Ambrogio knew them well and despised them.

They knocked with their gun butts on the door. Babbo was alone at home, working on his translation of Confucius. He went to open. *"Seguici, traditore."* He put the volume of Confucius in his pocket and followed them. With a joking gesture he made a noose around his neck with his hands as he stopped to leave the key with Anita, living on the ground floor. She asked the men: Where do you take him? "To the *commando* in Zoagli."

"Il Signore è un galantuomo, non stategli a far male" — in her Genovese singsong — he is a gentleman, don't do him any harm.

The previous day the Allies had arrived in Rapallo. Mamile had been to town early and heard they were setting up headquarters in a hotel on the waterfront. When she got home and told Babbo, he decided to go and report immediately — he had no feeling of guilt, and was ready to explain his ideas and actions. But by the time he got into town the Americans had moved on. No one had authority. He returned home to his translations. The following day Mamile went into town again to gather information and buy a paper. When she came back Anita told her "*due brutti ceffi*" — two ugly snouts — had taken the *Signore* to Zoagli. So Mamile walked down the other side of the hill into Zoagli. She was told he had been taken to Chiavari. She went on to Chiavari and was told: to the CIC in Genoa. And she went to Genoa and found him handcuffed in a waiting room at the CIC among a crowd of people. The American army, so generous with food, had forgotten to offer him a bite, so Mamile, who had not had time to eat, went out to find some *panini*. By evening the waiting room had emptied, but Babbo had not been interrogated. He was handcuffed, but not ready for prison. And there was a lady with him who refused to leave him until she knew what would happen to him, where they would take him. A guard told them they could spend the night in the waiting room. He brought them blankets and they slept on the benches. Next morning they were offered hot coffee and Babbo underwent interrogation. The CIC still did not know what to do with him. No orders had arrived from Washington. After three days — they had almost become adapted to living in that waiting room, grateful to have it all to themselves during the night and for the hot coffee and sandwiches they were now offered regularly — Mamile was called in by Major Amprim — I think that was his name — and told she must go home and keep herself at the disposal of the American authorities, ready to testify in case there was going to be a trial. Where, when? One did not know. Babbo was taken into custody; no one was to see him or communicate with him until further notice.

After a few days Major Amprim came to Sant' Ambrogio to look through Babbo's papers, and took a batch with him. He returned a week later and took the typewriter and more papers. Very polite and considerate but — sorry — he could give no information. Three weeks later — ? — Babbo was taken from Genoa to the Disciplinary Training Center near Pisa, driven through Rapallo in an open jeep, handcuffed to a Negro accused of rape and murder. Both were assigned to the death cells. But this no one knew till six months afterward. Ma' Magerna, the owner of the bar where Babbo had established his literary headquarters before the war and where friends and members of the family left messages, said someone had told her he had seen *il Poeta* on a jeep, driving at full speed in the direction of Zoagli. Mamile went back to Genoa for news, but could find out nothing. No one would tell her where he was, or reassure her that he was still alive. Those were days of hotheaded, senseless killing in Italy. Private grudges were settled by vendettas; the victims were accused of being Fascists, turncoats, anti-Semites, profiteers. There was some hope in the thought that Babbo had no personal enemies and was, presumably, under American care, though Major Amprim had hinted there was strong resentment against him for his anti-Semitic utterances.

There was nothing one could do, nobody one could turn to. I remained in Sant' Ambrogio for two days. It was no longer the place I knew. Light and space had vanished from the house. It was cluttered with furniture, trunks, books, but above all with tension and despair.

On his return to Rapallo in 1943 Babbo must have told Mamile that he had informed me about his wife's existence. The fact that his wife had actually stayed in my room at Sant'

Ambrogio for over a year was conveyed indirectly. "Dorothy had gone to see the old lady — that's why Babbo was alone when the partisans came to fetch him. When I came back from Genoa I found she had packed her things and left me a note saying she had gone to stay with the old lady." It seemed irrelevant. The main thought was: where is he, what will happen to him? And to us? Mamile was giving English lessons, had been keeping herself that way during the past year, teaching at the Ursuline school.

I was able to assure her that I had saved most of my salary and gave her the spare thousand lire I had with me. And she: "We must stand ready. We must be prepared. There will be a trial. His life is in danger. We must be careful what we say." Clearly my having worked in a German war hospital would be held against us, create a negative impression, damage Babbo. The yellow press might make a nasty story out of an illegitimate daughter and harm his reputation in the eyes of public opinion. Everything counts. Everything matters. It might be better for me to stay in Gais and never to appear at all.

Could such pettiness really carry weight? I was dismayed to the point of almost wishing I had responded to Babbo's summons and had escaped from the ease and safety of my town hall and hospital jobs and gone down to Salò to be shot by the partisans. Feeling as I did, I had little doubt that I would have provoked them to it. But these were unconstructive emotions. It might be wise to try and get a job with the Americans. The thought revolted me. After much debating, Mamile gave me an expired American passport and Babbo's seal ring. It was as though I had been entrusted with the Holy Grail. The significance of the gesture sank in deeply. I should go to the CIC in Genoa. Perhaps a young girl could more easily touch the officer's heart and he might tell me where Babbo was; perhaps even give me permission to see him. I had no luck. An impassible officer — Major Amprim was not there — who seemed neither to believe me nor to care whose daughter I was, said: "Sorry. I can tell you nothing." And he put no questions. I was dismissed.

I started on my way back to Cortina with the passport and the ring in a little bag around my neck. Handbags are easily snatched away, Mamile thought. But the nightmare of the pawing persisted. The ring was such a responsibility. Somehow it gave me a glimpse of how tenuous a thread tied me to Babbo. As a reaction perhaps to my insecurity I began from then on to idolize him. Now that I did not even know his whereabouts, he was no longer merely the Herr, il Signore, the Teacher, Tattile or il Babbo, but the hero, the victim, the righteous man who had tried to save the world and had fallen prey to evil powers. The Infallible. His having come from Rome to Gais to tell me the truth and confide his intentions and, as well as he could, his feelings, took on a great significance for me. I completely adhered to his ideas and ideals, as far as I could grasp them. But to the question of how I could help him, the only answer I could find was: Pray. Divine Providence seemed the only power one could turn to and trust since the world, or at least Italy, was in such confusion and one no longer knew who were one's friends or enemies. And my life in the war hospital, though I realized it might be held against Babbo, was the only thing that made sense. When it broke up and I went back to Gais, I received a letter from Mamile saying I should come to Rapallo with all my things as soon as possible. She still did not know where Babbo was, but she gathered he had been taken to the States and felt that we must try to join him there. Mamme was upset: "Wait, wait, how can you go so far, it makes no sense, stay here and help us, wait until you hear what has happened to him, wait until trains start running again, roads are not safe, you will be robbed."

The luggage was a problem indeed: it would have been relatively simple to hitchhike to Rapallo without it. After my first experience I knew one had to be prepared to walk now and again for long stretches. The Hawaiians had unfortunately moved on. At the American headquarters in Bruneck the sergeant I managed to see said they had no jeep that could carry a civilian. It took me a long time to find transportation. I must have alerted the entire valley, for one day a woman working in the pulp factory in Sankt Georgen said that every week a truck came up from Genoa to fetch a load of cardboard. I might try them. The day the truck was due I hung around the factory until I was able to speak to the drivers during their lunch hour. They would leave in the late afternoon, travel all night and arrive in Genoa sometime next day, depending on the queues on the Po where the bridges were all down. Yes, they would give me a lift as far as Genoa. It was a stroke of luck. I offered them each a packet of cigarettes. I had saved my rations; they were the most accepted form of currency in those days. No, there would be no space for luggage in front, but if it was not too bulky, a couple of suitcases could easily be put in the back. I should hold myself ready by 4 P.M. the same day next week.

I decided to put all my belongings in one big trunk, so big and heavy that no one could run off with it. If I looked helpless enough someone would always help me carry it, or else the bribe of cigarettes was sure to work. Inside it I placed my locked treasure box: Babbo's ring, my emerald ring and golden brooch that Grandfather Homer had given to Mamme and she had given to me, and the golden chain with the three cameos, as well as all the money I had saved from my salaries. The other treasures were a few of Babbo's books, the map full

[246]

of annotations and a few fragments of verses and my photographs. Also, knowing how short of food and money Mamile was, I packed lots of tins both from the German army — the surplus in the hospital canteen had been generously distributed during the last weeks — and American corned beef, peanut butter and shortening which the Hawaiian soldiers had given to Mamme. Although Tatte thought that my notion of the trunk was brilliant, Mamme all the while I was packing it wrung her hands and repeated: "I shouldn't go, I shouldn't go," and when Tatte drove me off in the cart she cried as though I were being driven to the gallows, "With two strangers, so far away, all night, with all you have, and then to America!" It was hard to tell which was the greatest evil.

Both Tatte and the horse seemed to turn homeward reluctantly, one skeptical, no doubt, about the company and the other about the vehicle. The truck was obviously constructed for long trips. It had a sort of cot built in behind the driver's seat all along the partition. But we started out all three sitting up: I was allowed to sit by the window. The drivers were two burly, taciturn types who cursed heavily against the war every time they came on a pothole. It soon started to rain. Depressing, and I was already depressed. My glowing prewar dreams of going to America with Babbo had given way to dread. Babbo would not be there proudly to show me his country, happy and full of zest as in the days we walked around Venice and Siena. It would be a dreary crossing with Mamile to see Babbo imprisoned and the great specter: to watch him led to the electric chair.

Shortly after Bozen I was jolted out of my gloomy thoughts by a sudden stop. It was by now pitch-dark and it rained heavily. Inexplicably the truck had broken down. The drivers pottered around for a while and then decided they would abandon the truck and walk into town to spend the night at an inn. There was nothing they could do in the dark and in the rain. What could I do? They showed no sympathy for my predicament. "Come and stay with us and tomorrow we'll go on." I did not want to sound afraid. "I can't leave my trunk!" Later on, reviewing all my mistakes, I blamed myself for having shown too much concern about that trunk. Perhaps they had decided from the outset that they would keep it? While I was debating whether I could spend the night in the truck by the roadside, another vehicle drove up and stopped to see what was the matter. The drivers shouted a few technical details and cursed and started the truck's motor again. "Stop, stop! where are you going?" "Milan." And quickly I thought: How lucky; we'll get there by daylight and I will be able to manage. — No, they did not expect to stop anywhere in between; and, yes, they would give me a lift. "Jump in the back." When the canvas flapped open, the flashlight of one of the drivers revealed people sprawled out. In the foreground the shiny faces of two Negro soldiers. An Italian voice that sounded drunk: *"Vieni pupa."* A shrill female voice cursed him. This looked bad indeed. I walked up to the drivers and asked whether I might sit in front with them. One laughed: "Yes, the girls might be afraid of losing business and beat you up." But again, no room for the trunk, that must go into the back. I begged the two drivers to unload it from their truck and lift it on to the new one. All right, but quick, they had had enough of standing around in the rain. I saw them take it off their truck and lift it on the other — in a hurry to move on: get in.

On the road along the shore of Lake Garda I heard a terrific bump. "My trunk!" I shouted, jolted out of my doze. The driver slowed down and stuck his head out of the window. "Must have been a pothole I did not notice." He did not seem convinced but drove on. Craning my neck out of the window

[248]

revealed nothing. Everything was dark and silent in back. I begged him to stop, but he said: "Don't worry, no one can jump out of a moving truck, and certainly not with a trunk." "Yes, but he could have thrown it out first and then jumped after." "Do you want to get off and start looking for it? I have no time to lose." I shut up. When in the early morning the truck pulled up in a square behind the station in Milan, after the bedraggled crowd of men and women and soldiers had jumped out and were moving off in all directions, empty-handed or with small cases, my trunk was gone. The drivers called after the people and a few of the men came back; they knew nothing, had noticed nothing, were asleep, never noticed whether a trunk had been put on or had been taken off. Yes, they remembered the truck had slowed down once, but that was all. The drivers expressed regret, shrugged their shoulders, all they could do to help me was to show me where the police station was. And there I waited among a crowd until the office opened. Eventually my turn came to go into a dusty office stacked with files. A sleepy policeman took down the list of contents. Suspicion? The two drivers of the first truck might have faked. It was dark; they might have simply lifted the trunk off their truck and instead of transferring it, lowered it on the other side knowing I would get in in front. And that bump along Lake Garda. The exact spot? Names? Addresses? Nothing, nothing. "I fear we cannot help you." "But surely," I said, "the police can find the ring, it's such a unique object, a red stone, with a profile, almost an inch long." "First thing anyone will do is wrench the stone from the setting and melt the gold." Hopeless. *Archiviato* — filed. What next?

I had only a couple of hundred lire on me, hardly enough to get me to Rapallo if I had to take a train. Besides that, a comb, a few packets of cigarettes intended as a gift to the drivers or a possible help in proceeding to Rapallo, and, for whatever emergency, the Italian identity card and the American passport.

I thought of Ludmilla's kind mother in Milan. When I got to the house a neighbor said they were away on vacation. So I made for Willi's house. His wife and sisters-in-law had been so friendly, perhaps I could at least wash up and rest long enough to think things over. Fortunately one of the sisters was at home and, to my surprise, Dr. E. had arrived in Milan the previous week. *"Poverina, poverina,"* when I told her what had happened. "Take a rest until lunch and when he comes he'll help you." Like his friend Willi previously, Dr. E. appeared radiant, and in civilian clothes! He must have guessed my surprise and explained that the letters I had carried for him had speeded up things. Two British officers had come to Meran to "free" him and drive him to his friends in Milan. His home, I remembered, was in Vienna. After I had told him my woes, he immediately pulled out a ten-thousand-lire note and handed it to me. It seemed a lot of money, and I said I could not possibly accept it. "I have plenty," he laughed, "and you have helped me more than you realized." He looked as though he disposed of lots of money, but it was really his assurance which suggested it. Even while at the hospital he had shed a sense of well-being and prosperity. And since he now was a civilian and the war a thing of the past and perhaps because I hoped that with his connections among British and American officers, he might even know something about Babbo, I told him who I was and that I had an American passport, though expired. It was his turn to be surprised. "But then you should have gone to the American police, not to the Italian. They are much more likely to help you, and anyway they will drive you to Rapallo." He told me where to go. Babbo's name meant nothing to him, and he had no advice on that score. He gave me to understand that his own release had been so prompt because he had been instrumental in saving Jews in Austria.

I followed his advice and went to the American Military Police. I had slowly decided upon a course of action. If possible I would ask them to drive me back to Gais. Perhaps it was only to tell Mamme how right her forebodings had been and gather the nerve to face Mamile, but in reality to collect my few discarded clothes and pick up some more food. And in the back of my brain crazy thoughts: perhaps we'll find the trunk along the road, or I might find out about the drivers at the factory, or meet their truck. This sounded reasonable to the sergeant who listened to me. O.K., I'll have two guys drive you home tomorrow. Go over to the Recreation Center, they'll give you a room and take care of you. And I was directed to a very comfortable hotel. I was astonished at their easy manners. All I had said: I am an American. They had not even asked me to show my passport. All I was told was to be in the lounge by seven next morning, and to have a good time. I went to bed immediately, glad to be finally alone, and cried myself to sleep.

In the lounge next morning two MP sergeants were waiting, one blond, reserved, thin and taciturn, the other dark, bald, roundish and jolly, stocked with Mars Bars and chewing gum. At some kind of headquarters in Desenzano we stopped for lunch. They positively stuffed me with food, thinking it would cheer me up. It almost did; but in Gais, Mamme pitifully wrung her hands and wept over tins and clothes and money, while my anguish was for the irreplaceables.

While I hastily collected my discarded belongings, the two sergeants were left in the *Stube* with Tatte playing host, quietly smoking his pipe and holding the latest foundling on his knees. The two MP's killed time by looking at the pictures

[251]

on the wall. The central paneling between the two windows had with the passing of years turned into a kind of altar of images; dozens of pictures pinned to the wood: Tatte as a soldier in 1917, wedding pictures of the various brothers and sisters, above all snapshots of the many children Mamme had brought up. Most of them were of myself at different ages. All these were arranged in a sort of halo around a big picture of the Herr. The effect was bizarre, but Mamme was very proud of her composition.

When I came in to say I was ready, Tatte whispered suspiciously: *Er schaugg gröt Ihm un.* The jolly easygoing sergeant turned raging dark eyes upon me and said: "Young lady, what do you have to do with *that* swine!"

"He is my father."

The blond sergeant blushed; to break up the embarrassment he said: "Ready?" I was of two minds, and still perplexed that anyone should have recognized Babbo. Above all at the rage. Fortunately Mamme and Tatte had not comprehended, though they obviously sensed something had gone wrong. The dark sergeant jumped behind the steering wheel and concentrated on speed. When they changed off, he sat glum, knitting his brows. Despite my hurt and disgust at his utterance I couldn't help being amused: he looked exactly like the perpetually angry dwarf in Disney's *Snow White.* The thought that perhaps he was sorry for what he had said occurred to me, but I ventured no explanation and was asked for none. They dropped me off in front of the Recreation Center, as though I were entitled to a free room once more. The blond sergeant said: "Take good care." I told the GI at the desk I would leave early next morning.

I took a train to Genoa. The surprise and relief at being taken care of was short-lived. Things were not as simple and easy as all that. I decided I'd take care of myself once more.

But that proved not so easy either. I found a seat next to a young man in civilian clothing, reading *The West Wind of Love* and with a pile of English magazines on the vacant seat. Very politely he lifted the suitcase for me, and because of his appearance and reading material I thanked him in English. Gradually we got to talking. Or rather *he* talked. Had I read Compton Mackenzie — *West Wind, South Wind, North Wind?* I had not. And he held forth on their literary merits, their philosophy: what an extraordinary writer! To this day I have not got round to reading him. I would have preferred looking at the young man's magazines. In Genoa it turned out that he too was going to Rapallo. Impossible to shake him off. He was too polite, carried my suitcase. And picked it up again in Rapallo as a matter of course. I was frantic. I could not possibly appear at Mamile's doorstep with a stranger: it was bad enough to tell her I had lost the ring. Perhaps it was the latter fear that deprived me of the necessary firmness to get rid of him. He kept up his whirlwind conversation all the way to Sant' Ambrogio. Mamile was, as expected, surprised to see me turn up with a stranger, but his appearance was so decidedly civilized — and British — that she asked him in for a cup of tea. But that was that, and he promptly left. Mamile commented: "I did not like the way he looked at our books, one has to be careful. Everyone seems to be a spy these days." Staring at me from the bookcase were Mackenzie's *West Wind, South Wind, North Wind.* —

And now the sad tale about my trunk unfolded. At the beginning Mamile was full of sympathy. Since I could not help crying she hugged me and tried to console me until I almost felt consoled. Then suddenly: "But you have Babbo's ring?" "No." I had not had the courage to say it at the beginning. She pushed me away: "Naughty, stupid, wicked child, I knew you couldn't be trusted! This is a sign, this is a sign."

And she started to weep. I felt scorchingly all the things she said and knew that by "a sign" she feared bad luck for Babbo. It turned into a haunting thought. A strained, painful six months followed.

And finally a letter from Babbo arrived. A short note in pencil. The address was typed on a brown envelope that had BASE CENSOR over it — or some similar imprint. He was — had been all the time — barely two hundred miles from Rapallo. At the Disciplinary Training Center near Pisa. His wife had been granted permission to go and see him. On the second of October permission was granted to his "minor child." We were elated, and apprehensive as to how we would find him, turning over in our heads what to say during a precious half-hour. The permit said thirty minutes once a month, in the presence of two guards.

The only military stationed in Rapallo were South Africans. A jeep was going to Pisa late in the afternoon and would come back next day: they would give us a lift. We arrived at the camp when it was already dark. The South Africans said they would wait for us, they had advised us to spend the night at the American Red Cross in Pisa.

Mamile handed the permit to the sentinel who shouted into a telephone: "Two young ladies." Then, having looked us over he added: "Pound's minor child at the gate!" We had feared Mamile might not be let in since the permit was only for me, but either because it was assumed that a minor must be chaperoned, or, more likely, because under dramatic circumstances, she automatically turned into an irresistible force, we were both led into a big tent. As far as I remember there was a desk and three iron chairs in it, but my memory is vague; my eyes must have been fixed on the opening of the tent and then on Babbo.

I had last seen him in Gais weary and full of dust, with crumpled clothes, so his appearance was not too surprising. He had aged a lot and his eyes were inflamed. It was the dust and the light, he said, but now he was getting treatment. He sounded grateful, he had kept his trait of being most appreciative of small kindnesses and he made the medical care and the tent that he was allowed to sleep in sound like great blessings. In the *gabbia* he had collapsed. A severe sunstroke, he thought. He used the Italian for cage, and since we had not seen the cages we did not have a clear idea of what he meant. It was only years later when I visited him in Saint Elizabeths Hospital in Washington that he described the gorilla cage in detail and how he had felt threatened by the sharp iron spikes. He had been deprived of belt and shoelaces to ensure that he could do himself no harm; and yet when, for no apparent reason, they reinforced his cage with stronger iron netting, they cut the old netting about ten inches from the ground so as to form a low hedge of spikes all around. He had interpreted it as a not-too-subtle invitation to suicide: the easiest way to slash his wrists. I realized that during certain hours of despair the temptation had been great.

Of his life in the DTC he himself has left us the best record in the Pisan Cantos. Despite his walking tours and his familiarity with the hills and the sea, never had he lived so close to and been so dependent on nature as while in the death cell, and in the drenched tent, under Mount Taishan at Pisa, where the sight of a lizard upheld him; when

> the loneliness of death came upon me
> (at 3 P.M. for an instant) . . .

and

When the mind swings by a grass-blade
an ant's forefoot shall save you . . .

He told us he was now allowed to go into the infirmary
after office hours and use the typewriter. He had not lost his
humor: "because of exemplary conduct," and he winked mis-
chievously towards Mamile. He also apologized to her for his
untidy appearance, pointing at the unlaced shoes. As ever he
tried to express more with his eyes than in words. A guard was
standing by the entrance of the tent; he looked embarrassed
at having to stand there and made up for it by allowing us to
stay almost an hour. When he could concede no more he said:
"Time to go, Mr. Pound." And he left us alone in the tent to
say goodbye. 'Nothing. Nothing that you can do . . .' — it
was reciprocal.

Aside from the tent and a few guards, I have no memory of
the DTC. The image of Babbo, grizzled and red-eyed in a
U.S. Army blouse and trousers, in unlaced shoes without
socks, with his old twinkle and bear-hug, stands as on a huge
screen in the foreground.

Shortly after our visit the first batch of Pisan Cantos arrived. He wanted me to type them up and make several
copies. For the Base Censor to allow them out he had written
a note to the effect that they contained nothing seditious, no
private code or personal message. But for us they contained
more than all this. I was overwhelmed by the responsibility of
the typing. What if I misspelled? I remember pondering for
hours over *Vai soli,* not knowing the origin of the quotation, I
felt sure it must be *Mai soli,* but dared not alter it. And fountain pan? — dust to the fountain pan
It was only after I had detached myself from the chore and
responsibility of the typing that slowly the entire passage crystallized and I could see the rose in the steel dust

[256]

participating in the poet's vision:

Serenely in the crystal jet
      as the bright ball that the fountain tosses
(Verlaine) as diamond clearness
        How soft the wind under Taishan
            where the sea is remembered
        out of hell, the pit
        out of the dust and glare evil
        Zephyrus/Apeliota
This liquid is certainly a
      property of the mind
nec accidens est   but an element
                  in the mind's make-up
est agens and functions   dust to the fountain pan otherwise
      Hast 'ou seen the rose in the steel dust
               (or swansdown ever?)
so light is the urging, so ordered the dark petals of iron
we who have passed over Lethe.

We who have passed over Lethe. For me he had by then entered into the dimension of the Beyond. This feeling had
nothing to do with hero worship or morbid attachment. It was
respect. Transcendental. I did not go as far as sewing fragments of Cantos into my clothes, but I certainly wrapped
them tightly around my mind. I suppose it was because of the
intense enjoyment and insight certain passages offered that
the Cantos slowly became the one book I could not do without. My "Bible," as friends have often teased me.

    But I was not the only one to have strong feelings about
them. Never have I seen Mamile cry so unrestrainedly as
when she read Canto 81:

Pull down thy vanity

And the cry of AOI is an outburst more personal than any other in the Cantos and expresses the stress of almost two years when he was pent up with two women who loved him, whom he loved, and who coldly hated each other. Whatever the civilized appearances, the polite behavior and the façade in front of the world, their hatred and tension had permeated the house.

Les larmes que j'ai créés m'inondent
Tard, très tard je t'ai connue, la Tristesse,
I have been hard as youth sixty years

Until then the attitude toward personal feelings had been somewhat Henry Jamesian: feelings are things other people have. One never spoke of them or showed them.

In the last six months we had tacitly resumed the pattern of our life of 1941–1943, with two sad differences; no Babbo, and instead of playing the violin, Mamile gave English lessons to earn our keep. For me, improving my English was still the main task, now with an added scare: should we be called to the States it would make a very bad impression on people if Pound's daughter did not know English! Father Chute, who during the last two years of the war had been interned by the Germans in some forlorn place in the hills, had returned to his villa. He gave me no longer lessons, but work. He was editing Eric Gill's letters and asked me to do the typing. The handwriting of the originals was exceptionally elegant; one saw his preoccupation with beautiful lettering.

Another little job I got with Mrs. Riess, a longtime member

of the English colony at Rapallo who had been interned in the hospital in Sterzing during the war — a delightful old lady, except when she spoke of her son, against whom she had some grudge. Her feelings may have been justified, but in expressing them she became frightening to look at: the composed, almost Buddha-like face became hard and ugly and her language absurd.

I was to put her books in order, read out loud to her and play bezique. I also answered the doorbell, made tea and sometimes prepared a very light supper for her. She was plagued by severe arthritis. And old age of course. Aside from a little pocket money I picked up a few useful notions: how to make six omelets with one egg, various cross-stitch patterns and the valuable William Morris dictum: Have nothing in your house that you do not believe to be both useful and beautiful.

One day a tall thin figure stood at the door: small face with steel-blue eyes under a cumbersome, dark, homemade-looking beret, head held high. Her ample cloak seemed like draperies stitched together, rather than a cut and sewn garment. It gave her a willowy, flowing appearance, not unattractive, but distant and almost unreal. "You must be Mary," she said, but did not introduce herself. "Would you kindly return this book to Ma Riess and tell her Mrs. Pound did not like it at all. I shall look in on her some other time. *Au revoir*." She turned abruptly and slowly descended the stairs, clinging to the railing.

Mrs. Riess was very deaf. I delivered the message at the top of my voice, but failed to convey the fact that I did not know who the visitor had been. She assumed I knew, so I learnt more than I wanted to, though I am sure she did not mean to gossip. My grandmother it seemed, had very decided literary opinions.

When I told Mamile about the encounter: "Her! An excuse to see what you look like!" — and it was as though Dorothy, Babbo's wife, by showing up, had opened the floodgates of Mamile's discretion and restraint.

My vision of Chinese Imperial customs and order was smashed to pieces. Mamile had been wronged, it was tough, but all I could think of was: poor Babbo. His wife and his mother on one hill exchanged polite notes with the mother of his daughter on another hill, a much higher one. Ma' Magerna's café served as our private post office. No one met.

The time for our second visit to the DTC in Pisa was drawing near: half an hour once a month, the permit had said. And we went into town to make arrangements about transportation. The South Africans were again willing to take us in one of their jeeps. But when we bought a paper we read that Ezra Pound had been flown to Washington to be tried for treason. Illa dolore obmutuit, There was no further need for transportation.

At Ma' Magerna's we met John Drummond, an old friend of the family's who used to live in Rapallo before the war, but was now in the British army. Whether by design or by chance, a very young American soldier came into the bar. Dark, spectacled, he looked frail and shy. Drummond knew him; confusedly he muttered introductions: So this was Omar! Dorothy's son. I wondered: does he realize who I am, shouldn't we embrace?

No ice was broken. We evidently had nothing in common.

Omar, on a visit to his mother, had stopped by the Pisa camp and had been told the news the previous day. On the way home Mamile said: "It is a very good thing he has joined the American army. It will be of great use to Babbo." Yes, no doubt, whereas my having worked in a war hospital with the losing side would harm him. It hurt. It did not tally. And I was not mature enough then to realize that Mamile by speaking thus was merely trying to keep her own inner furies at bay. AOI! AOI!

Babbo was gone. There was nothing left. I would return to Gais, to my brothers and sisters there who were not my brothers and sisters at all, but at least there was no pretending. Needless to say, I hated the American officials for not giving us notice: hadn't they known three days before that they were going to fly their prisoner to the U.S.A.? Couldn't they have let us say goodbye to him? It had not been ill will on the part of the guards at the prison camp; they had all been kind. But the anonymous power, because it is anonymous, has no heart.

So I decided to turn my back on a situation I did not accept. At the time I thought I had freedom of choice. I felt sure of what was right or wrong, true or false, sincere or devious. "Listen to your own heart and then act." How? My confidence in Confucian ethics was unshakable. I could not go far wrong. The world of which I had had a glimpse in Venice, Siena and Rome had obviously collapsed. The society of great minds in elegant surroundings for which I had fostered vague hopes, had been dispersed by the war. America: a big question mark, holding Babbo in its tentacles and me in the dark. It frightened me. But Rapallo too was devious and treacherous. I was bored and unhappy. I wrote bad poetry and grew fat, and was of no help or consolation to Mamile. I hated myself.

Finally I took courage and announced I would go back to Gais. "That may well be the best place for you, but first finish your job. And read this." A typed will. I read it carefully but did not realize its importance and far-reaching effects, nor what literary executor implied.

My job consisted in making an inventory of Babbo's papers and books. As soon as we heard that he had been taken to Washington Mamile decided we must put all his papers in order and seal them up and sort out and list all the magazines and books, marking those which had items by him, etc. And so for weeks I tied strings around the Moriondo chocolate boxes where he kept his personal letters and sealed them, and the files where he kept his carbons and letters from literary and political correspondents. I assembled and sorted newspapers and magazines and tied them up in parcels, numbered and labeled. Pamphlets, Baedekers, broadsheets, each scrap of paper had assumed vital importance: one stray sentence might help his cause. I liked doing this, for it kept me in touch with Babbo's work. But there was also a feeling of doom in the whole process: a sealing up and saving for eternity every single word he had read or written.

I stopped eating peanut butter and writing poems. Rigorously I worked out my own future. What weighed on my conscience was the loss of Babbo's ring. Whether I could have avoided the theft by greater care or courage was doubtful, but the fact remained: I had been entrusted with the ring and must replace it. I interpreted

> and another Bacher still cut intaglios
> such as Salustio's in the time of Ixotta

as a pointer to remake it myself. — Though I had absolutely no talent for drawing, I practiced for hours copying Babbo's profile by Gaudier-Brzeska. I would go back to Gais and ask Herr Bacher to take me on as an apprentice. I would learn how to carve and make intaglios. The idea of becoming a sculptor inflamed me. I had never been able to make up my mind which was my language; in whichever I wrote the results seemed worthless. I was incapable of mastering words. I would no longer depend on words to express images and feelings. So I got enthusiastic over the Vorticist manifesto and

[262]

started to read everything I could on sculpture and painting. Eric Gill's letters may have been instrumental in awakening my urge for a craft. But the greatest influence was undoubtedly Ronald Duncan's *Diary of a Husbandman*, for it showed how one could practice agriculture and a métier at the same time. A book full of good sense applied to the only field I had some experience in: farming. I knew I would have to earn my living. Duncan described how one can be self-sufficient on two acres and have a part-time job. I knew it was not enough for me to say: I will go back to Gais and study sculpture. As long as I lived with Mamme and Tatte I would have to live their life. I had found it hard in 1943. Working in the fields at their pace entailed complete participation in the village life, including churchgoing, dancing and conforming to village customs.

Behind the Bacher mansion was a small cottage. It had burnt down once when I was a child. I had been frightened: from our bedroom window we had seen the glow on our neighbor's farm and for a while we could not figure out what it was, it looked so ominous and supernatural. When we came out of the house, we smelt the burning and ran, half dressed, amidst a great clatter of powerless firemen. It was midwinter. The river was too far away to get water from, the fountain frozen. I remember watching two empty bottles on the kitchen windowsill slowly melt like candles, spellbound by fire. But then I threw snowballs like everyone else on the Bacher woodshed. The crowd threw snow against the neighboring barns to prevent them from catching fire. The firemen shoved snow into the flames. By dawn the house had been reduced to a few crumbling walls. It had been a very old cottage and had stood empty for a couple of years. Before the war it was rebuilt and rented to the roadsweep. The land around it was not sufficient to keep a family. I had little doubt that Herr Bacher would prefer me as a tenant since he was notoriously on bad terms with the roadsweep. I became convinced that the place had always been waiting for me. The lawful owner had left the village the very year I was born and had never returned.

I knew how to grow vegetables, wheat and potatoes, how to milk a cow, cut grass, make hay. I had raised sheep at a profit and kept bees. My sole capital consisted of the ten thousand lire Dr. E. had given me in Milan. But I was sure Tatte or one of Mamme's brothers would lend me a cow. My existence seemed to depend on a cow. And since obviously I could not hope to produce a fine intaglio at the outset I would practice by carving all my tools and crockery, sticking to the William Morris principle. Babbo had advocated self-reliance and self-sufficiency: I would put his ideas into action down to the minutest details. I would improve my spinning, perhaps learn how to weave from one of the two weavers I knew. Everything essential was produced and made in Gais.

For three months I nurtured my dream and made plans. Babbo seemed swallowed up in distance and silence once more. One letter had arrived from Gallinger Hospital, but it gave no details about himself. Mamile had been urged by friends to be patient, keep quiet, stay put and above all not to try and go to America because that might stir up rumors. It was suggested that perhaps if I tried to be put on the immigration quota, I might eventually get accepted at an American college. For some inexplicable reason the word immigrant was most distasteful to me. Also I thought the American college system was the same as in Europe, which would have meant for me another five years schooling since I had no degrees. Absurd to go back to school at twenty, I thought. I had to earn a living; besides, I had never heard Babbo recommend a college education for me.

Mamile was being hurt and humiliated from all sides. I felt

sorry for her but helpless. She lashed out against wives and humbugs. She was right, and I was distressed. Finally she proposed going back to Siena if the musical academy reopened. Perhaps Count Chigi could offer me a job. No. I stuck to my resolution: farming and sculpture. Mrs. Riess approved of my plan. She gave me a few books and a cross-stitched tablecloth for my cottage. She must have told Dorothy that I was going back to Gais. One day we saw each other on opposite sidewalks. Dorothy crossed the street and said: "I hear you are going back to Gais. I shall soon be leaving for America. If there is anything I can do for you, you must let me know, you must think of me as your stepmother." Did she have tears in her eyes? I forget whether I managed to say anything except thank you and goodbye. I felt no need for a stepmother. For Christmas a parcel had been left for me at Ma' Magerna's with a note signed DP. She and grandmother had heard of the loss of my trunk. Dorothy sent me three books of Babbo's almost completely decayed; she apologized for the condition they were in, they had been buried in a garden during the war. And grandmother sent me a few bits of fur. I would have preferred an invitation to go to see her. Grandmother wanted at all costs to go to America. Our informant was Father Chute. He did not approve of my decision of going back to Gais. He thought I should stay with Mamile. I agreed in principle but said I did not feel like being a financial burden to her; my company did not cheer her up, and I was of no use to anyone. And then he said a strange thing: "Remember that in the eyes of God, according to our Catholic faith, your mother is your father's true wife." The war had mellowed him, had taught him to devote himself primarily to the alleviation of human suffering. He had lost his excessive reserve.

By the beginning of March all Babbo's papers were neatly tied up and sealed, all his belongings listed. His writing table was tidy, pencils and rusty paper-clips waiting for his hand to pick them up again. His hat on a hook by the door, the wine-red peignoir on a hook by the bed, worn out slippers and sandals lined up on the cupboard floor, old underwear neatly darned and stacked, strewn with mothballs and eucalyptus. The bassoon, the tennis rackets and walking stick, everything. Embalmed. Deadweight. Unbearable. Light and lightness had fled from the house, hovering, shrouded, and sighing, among the gray olive branches outside. The dark almond tree by the window burst into white tears as I left.

Courageously, obstinately Mamile clung to and defended the shrine, against rain and theft. To no avail. Maxims pegged for memory over the doors: dead letters. *"Vivere così che i tuoi discendenti ti ringrazino"* — "Live in such a way that your descendants will be grateful." Are they ever? And locks? To no avail. The spirit had left. The profile by Gaudier, on the whitewashed wall over the bed, underlined the chill that had entered that room. Too many people had been unhappy in the house for too long. The air was poisoned. The holy ground sealed up.

I was eager to start out on a life of my own, free, with clear and high ideals, and, to be sure, an overdose of pride. I thought I was rejecting all the lies and pretensions and compromises, Mamile's dark resentment, grandmother's stubbornness, Dorothy and Omar, whatever, whoever they were. I was leaving everything behind. All I wanted to keep was something to believe in — the freedom to live the kind of life I thought Babbo had meant me to live — simple and laborious. I set forth, with no regrets other than Mamile's disappointment. But in reality, far from cutting myself loose neatly, I was setting out to build castles — castles in the air turning into a castle on the rock into which slowly streamed everyone and everything with all the clatter of outlived feelings and discarded belongings and all the papers tied up and sealed for eternity, tossed and torn and disrupted by a horde of disciples and publishers scholars secretaries and collectors — hogs after truffles, greedy widows and fearful wives, chucked from attic to attic from truck to truck in a whirlwind . . .

And all because Mercury — for the fun of it? — had withheld a telegram for over a year.

At the bottom of the hill-path, a few days before my departure for Gais, a swift boy from the telegraph office holding a bicycle, handed me an impressive bundle of papers. Half a dozen wrappers from Red Cross stations, German Commandos, post offices, and inside it all simply: *"Buon Natale e Felice Anno Nuovo. Boris."* Happy New Year!

The boy whom I had met at that April picnic outside Rome with Princess Troubetzkoi had no friends or relatives in the North when in 1944 the Italian Red Cross distributed free telegraph-forms for Christmas greetings from the South to the North, so he thought of me.

That April in Rome with Babbo belonged to another era, but the urge to communicate and for some intellectual contact was strong. There was no one in Gais I could talk to. So letters started to fly back and forth: my correspondent was intrigued by a girl who had set out to start on her own, farming of all things. In his surroundings there was nothing so clear cut and solid. He would like to invest 100,000 lire in a cow, he wrote. Could he come and see me?

I was still staying with Mamme and Tatte. I had spoken seriously with Herr Bacher. "So so, so so . . ." and he scratched his head and laughed: *"Interessant, interessant."* The renting of the cottage seemed feasible enough, though it would mean waiting until Michelmas, when contracts expire. But as for starting right away as an apprentice in his workshop — *Ja ja*, he would think it over. I could see that the idea amused him. And I waited. It was time to put in potatoes; we were very busy, and one gets pretty tired and dirty pacing all day long the cloddy newly plowed furrows, stooping to place the "eye" at regular intervals. Finally the end of the week came and we had finished and I was bicycling homewards thinking only of washing and the Sunday rest. In Gais things always happen when the furrows are opened for sowing or for reaping. When Tattile came out of Rome in 1943, we were reaping. When a young boy arrived in 1946 out of Rome — the Eternal City — we were sowing.

A slender boy with the face of an angel was stretched in the grass outside the house. "Your guest from Rome," Mamme said. I had not expected him so soon. We would hardly have recognized each other; he probably had not thought I was so radical in my decision to work in the fields. Evidently we both had not taken each other's letters too seriously.

To ease the mutual embarrassment I immediately took him to see "my" cottage. He was not impressed in the least. But he raised his eyes: What a wonderful castle! Yes, Neuhaus. The Schloss and the chapel and the farm. They were in the picture. One could not look at Sâma, my home, without including them in one's range of vision. And as for my cottage, at the edge of the wood, at the foot of the mountain, it stood right below and was called Schoutna — in the shade. The name of the cottage had always appealed to me, I liked the idea of living in the shade, symbolically, of history and art. Bacher's house shielded Schoutna from the road.

By the Italians Neuhaus had been called Castello di Casanova. I knew it inside out, its legends and history. Three times a year one went up there in procession. The white baroque chapel was perched on a grassy slope at a stone's throw from the castle. In between stood the farm. During my childhood it had been a pub; I had gone there with Mamme

[268]

and Tatte on Sunday afternoons. At present the property seemed to have no owner, an aftermath of the political options of 1938. A German ex-officer was living in it, quasi-clandestinely; clearly a *Hochstapler*, in front of the village claiming he had a right to be there because he was engaged to the Count's daughter and had been entrusted with the sale of the castle. Boris promptly declared he would get his father to buy it for him.

"What would you do with a castle?"

"Oh, invite my friends."

"To do what?"

"Paint, write, study. Besides, I want to reestablish the Order of Canossa; I need a seat."

"What's the Order of Canossa?"

"Haven't you ever heard of the Order of Malta?"

"Of course, I have even looked at Saint Peter's through the keyhole of their portal. I know about the Templars and the Albigenses, in The Cantos. . . ."

"Yes, and in my family the crusader Raimondo in 1289 founded an order in honor of his ancestral aunt Matilde di Canossa; in the illuminated parchment of the twelfth century that is kept in the Vatican Museum, Donizone gives the whole history. We are descended from Rothar, who married the daughter of Teodolinda, legitimate heir of the Longobard kings, despite the *lex salica*, through alliance, her brother having been dethroned. In the year 900 Sigifredo still governed Lombardy . . ."

More or less . . . How can one remember so much history flung in one's face still smelling of earth! But I was interested. This was almost like the Cantos; I had not heard such topics mentioned since the days I walked on the *salita* with Babbo.

"And the motto is *Canusiae cuspis caesim caedit* . . ." *Canusiae cuspis* . . . his eyes too, his grace, his charm had

[269]

slain me suddenly. I felt elated. I thought: "Intelligence, the glory of God," stands before me. Finally someone I could talk with. And he quickly grasped Babbo's ideas and poetry; and although his activities after 1943 had been with the Allies, and one of his best friends killed in the Fosse Ardeatine by the Germans, he was full of sympathy.

"*Atto fuit primus princeps, astutus ut hidrus;/Nobiliter vero fuit ortus de Sigifredo* . . . later entered The Tale of The Tribe:

Lupus comes itineris, Rothar arianae haeresios —
           edicti prologo
. . . got some laws written down . . .

A new dynasty came in through the Edictum Rotari. And goes back? — through Obthora to Odin who hung in the wind for nine days to learn the runes. They are all there in the background: Authar and his marvelous reign; Teodolinda with the iron crown and aunt Matilde at whose door the emperor had been kept waiting; and the crusader Sigifredus and on the other side the Cossack and Mongol grandmothers and the architects of Petersburg. But the lands? Gone to the Church. The homes? To the State. The crown? La corona di ferro in the Monza dome. The castles? Castiglion de Barattis a ruin. Ruins and debts and crumbling *cimeli*.

But the Geni? Oh, the geni are livelier and stronger than ever. And I wrote to Babbo: We have mated. I wanted things to be clear. And from the hell-hole: Make sure he is healthy. Mamile had a few happy moments visualizing the wedding ceremony in Count Chigi's chapel and described the clothes she and I would wear. But she cautioned: Wait, there are signs. Wait and see if the father does buy him the castle.

The father came to Gais. I asked Tatte if I could harness Fuchs and drive to meet him. *"Wenne moansch . . .* if you think his wallet is so heavy he can't walk from the station to our house . . ."* Over the bridge the horse shied. He pranced on his hind legs and kicked sideways as though he wanted to throw me into the river, cart and all. I had to get off and lead him back home; he kept nudging my shoulder as though he were pleased. One cannot be angry at a horse for very long. Father and son followed on foot. I did not like the father. He said after dinner, as we were watching the stars: Let's keep a happy memory of this visit.

Memory? Oh no, this wasn't something to be remembered. This was the future. It was love. And I had been told: I'll marry you. They departed, for there were exams to be taken.

After two months I thought I could endure the separation no longer. I forgot all my resolutions, broke all promises to myself and took a train for Rome. I was twenty-one.

Coda. My marriage to an Italian, though half Russian and though we were careful to speak English in public, had broken my bonds with Gais. He came from *untn aua,* from Rome, from the despicable "down there" where for Tyroleans all evils come from.

But I soon discovered that nationalistic prejudice was a bagatelle compared to religious prejudice, in those days. Grandmother Isabel was not a Catholic. To marry an Italian — well, it had happened before, but to bring a Protestant to Gais, and an old lady who would surely die there — not even Mamme could forgive. She wrung her hands and entreated me not to do such an *Unsinn:* "It will take hours to get a doctor and who knows if in winter you can get one up there at all. The priest can't give her the Sacrament and you have an innocent baby in the house!"

What about kindness? What about the dream of building up a strong family with descendants and ancestors and one's duty to the aged!

They won't bury her in sacred ground. What a *blamage!* — under stress Mamme had a way of overflowing with historically charged words, or interlingual root-words, left behind like driftwood by the flood tide of some foreign army. — "What a *blamage,* if she dies they won't even ring the bells for her."

Bells! Bells! What arguments. We had a chapel of our own with a steeple and two bells.

And how they had rung clear and festive over the glittering snow in the valley at midday the first Sunday after we had entered Neuhaus.

It was the custom: when the owners were in residence, the tenant rang the bells on Sunday. But the tenant did not go to ring the bells for us. Although he had received orders from the Count to give us the key to the castle, he looked upon us as mere intruders, two children and penniless at that. Moreover, he wasn't sure that the Count had any rights either.

"Let's ring them ourselves!" And Boris climbed the swaying stairs in the belfry and rang long and loud, long after the bells of the village church had stopped. And I stood in the arched castle doorway laughing and crying with sheer joy. We had won. We were in residence. A few weeks later the priest came to pay us a visit and said we should occupy the pew by the altar; it was the privilege of the *Burgbewohner.* Thus privileges and burdens started and we had to go to church and ring the bells even when we did not feel up to it, because:

"Tot has made good!" — how could I disappoint him. He had been the only one who hadn't inveighed against the folly of our marriage, who had understood and sent his message under the letterhead "J'ayme Donc Je Suis," from St. Liz:

> Such beauty hath thy house.
> That walks with him, as an hibiscus bough,
> So fair, so fair,
> > Lady of Chiang.
> The little sound
> of gems that from thy girdle hang
> Shall last
> Till all times past,
> For thy sincerity . . .

"from the Odes of Chêng, for M. and Boris Ivanovitch or whatever the name is." Despite his feelings: "Russians!! Am I never to hear the end of these Russians!" — Whereas family and friends with rickety titles, old relics in Capri who hadn't stopped gossiping since they had fled from Petersburg, and old relics in Rome whose only claim to authority was a pair of emerald earrings (if anything, a certain connection with Franz Liszt might have carried weight) kindled rumors in the palazzi in Siena, in Venice, in Rome among aunts and retainers: "Olga beware . . . *le père n'a pas le sou* . . . *très bien élevé, charmant* . . . *mais, mais* . . . *il n'a pas l'étoffe de l'homme* . . . *la pauvre petite* . . ." But *la pauvre petite* didn't have *le sou* either — not the American heiress that they'd need — no, no — a peasant from the mountains — no, no — she's the daughter of — they say her father — a traitor — insane.

And Mamile came posthaste to Rome with Babbo's walking cane and said: "Boris, no need of you." And Boris bowed and said: "Madam, we are going to get married as soon as Mary's papers are ready." And at Cook's, when she said: Two tickets for Rapallo, I said: No, *one*.

And Boris and I walked up to the Campidoglio and sighed with relief on seeing our marriage banns posted, and laughed over the ridiculous fuss and clamor. It seemed funny, but not for long. We were stranded.

Slowly Boris sold the furniture of his studio, along with his phonograph, radio, camera, and we went back to Gais.

Neuhaus stood empty. It belonged to no one. Was the Pustertal going to be annexed to Austria or to Italy? Negotiations were still going on, quibblings over frontiers, over property, over citizenship. No need to buy since no one could sell. No need for money. We were granted permission to live in it: rent-free, until —

And so, on Christmas Eve 1946 we moved into our new home, with a loaf of black bread, a bottle of milk and a Christmas tree. It now seemed natural that if on my own I was to have a cottage, the two of us needed a castle. Fortunately there were big majolica stoves and a vast supply of dry wood and Mamme doled out milk and bread and eggs.

As soon as we were in the castle we had a fine life. Nothing to do but keep alive and warm. January, February, March had flowed by gently, muffled in deep snow and silence. Sometimes we walked down to the village hoping to find a remittance from Boris's father and in quest of more milk and black bread from Mamme. On Sundays, after Mass, she gave us a good lunch.

Ling! Ling! Boris seemed to know the proper procedure, forever dancing gracefully under heaven, waving Shaman's sleeves, dreaming things into being, creating with ease, forever flowing, never rigid, unattached, non-possessive, ingenious. Where I would have spent a day to build a barricade in front of a missing door or window, hammering, carrying weights — he placed a few empty bottles at each side, tied together with a thin thread. If anyone wanted to do us harm, he'd take flight at the noise and we'd be alerted by the noise of the bottles falling — no one would suspect a thread.

I was impressed by such ingenuity. We were a bit scared and slept with an axe by the bedside. The castle was so very big, so very empty and cold; each bird cry or fox cry, each creaking board or banging shutter so very sharp against the deep silence of the white shrouded trees. But we were happy and peaceful and warm in our wood-paneled room with the big stove and high window. Boris read out loud to me the Russian classics, while I hemmed diapers from war surplus material, a bale of gauze from the German hospital. And on walks to and from the village he told me stories of "Fiammiferino," his childhood hero. And because I was no good at games he played chess by himself while I pottered with chores. He experimented with the planchette, drew Egyptian hieroglyphs, studied *The Book of the Dead,* and Guicciardini and certain other texts required for a course in Vatican Diplomacy.

On the first of April we left for Meran. Food was still rationed and I had to go to the doctor for a certificate to get more sugar. I knew the baby was due at Easter, but the doctor said no, earlier. I had felt fine ever since leaving Rome, but he said my muscles were not strong and it would be a difficult delivery; I couldn't have it at home.

Why did we choose Meran? Probably the doctor's suggestion. It's a mystery to me now, except that the Bruneck hospital was so very dreary and they had no room anyway. The moon was still up as we walked down the mountain for the early train. The landscape still wintry. I felt a tight pang looking up at the castle, a pale blotch, almost unreal, against the massive fir-wood. I was not afraid, but couldn't help feeling that I would never return to Neuhaus, that I was losing it; and in a sense it turned out to be true.

It was spring in Meran. The Clinic Martinsbrunn seemed heaven. Tea with cream in tiny silver pitchers and dainty *kipfels* served by smiling white nuns. For two or three days I enjoyed it to the full, then panic over the bill started to loom bigger and bigger. I walked among apple blossoms blessing God for so much beauty. I walked for hours on the Tappainerweg pleading with the baby to please come quick.

On Easter Sunday Boris returned and we went for a long walk. He wanted to visit the castles one saw from Martinsbrunn, especially the nearest, the one right under Schloss Tirol, that looked so strange. All I wanted was to speed up the baby.

We reached Brunnenburg in the late afternoon, having walked around it in a wide circle: Thurnstein, St. Peter, Schloss Tirol, the village and then down a steep path. The outer gate was bolted. A woman came out from the farm and shouted in Italian that we mustn't try to go in, it was forbidden and very dangerous. And then looking at me she added: and you shouldn't be on the road in such a condition. Dangerous? Yes, the roof, the walls may collapse any minute. We thought she was mad and skirted the outside, intrigued and thrilled. The walls seemed very solid to us. The only trouble was: absolutely no way in except through the door. We noticed there was no glass in the windows. Quite clearly the place was abandoned. A strange coincidence: Brunnenburg stood over Martinsbrunn just as Neuhaus stood over the cottage Schoutna, so that whenever Boris had lifted his eyes from where I was or wanted to be, they met a castle, uninhabited, waiting for an owner.

The nuns were appalled when they heard how far we had walked, but knew little about Brunnenburg. They thought it belonged to the government, no one had lived in it for over twenty years, people said it was haunted.

That evening the pains started and next day, Easter Monday, as the sirens and bells announced midday, our son arrived with loud yells and I felt happy beyond imagination. Guilty perhaps of thinking more in terms of a grandson for my parents than a son for my husband. But Boris had his reward naming him: Sigifredo Walter Igor Raimondo — after his most glorious ancestors. Only Walter was father's choice, in honor of Walther von der Vogelweide.

As soon as I could get out of bed I went to the window and saw the big magnolia in the garden underneath had burst into flower and I rejoiced for the beauty and the good omen. The open magnolias looked like lotus flowers, inside me shone the picture of my son, and now in my memory lives a Baby Bodhisattva kneeling full of sweet austerity upon the flower of the lotus.

Then the worry over the bill took hold again — that extra week, a minor operation, and because I had a slight temperature the doctor wouldn't let me go home. Another week, no longer walking under apple blossoms but kneeling in the chapel: Dear God, until we can earn our living, send us some money! And then one evening, as I came out of the chapel red-eyed, a nun handed me a telegram from Boris: EZZA MONEI. Saved by Babbo's wedding present: one hundred dollars, mercifully held up by bureaucracy until the moment of essential need.

One has so much courage in spring with a newborn baby at the breast and feeling fine. It seemed to me I could take the whole world on my shoulders, never thinking another winter would come and that I would feel weary.

My plans for carving intaglios had come to nothing. There was much work to be done to turn the castle into an inhabitable home. In place of the lost ring, Babbo was presented with a grandson. And he wrote: BANZAI. He enjoyed his role of "granpaw" and forgot about his surroundings. Banzai. Tot has made good! — If this was his belief my job was to give it substance, build it up, keep it up, make it good.

He immediately set out to populate the vast halls in which Walther von der Vogelweide had allegedly sung (historically disproved) and where Oswald von Volkenstein had been kept a prisoner. He acted once more like a lord; his vigor had come back to him. Letters flowed in, seething with ideas. Our dreams soared high: we would achieve extraterritoriality, we would fight for his extradition from the U.S.A., and he could rule over a domain populated with artists. He would finally get the *palazzo* for which he had clamored in *Exile*.

The way to keep up a castle is to take paying guests. After the baby was born I laid out a long narrow kitchen garden under the south wall.

And then our first guest arrived: proud Hermione. Grandmother Isabel had been left behind. Dorothy had gone to America without her. She had a broken hip and a broken arm and her back full of bedsores. But her spirit was intact and she kept fighting: this time the Rapallo Hospital. She was glad to find a home.

She had not been allowed to play to the full, and enjoy, the role of the Poet's Mother. Now her son was offering her a castle to preside over, and a great-grandson to whom she might, in due course, read Longfellow, Wordsworth, Tennyson and Byron.

Mamile rose to the occasion; she laid aside old resentments. She drove with the old lady up from Rapallo in a black car, to the foot of the mountain. Once again the haymaking in the village was disrupted. Tatte rallied the peasants from the fields. They improvised a sedan-like contraption by passing the long poles of rakes and pitchforks between the slats of a deck chair. The old lady would not hear of a stretcher.

Heiho! They hoisted her on their shoulders and slowly carried her up the mountain, stately, erect, like an Empress Dowager, followed by more men carrying trunks and all my little Gais brothers with cushions and bags and baskets. The old lady talked incessantly, though her words were hardly audible because of the rushing mountain stream. The woods, the stream, the red painted floors reminded her of Idaho and the locks of her great-grandson were as golden as Ray's. And he was just as ready to look up as the Infant Gargantua had been. And very enterprising, yes, very enterprising, the old lady kept saying, since he protested loudly against any enclosure, be it cradle or playpen, and at the age of six months had tried to turn the big wheel by climbing it.

— The big wheels of the monumental chair where grandmother Isabel spent her days reading and rereading *Don Quixote*, instructing me how to poach an egg to perfection, how to run a house the American way; planning a canal from Venice to Milan, big enough for big boats to navigate with their cargo. Remembering.

As we walked up the mountain after Sunday Mass, Boris announced solemnly: *Il mio cuneo batte su Brunnenburg.* I laughed heartily, it was such a funny way of putting it: His mind was bent on Brunnenburg. The territorial domain of the Longobards had extended as far as Maia, his ancestors had once owned that part of the world, hence Meran was the place for us to settle down in.

But I no longer had time to follow his dreams. I had my hands full with the baby and grandmother. I was pleading for help. And one day Boris turned up triumphantly with a handsome young Italian who knelt down and kissed the hem of my skirt: Principessa, your humble servant!

I was furious, but not for long. "I need a woman to wash sheets and diapers, not another man!" There was Boris and his younger brother Igor and my cousin Peter, the baby and grandmother in the wheelchair with me alone in the kitchen and behind the washtub.

"I will do everything, wash, cook, sweep — just room and board."

Irresistible. And his name too: Pilade Soave. He was the stationmaster in Gais. On Mariahimmelfahrt, in honor of the Mother of God, he had given out free train tickets. The railway administration hadn't liked it.

I turned to grandmother. She was delighted with the idea of a manservant. One had menservants in Idaho. She loved Pilade Soave and he baked bread and cooked gnocchi that tasted absolutely delicious and used up in a week what I had to make last a month. His energy and imagination were boundless. As though the forest at the back of the castle were not enough, for a surprise he planted over a dozen fir trees right in front of our entrance. We could hardly get out and had to ask him to remove them again because of the forestry laws.

The excitement did not last for very long. A rich widow had apparently answered his lonely-hearts advertisement in a paper and he went home.

After the experience I was glad to be alone again. Boris and

Igor were put in charge of the water. With the first frost, the trickle in the fountain had stopped. The tenant said this had happened before and there was nothing to do about it except go and fetch water from the river. A frozen brook, an icy path, two pails on a sledge, and an axe to chop the ice off the edges. I had to be very parsimonious with water; Boris and Igor were city boys more interested in Egyptian hieroglyphs and in Chinese radicals than in pioneering. Cousin Peter, who had come to live with us as a p.g. to study Italian, was more helpful and kind; he chopped and carried wood, lit fires and emptied the ashes.

It was a very rough winter. Soon after Christmas grandmother had a stroke. I had great difficulty in making her eat. Mamme's forebodings had come true. No one would come to help me nurse her. The doctor did come, several times, but there was little he could do. Even the priest came once, about a week before she died, and she had seemed glad to see him. I left them alone. Next morning she was almost cheerful and said: "Homer came to me last night and told me to give up." And as though she had willed it she went into a coma and never came to again. On the ninth of February she died, aged eighty-eight.

Tatte brought us the coffin, but did not want to enter her room. We had to bury her ourselves; they couldn't have her in sacred ground. Mamile came. We laid grandmother out in a precious cashmere shawl. She looked very majestic and serene. The tenant helped dig the grave by the chapel. The soil was so frozen we had to be contented with a shallow one. He helped the three boys carry the coffin. Peter recited the Lord's Prayer. We did not ring the bells.

Babbo wanted Herr Bacher to do an intaglio for his mother's grave and sent the drawings and wording for it. I was exhausted. Uncle Teddy offered hospitality in England and Peter took me and the baby home with him.

After my two months in England, I did not return to Gais, but to Tirolo. It had become clear that we could never buy Neuhaus. With the castle went a farm, land and woods. Besides, Boris had liked Brunnenburg much better, despite the fact that it was uninhabitable. Being a ruin, it had one advantage: we could afford it. Juvenile recklessness, of course: little did we suspect how much it would cost us over the years in worry, work and money. But for the moment we had our tower. A Roman tower of our own. With the most splendid view over two open valleys and endless ranges of mountains. The climate was much milder. One was not driven into hibernation and handicapped by ice and snow.

After a few weeks at the village inn we were able to camp in the highest room of the tower. The village carpenter and his son moved into one of the ground-floor rooms with all their tools and set to work repairing doors, floors, and ceilings. A Neapolitan engineer gave us advice in exchange for a sojourn in good mountain air, and directed the works: he was the right man for us at that moment, an expert in propping up, mending, shifting, making do. The tourist boom had not yet set in. Labor was abundant and cheap. And the spirit moving us was *dos moi pou sto kai kosmon kineso* — give me a place to stand and I will move the universe. Our faith and euphoria spread to the young people in the village. All the girls wanted to look after our son, and the boys were eager to help tidy up the place which in their schooldays they had stormed in imaginary conquests. One old woman with shiny eyes thanked me for having put some light back where it had been dark for so long. I think all the superstitious peasants were relieved that the place was no longer so sinister and haunted. It was re-assuring to look down from the village on our lit-up windows.

Boris's appearance and his lack of spoken German were something exotic. Rumors about his connections with the Tsars and the Kings of Bulgaria took root: the importance of being Boris. As for me, with my dialect, I was easy to understand by peasants and workmen. They liked me and told me of their *Nannerls* — all the Habsburg princes seem to have had a penchant for fair farmers' daughters and sometimes they even married them as in the love story of the postmaster's daughter in Marling. Because I came from the Pustertal I was perforce the daughter of a *Holzhändler*: for the *Burggräfler* with their vineyards and apples the Pustertal means lumber and potatoes. Well, the family fortune and money had been founded on lumbering before.

Dorf Tirol seemed eager to have their own *Gräfin*. It had little sympathy for the Austro-Hungarian-Empire counts and barons and morganatic wives who lived in Obermais, stuck-up and impoverished, they said; they did not take part in the village target-shooting, as Franz Josef had; did not come to drink tea at the Rimmele like Empress Elisabeth. In truth the shooting had stopped and the Rimmele had been closed since the end of the First World War . . . Negligible details to whoever is bound to Schloss Tirol — the old capital that had given the name to all the Tyrol — and to the descendants of Friederich mit der leeren Tasche and Margarethe Maultasch . . .

In town they pricked up their ears. Soon the local paper carried the headlines: *"L'ombra di Margaretha Maultasch si aggira nelle sale di Castel Fontana."* The Ugly Duchess's ghost moves in the halls of Brunnenburg — it also said that we slept on straw, which was slightly exaggerated. And we laughed and kept busy, scrubbing, mixing our paints, looking for door-handles and hinges among scrap iron; calculating glass, wood and plaster by the square meter, getting acquainted, poking around barns and attics for Tyrolean furniture.

For my birthday, Boris had ordered dinner at the inn. Towards the end of the meal, in came the children of the owner dragging a cart full of flowers and behind them three old men with zither, *Raffl* and guitar, and as soon as music was heard more people came and we danced and drank wine and were merry. The three musicians happened to be three very big farmers. For the next ten years the celebration grew; they lit up the battlements, they lit up the road from the village to Schloss Tirol. The inhabitants of Dorf Tirol were then a people of leisure, or so it seemed to us, young and eager:

Ah ritorno età dell'oro,
alla terra abbandonata
Se non fosse immaginata
Nel sognar felicità.

Non è ver quel dolce stato,
non fuggì non fu sognato
Ben lo sente ogni innocente
Nella sua tranquillità.

Age of Gold, I bid thee come
To this Earth, was erst thy home!
Age of Gold, if e'er thou wast
And art not mere dream laid waste!

Thou art not fled; ne'er wast mere dreaming;
Art not now mere feignèd seeming.
Every simple heart knows this:
Candour still thy substance is.

[285]

True, towards the end of the first winter I had to run away because the banging on the door had become too loud and insistent: the plumber and the electrician wanted to be paid. We had been, wisely, reckless — had had water and light installed. Having been shown by our deaf and dumb neighbor in his field a spring that by right belonged to the castle, we had proceeded to *Quellenfassen* — to catch the spring — and then built a small reservoir for pressure. Major jobs, undertaken by firms in town.

Boris was in Rome attending classes at the Biblicum and trying to raise money.

This was at the time of the Bollingen award to Ezra Pound in 1948. Mamile too had gone to Rome, to rally old friends. It seemed as though Babbo might be released any moment. I was caught in the flurry. But I remember mainly the pain and the rage over certain ungenerous statements by American literati, and my own worries: what about my home that was to be His *palazzo?* — Pa'-in-law gave me the money to return to Brunnenburg. With a seed parcel from UNRRA, I laid out a vegetable garden. There were several patches of ground inside the walls and also a white cherry tree and some plum trees with delicious fruit.

Again the only way to make a living was to take in paying guests, and again it was Babbo who sent them. The first was Mary Barnard, a young poetess who had corresponded with him before the war and had been to see him at Saint Elizabeths. She came to Europe on a Cantos-itinerary. And then Signora Agresti Rossetti, who had expressed concern for the lungs of her adopted niece. Babbo wrote to her she should bring the girl to me for good mountain air, and paid for it.

We had little comfort to offer as yet, but much beauty, of the kind people respond to and enhance. Signora Agresti, who seemed to me then a very old lady, sitting on a tree stump on our verandah, for lack of chairs, a rosary in her hands, gazing serenely at the Mut, is a sight I shall never forget.

And then Patrizia Barbara Cinzia Flavia was born. This time it was easy. I ran down the mountain to Martinsbrunn and two hours later she was there. The February new moon had brought her, on Ash Wednesday. Next morning we were snowed in: her little hands and feet were as delicate and perfect as the snowflakes that kept falling. Lots of auburn hair and silence, contentment, reserve.

I had always joked: twelve boys is what I want. But the joy of one little girl seemed to make up for eleven boys. Two years later we took on a baby girl without parents — Graziella, gay and good-natured. There was enough space and energy and food and warmth in our home.

On March 1, 1953, I left for America. Mamile took care of the children in Sant' Ambrogio. It was due to her efforts that I was issued an American passport, and it was she who raised the money for the outward journey.

"Don't you want to be popular?" — It sounded as foreign as years earlier the GI's "relax."

Hadn't I noticed that the two young women seated at our table had been transferred to cabin class? — The tough guy stranded with diffident me aggressively moved to another table. I was left alone to view a mass of ordinary, ugly people. I couldn't eat my food and so just stayed in bed, pathologically seasick; a nuisance to the three garrulously aging ladies who shared my cabin on their way home from a visit to Israel. At first they had tried to cheer me up by describing all the gorgeous things one can buy in New York.

— New York — New York — the dream of long ago

My city, my beloved, my white!

What was I heading for? A junk shop and then a madhouse? On the high seas, seasick, with nothing to do but shuttle my thoughts back and forth, back and forth, back to that other dream: "of a cottage / my hair, like yours, will be white / when he comes . . ." One of the many bad poems I had written at twenty. Back and forth, back to England in 1948 — walking along the Thames, past Tennyson Mansions on a misty spring afternoon, I thought: what a suitable area for a poet to live in. I was on my way to call on Mr. Eliot for news. He had visited father in St. Elizabeths, was the best-informed and most authoritative of his friends.

Tall, thin, stooping, with a sad enigmatic smile, he opened the door and led me into his study: ". . . you must forgive . . . a better welcome . . . I am just out of the hospital . . . we are alone in the house." I was struck by the austerity of the room. An imposing desk behind which he sat and behind him a blocked-up fireplace. A small electric — perhaps gas — stove burning. I felt awed and yet sorry for him, he should have been sitting in front of a blazing fire, that's what he needs, I thought. The room and his words felt chilly. After a while he went to fetch some tea: "Oh let me . . ." "No, no, stay where you are." *Inchiodata*. And stooping, he returned carrying a small tray with two cups and a tiny plate of very thin, very dry Saiva biscuits. And I inwardly: I wish I could give him some bread and butter . . . He talked. Gently, uninterruptedly. Twice I dared put a question, he raised his hand and said: We'll come to it later. We never came to it. It was time to go. For viaticum he handed me, Pandora's box? Gianduia chocolates for my son.

As we moved towards it, a letter was slipped under the door of the study. I promptly picked it up — he had tried — and gave it to him. He blushed and whispered: Is it for you? Did I knit my brows into a question mark? I took leave in a hurry.

Alone in the house? No matter. I had met a great man and Loneliness.

. . . And now, on high seas, his words lingered: "I fear your father does not want to accept freedom on any terms that are possible. The idea that you should be sent over to persuade him to sign a statement that he is mad, is a travesty." A travesty — and even if it were the only way out, I of all people should suggest it?

The Statue of Liberty and the excitement of the Manhattan skyline dispelled my forebodings, and my dark resentment against America almost faded.

and there are also the conjectures of the Fortean Society

Tiffany Thayer, editor of *Doubt*, and his beautiful wife were on the pier and took me to their flat in Sutton Place. I was dazed from the voyage, from the surprise: the ease, the comfort, the elegance; the beauty of the view over the East River, and then dinner at a Japanese restaurant with a vegetable flower in the depths of clearest soup in an Oriental bowl, and the drive down Broadway in the glitter of changing neon. I couldn't believe my eyes: my city, my beloved, a mirage? Tiffany smiled: You haven't seen it in daylight. But this too is America. America my country — and I remembered how my little son, when I took him back to Gais for a visit after a year, wrenched loose from my arms and ran towards Mamme who came running towards him with open arms, full of trust and joyful although he did not know her.

But I had come with the firm intention of taking Babbo away from this country, to take him home, to Italy. James Laughlin came to Sutton Place and we talked of ways and means. "You are the only person who could influence him

. . . if you can get him to sign certain papers . . ." Ah, the travesty. No, I couldn't do that, nor would I succeed.

Laughlin arranged a meeting with Julien Cornell, father's lawyer, and Cornell took me to lunch with Arthur Garfield Hays and Osmond K. Fraenkel, counsel and associate counsel to the American Civil Liberties Union, at the Banker's Club.

I had no idea what part of town we were in. From the subway to the skyscrapers, New York even in daylight enthralled me. Whenever I lifted my eyes I saw the tips of tall buildings high up in the sky dance and bow to me. The swift ride in an elevator made me feel dizzy. I was glad I was with Cornell, I liked his reserve. Although at first I had felt impatient, almost reproachful, I soon realized he had done everything in his power, everything, that is, within the power of a good conscientious lawyer. But my urge for action transcended legal reasonings and professional codes. He briefed the two other lawyers with clear, crisp sentences and then kept quiet. I have no recollection of the faces around the table, but the atmosphere seemed friendly. ". . . He has not betrayed America. He tried to stop the war. It may be crazy to go beyond one's duty, but he knew what he was doing. Why should he be punished because his insight and courage were greater than those of most citizens in the United States? . . . He came here in 1939 and said then to congressmen the same things he repeated over the radio. In his letter to the Attorney General, as soon as he had heard he was accused of treason, he explained his motives for speaking over the Italian radio and made certain distinctions. Whether one believes a poet is a seer or not, his achievements, and his long sojourn in Europe and especially Italy, did make him "qualified" to express an opinion and free speech without free radio speech is as zero. All right, it was an Italian radio, but he was broadcasting his own propaganda. As for technical errors, what about the government official who had no business to be rude when he tried to go back, and of the army officials who inflicted upon him such inhumane treatment — all protected by their official status and anonymity, while he shouted: Ezra Pound speaking — any person in good faith must see that certain aberrant phrases were the result of strain and exasperation. And why was he denied the privilege of habeas corpus, why was he kept incommunicado? Why?"

Such were the themes I repeated every occasion with more passion than reasoning. I thought I had convinced Mr. Hays; as we left the room he put his arm around my shoulder and I interpreted the gesture as a promise to help. Mr. Cornell too seemed to think they could carry the case through and I went down to Washington with some hope.

Caresse Crosby, whose guest I was for the first week, drove me out in a taxi to St. Elizabeths. Cheerily she said: "Hello, Ezra, I am off to Europe," and left us alone while I was still straightening out my cap, displaced by the powerful bear hug, and blowing my nose.

So here finally we were. For two days he had received no visitors. Waiting. He had not expected me to stop over in New York, was not interested in Cornell and in Garfield Hays. I felt terrible, no excuse, I should have come to him straight off the boat, first things first. "No use being sorry." "Yes, I know." I remembered his lessons and all was well. And he wanted me to fill in the gap: ten years, except for that brief visit to the prison camp in Pisa. I knew he was proud and amused to be a "granpaw," his kindness and curiosity were boundless. When I told him of his hand moving "Divine Providence" and enabling me to leave the clinic he looked the happiest of men. "Thank God you have taken time to produce a family and lead a sane life." And it never bored him to listen to accounts of Boris and the children and of our efforts with the castle. But whenever I tried to lead the conversation back to "What can we do to get you out of here?" he became tense and impatient: "All you can do is to plant a little decency in Brunnenburg."

With the passing of days the bleakness of the outlook became clear. I had come armed with letters of introduction from his old friends in Italy, Pellizzi, Villari, Signora Agresti, to their friends in the States who might have some influence or advice. But father shook his head: no good. Well then: "If you would sign certain papers . . ." Did I have a clear notion of what it would involve? "Not clear, but vague — a device which you can repudiate once you are free and back in Italy." But his sharp glance made me feel ashamed. No — for mere impatience pretend guilt or incapacity — not in keeping for a man who had harped on responsibility. "Stand trial and you'll be acquitted!" Was Garfield Hays's price exorbitant? "What's the point in my being free if the family has to go bust and one has to pass the bowl around!"

Caresse Crosby's lawyer obtained an appointment for me at the Department of Justice. I was promptly dismissed: "If you want a piece of good advice you better not insist that the case be reopened; you might land him in the electric chair." The same chill as years earlier: "Young lady, what have you got to do with that swine!" — So it was true. They hated him.

At social occasions, as long as I was the charming young princess with a fairytale castle in Italy, everything was fine. But this role reminded me too much of 'Jap'nese dance all time overcoat' . . . a convenient cloak to meet le beau monde in, but as soon as I met anyone I thought could help Babbo, I was impatient of trappings and chitchat. An unpardonable breach of etiquette. The prominent lady novelist: "Yes, yes, I know" and impatiently turned to the partner on her other side. And Francis Biddle, the former Attorney General — as I was thanking the stars for the meeting, the man who surely must know more than anyone else — ". . . you know at the Bollingen Award . . ." "Yes, but that was four years ago and he is still . . ." and he with a disarming smile: "Let me get you a drink." A good thing I was not pining for a drink, for I never saw him again. And at St. Elizabeths? I went to see the director of the hospital, Dr. Overholser, but he was away. A few days later he came, ostensibly to lend father a book, and said: "I am sorry I missed you, come by any time you wish." After he had left, Babbo said: "No use bothering him, he is already overworked. There is nothing you can learn from him."

Every day from his window he watched out for my arrival and was right behind the door when it opened, ready to go out on the lawn or to lead me down the long corridor, leaning on me heavily as he used to for fun in Venice and in Sant' Ambrogio. He introduced me with pride to the attendants and if they said something nice he bowed and smiled as though he had heard "*Che bea putea.*" Oblivious, it seemed, to the heavy bunch of keys at the end of a chain, to the poor driveling empty husks rocking with vacant stares in front of blaring televisions, to the frightful leering of younger shades.

After my second day Dorothy was usually present, sometimes also Omar; and after the first week his regular visitors returned. My role became that of a spectator. I was to be further educated. At first I was intrigued, then indignant, then depressed, then amorphous. I remembered: ". . . Mr. Pound is here as an anthropologist" and thought he was merely appeasing his curiosity. To me, at that time, the young people who came to see him were a new species of human beings in appearance and behavior: sloppy and ignorant. "*Il nemico è l'ignoranza*" — he is fighting ignorance — "They all need kindergarten" — but what a waste of his fine mind. It seemed to me no one had read or seen anything, certainly had not read much Pound. There was no conversation. They came with tidbits of political information and racial bias in the nature of what bums might fish out of garbage cans. Vapid jokes. And if father threw a new name at them they ran off with it like crazy dogs with a bone and since it was all they had in their mouths they declared themselves experts: of del Mar, Agassiz, Benton. Not that I would deny their importance, but in perspective. When I questioned or tried mildly to remonstrate, he said: "In times of war" . . . yes, yes, Confucius had said "make use of all men, even dolts."

The sad fact was that there was no one else willing or able to keep him company regularly and he needed an outside audience as an antidote to the inmates. The *beau monde* used that "funny crowd" as an excuse for not visiting more often, but in truth St. Elizabeths was a very disagreeable place to go to and Pound was not yet a fashionable topic. Also, the times were unpropitious. A powerful witch-hunt was sweeping over the country. McCarthyism was in full swing. Alger Hiss had been convicted, treason had been located in the Department of State. But all this did not help Babbo. He seemed to be skeptical about McCarthy. People who might have moved in his defense lay low. The defenders of civil liberties and the defenders of the Constitution — who, in my ignorance, I thought should stand for the same values — were at opposite poles.

The only saving element was a group of professors from the Catholic University, foremost among them Craig La Drière and Giovanni Giovannini, who had not only read Pound in their college days, before the war, but had the patience and the intelligence to acquaint themselves with the facts and circumstances of the broadcasts so that they were able to state the case clearly in print on several occasions. They were not among the crowd who ultimately claimed credit for Pound's release, yet I know they have to be thanked for more than that. They were men with an education and manners — *éducation du cœur*. But out on the lawn or behind the windscreen in the rank overheated corridor these gentlemen were outnumbered by the "disciples" who, as often as not, would tease them about their political and racial non-commitment. "Their asperities" still amused Babbo. He himself was without malice. And yet why did he allow this farce to go on in his presence? Why didn't he teach these young people manners! And then I saw the caged panther, the boredom, the weariness of the man hit by history full blast.

There is fatigue deep as the grave.

How could those who called him "Maestro" understand the burdens of "Kulchur" — or of the lack of it. And I was myself so ignorant about America and the new generation sloppily sitting there gobbling up hardboiled eggs which he had saved from his lunch or munching peanuts destined for the squirrels. I thought: they should all go on a hunger strike and call attention to the infamy of keeping the nation's greatest poet locked up in an insane asylum — if they have a taste for rabble-rousing, let them rabble-rouse for a good cause! But it seemed to me that to the lot of them what mattered most was keeping him exactly where he was, to prove their points, to serve as illustration of their private petty ends. And even some professors who were humane and well-intentioned said: "But going back to Italy would expose him to danger." Danger? "In Italy no one is afraid, people speak up and attend to their business." And for that matter, even before and during the war — granted I was very young — I had never witnessed the kind of senseless fear that was hovering over Washington in 1953. All the slurs pinned on Italian Fascism I sensed only now, in Washington, where, at behest of *usura,* the best cultural coin was kept out of circulation.

And so I just sat and watched: Babbo had put on weight, but he was very vigorous and his movements swift. His features seemed to have lost their sharp outlines; I did not like the tripartite beard although it gave him a Chinesey old-sage look — it was not his look, the one point suited him better.

The sense of stagnation increased with the first warm humid days. Inertia and not earning my salt slowly turned my urge for action into depression. The long bus rides and the soft lulling music everywhere grated on my nerves. At Lexington Avenue, near the Department of Justice, about halfway between Webster Street, where I lived with a charming Chinese girl, and St. Elizabeths, I changed buses and had a lunch sandwich and a glass of milk in a conveniently placed drugstore. When I mentioned this routine to Babbo he said he could give me a better sandwich than any drugstore. I saw he was eager to feed me, and I couldn't refuse. Also I was very short of money. Babbo had a tiny purse where he kept some coins for peanuts to feed the squirrels. "This is all I am allowed," he said, showing me the contents. And I had to bite my lips hard and smile and hold back the weeping until I left the grounds — the Herr, il Signore, who with lordly gesture would pull out a handful of coins and allow me to give them to the beggars, who would shove all the change my way in the Banca d'America e d'Italia, reduced to this ridiculous little purse — a woman's.

To combat this dreariness I realized the only way was to concentrate on poetry, on history and economics — things as far removed as possible from his daily life. I lost the courage to mention any practical matters, to talk about ways and means of getting him out. I think it was essential for him to forget about it or he would have gone mad. The strong live man, with his mind entire — I never saw the dining room except in my mind as I chewed and chewed on those sandwiches — standing in line, sitting at table with madmen, avid damp hands clutching food, toothless mouths slobbering — he who had liked his passionflower in the fingerbowl, who had chosen food with such care, who, even when all he could bring were but a few roast chestnuts, offered them as though they were *marrons glacés* strewn with candied violets — sitting, standing among the criminals and the insane.

And I had to leave him there. It was time to go home. Ten weeks had seemed an eternity and nothing had been accomplished. As I left, father seemed concerned primarily about the *Confucian Odes.* I was to stop over in New York only "to put the fear of God into Jas about getting out a proper trilingual edition and fast."

I left America bewildered and discouraged. The legal and physical morass in which father seemed caught up was a nightmare. I couldn't help sighing with relief as the boat — an Italian boat — entered the open sea.

Babbo's liberation must be obtained from Italy — this was the firm conviction I came away with. While I had been busy "building up the homestead" and raising the children, Mamile had relentlessly worked for it, starting in 1948 with the collection of signatures from the Rapallo citizens to testify that Ezra Pound, a resident of Rapallo since 1923, had never engaged in Fascist activities; was never present at party gatherings; despite his open sympathy with certain aspects of social economy, his activities were entirely cultural. From his way of life during the war it was evident that he had not enjoyed any privileges, but suffered hardships. His behavior had always been exemplary and never had he wronged any Jews, hence he was respected by all who knew him even by those who did not share his political opinions.

And the signatures ranged from the mayor to the doctors, from the shopkeepers in town to the peasants in the hills.

Whatever time she could spare from her job at the musical academy in Siena she devoted to writing letters to old friends, often too much in the tone of: Whatever you are doing, stop it and think of Ezra! Which, if it so happened that they were having a fine time, tended to annoy them.

While I was visiting St. Elizabeths, Babbo had received a letter from the seventeen-year-old son of his old publisher and friend in Milan, Giovanni Scheiwiller. He was about to take over his father's "hobby," mini-books, and wanted to start out with publishing something by Ezra Pound. Babbo was pleased and told me to look into it and to "educate" the boy. I was from now on to act as his literary agent in Italy. Thus the triangle Milan-Verona-Brunnenburg was formed and, with the help of the Principe dei Stampatori, Giovanni Mardersteig in Verona, the stream of small and big Poundiana started to flow, not into the market but at least into the houses of friends and enemies and collectors and reviewers. The start was tempestuous: *Lavoro e Usura,* an outsized book and an unusual topic for the Pesce d'Oro.

Mr. Hoepli sent a small brochure to Svitzerland
        and his banker friend replied *'urgente':*
'destroy it e farlo sparire.'

Vanni Scheiwiller received stern advice from his father's uncle Hoepli, the big publisher. Pound was not a safe venture. But we continued and after a year Babbo entrusted to us the manuscript of *Section: Rock-Drill* and then *Thrones,* an apotheosis of LING, sensibility; PEN YEH, the family profession; and KATI; A man's paradise is his good nature. Boris, with his translations of ancient Egyptian maxims and love lyrics, had opened new quarries. And we all worked, with *Hilaritas*. From St. Elizabeths father was harping on HILARITAS.

His spirit was hovering over Brunnenburg, but we couldn't forget that physically he was far away, locked up, and the aim of all we did was to get him out.

By spring 1954 Boris had "stormed" the Vatican and Jose V. de Pina Martins, Professor of Portuguese at Rome University, gave a speech over the Vatican Radio: "Ezra Pound: Prometheus Bound" — an appeal to America to free their poet. This was soon followed by another appeal, presented to the U.S. Ambassador, Mrs. Luce, by all the Italian writers, from Bacchelli to Zavattini, Moravia, Saba, Silone, Montale, Quasimodo, Ungaretti, Valeri. Giovanni Papini and the then famous Sindaco of Florence, La Pira, made further appeals and the Ministry of Public Education, and the Onorevole del Bo in Parliament, asking that America send Pound and not Lucky Luciano back to Italy. By 1956 *Life* magazine carried an editorial advocating that quashing the indictment against Ezra Pound should be seriously considered. The editorial pointed out: "Our European critics use the Pound case to argue that American civilization is indifferent to its own poets . . ." In Italy the outcry was loudest — and most audible to Mrs. Luce, the Ambassadress. But in Germany Eva Hesse assiduously translated Pound's poetry and worked through the radio and press, and in England a growing number of Poundians signed petitions, wrote pamphlets and letters to the editors. And, in frustration "pestered" Mr. Eliot for more action. Even Dag Hammarskjöld called attention to "the seer."

And slowly "the Tribe of Ez" passed through Brunnenburg, mostly at Babbo's recommendation or invitation. Some stayed as tenants for years, some as p.g.'s for months, some came on vacation and some overnight. Brunnenburg had been "put on the map" and we kept open house for Babbo. "*Una casa senza maniglie alle porte*," Quasimodo called it.

From our first top room in the tower, we had slowly expanded to twenty rooms, divided into different apartments, on six floors, or rather levels. The Roman tower stands on the highest rock. To the south of it, on a lower level, the outside walls of an eleventh-century castle built to defend the capital: Schloss Tirol. (In every war that the Ugly Duchess fought, mostly against previous husbands, — the poor creature having been married off at the age of twelve for the first time — it got dismantled, earning nonetheless the title "Defensor Teriolis.") The army was housed there. At the end of the last century a crazy Freemason from the Rhineland tried to turn it into a Wasserschloss, adding turrets and wiggly-waggly terraces and cement balconies encompassing the entire mountain. From the symbols and mottoes we found painted on the walls it seemed that he had in mind to establish a Masonic stronghold. He spent a fortune on granite and steel, ran out of luck and money, and after the First World War the property was confiscated by the Italian Government and reverted to its state of ruin. He was allowed to live on in it and died in 1925, alone and poverty-stricken. In 1904 he had thrown his wife overboard. *Casus est talis:* or rather, Both sayings run in the wind: "Frau Maria was seized by dizziness and fell off one of the high balconies as she was watering flowers"; or "Herr Karl aided her in falling and took a young niece unto him." These the latest legends. The earliest speak of giants holding watch over great treasures, a golden calf with a red silk ribbon around its neck; of temples with emerald columns, nine bowls full of gold dust — the deposits of underground streams. And so on and so forth.

Whitsunday, Patrizia's First Communion. A day of great clarity and contrasts: blue mountain ridges laced with snow, little girls in long, full white lace and long loose curly hair on the green meadow under flowering cherry trees. In their midst one tall handsome Negro lady — click-click — taking pictures of all the whiteness staring at her. Mamile had come with a friend, an American Negro composer. And on that same day I was to meet Archibald MacLeish. I had hoped he would come to the castle. I thought: If he sees the place at this time of year and the children, he will move heaven and earth to help Babbo get here. But his time was short, he asked me to have dinner with him and his wife at Sirmione.

Sirmione has its advantages over Brunnenburg in poetical tradition and associations, and soft air, soft fragrance, soft sound of lapping water at dusk. A tall gentleman stood in the hotel garden. Beautiful manners and kind voice. I was excited and afraid at the same time. His wife joined us and put me at ease.

Did I talk? I became aware of myself only when Mrs. Mac-Leish said: "You know, my husband is a lawyer, and a very good lawyer, too." I hadn't thought of it — I saw only the poet. And the man who had been challenged while holding an important position in government during the war, who had brushed politics aside and stood by his old friend in trouble, who spoke with respect and admiration of the Cantos. The strange conviction: here is a man with a golden key in his head.

Mamile was urging a second visit to Washington. I said: "With Boris and the children." "A tall order!" I had more faith in Boris's and the children's power of persuasion and charm than my own after my previous failure.

By then quite a few scholars had been to Brunnenburg on research grants from American foundations. I took courage; I had several translations in print and was working on the translation of the Cantos — the elucidations Babbo might give me could help scholars. But how does one go about applying for grants without proper qualifications? Ford turned me down. I turned to Norman Holmes Pearson. He wrote: "Try to get the lines and the half lines established" and sent me the money for our trip. All set. But Babbo: "St. Elizabeths is no fit place for the children to see their grandfather in. And there are rumors: granpaw might get sprung."

Not only rumors. Things had started to move and something had started to move in Babbo's head. I was ready to return the money to Norman . . . he wrote: "Use it on the castle and for your father's comfort, you can do the work when he is there." We were holding our breath. And I remembered Babbo's first wish when we got the castle: a room for his Gaudiers. So in came the masons and painters. A permanent museum, I thought. We had organized shows in Milan and in Meran: I knew how beautiful all the drawings and sculptures looked in one room. And for Gaudier's head of Babbo in the garden I planted an olive, a laurel, and a magnolia tree. Only the olive has survived, but it seems to achieve no height. Years later one of our tenants planted tulips and daffodils around the base of the monument — she thought it looked very beautiful and gay. It reminded me of a Tyrolean grave.

By now it was clear: Babbo was coming. He was worrying about the logistics of the place. I thought I had solved that problem. Since 1954 the castle had been his house: I had been told to bring all the belongings from Via Marsala and from Villa Cerisola, where my grandparents had lived. He must have all the beauty and space and comfort to recompense him for the DTC, the hell-hole and St. Liz.

Then, one evening, by chance I heard the late news over the radio: *Il poeta Americano Ezra Pound . . .* the indictment is dismissed. Oh Lord it's not possible! I waited for the last newscast. Yes, it was true, but again I said: it's not possible! And slowly the refrain in my head: They are giving him just enough rope to hang himself! The conditions he had accepted were a great shock: not free, but in custody. The magazine *Doubt* commented: "It looks like a victory for the poet. The facts are not so clearly cause for jubilation. Ezra could have left St. Elizabeths five years ago on the terms he has now accepted . . . One trusts he will not regret it." As usual, news items are presented in forms too simplified.

Juridically nothing had changed except for the worse. What had changed was Babbo's feelings. And public opinion. To this he himself had contributed the most by disregarding all yatter and clatter, tears, pleas, and threats, taking no apparent interest in his situation and not wasting thoughts on how to change it, but keeping at his job — poetry: *The Odes, Trachiniae, Rock-Drill* and *Thrones,* the major accomplishments. All proofs of his sanity. And of a wise man intent on fulfilling his destiny, not fighting it.

As for *"the white stag, Fame,"* and the force behind it — it always brings to mind the plot of a Noh play: "In Dojj a girl is in love with a priest who flees from her and takes shelter under a great bronze temple bell, which falls over him. Her sheer force of desire turns her into a dragon, she bites the top of the bell, twists herself about the bell seven times, spits flame from her mouth and lashes the bronze with her tail. Then the bell melts away under her, and the priest she loves dies in the molten mass."

Whether Babbo could really have been released earlier will have to remain an open question, as will the motives which induced the Committee to drop the appeal in the habeas corpus proceedings in 1948.

In his letters Babbo did not sound angry at the terms, he seemed in control of the situation, so I quashed my forebodings as unworthy. After all, even I had said in 1953: mere formalities which you can repudiate. I attended to business: household matters and gardening, the ten thousand details obvious to the people who do them and meaningless to those who don't. Walter had been sent to Gais for a change of air after school and to learn work in the fields. The day Babbo stepped on the *Cristoforo Colombo* in New York, the child was run over by a motorbike and landed in the Bruneck hospital. I had the consolation of learning that Walter had instantly jumped up after the collision, and clasping his torn thigh, run towards the man under the motorbike to ask if he had hurt himself. No, he hadn't.

But by the time Babbo arrived Walter was home again and limped to meet him and was bear hugged, and wept with joy. For how many years I had prayed for just this meeting . . . Babbo coming down the path! We were all swept off our feet and too happy. Only Patrizia, at least outwardly, kept aloof and watched with sidewise glances and a shy smile. She laid the table, wrote out the menus and decorated them with cats and flowers, and for the rest attended to her business.

After the first evenings and the great welcoming party to which the villagers had brought flowers and music and torches and drums, when everyone had retired to their rooms, Babbo would sit up in the dining room, under the pictures of his *aïeules,* and talk to me for hours, as though it were now his turn to "fill in the gap" — the years at St. Liz. It was strange, almost eerie to hear him talk about himself and I felt grateful, but, blinded by his glory, I did not see all his needs. The family had been trained for a demigod, and as such he came. With his wife Dorothy and his secretary Marcella. Committee and bodyguard.

I went to meet them in Verona. By the time we had eaten our lunch, at the Greif in Bozen, I had realized I was up against something beyond Babbo's control. He expected me to help him be just the lovable human being he is, in great need of shelter and tenderness, so that he might write Paradise.

And for one beautiful day there was peace

Oh, more than one and so beautiful were the days that all later suffering is forgotten. Yet something went wrong. The house no longer contained a family. We were turning into entities who should not have broken bread together.

I became convinced I should have insisted on my original plan for logistics. The existing division of Brunnenburg into separate, autonomous flats should have made the *Verkehr* easy, according to his principles of clear demarcation.

But to hitch sensibility to efficiency?

Slowly the vision withered, all the high norms and the poetry turned into dead letter. The letter kills . . . and kills the worth of every action performed by it. I felt as though my skin were a bag full of stones. Dead weary. And Babbo said: "I thought you were solid rock I could build on." "I had thought so too, but all the *acque chéte* have corroded the foundations. *Stille Wasser graben tief.*"

My audacity did not last into fortitude. In Sirmione I had said to Mr. MacLeish: "He has a right to do whatever he likes, anything that makes him happy. Whomever he wants to bring is welcome. He makes his own laws and I accept them." He had been honest with me but we did not see eye to eye on what was "good for him." Strictly speaking it was none of my business. *Aoi! Aoi!* He was not happy.

On Christmas morning I found the Christmas tree lying on the floor. A bad omen, I felt. Babbo said the altitude oppressed him. "And the first duty of a *capostipite* — ancestor — is to keep alive." True enough. And they moved to Rapallo. But by the following October he wrote: "I want to come back to Brunnenburg, to die."

He was quite strong and active for a while, though plagued by all kinds of remorse. Mr. Eliot was one: "I should have listened to the Possum." And we all had to read *After Strange Gods*. I wrote to Mr. Eliot begging him to come and see Babbo. He sent a birthday telegram saying: "You are the greatest poet alive and I owe everything to you" — or words to that effect.

Then he worried we would not have enough to eat and not enough fuel and Archibald MacLeish sent a check to keep Babbo warm.

We still talked a lot and I suppose it must have been trying for him to have me continually quote the Cantos at him.

Eventually he summed up my frustrations in Greek: "ou tauta pros kakoisi deilian echei." "What are you talking Greek for, I don't understand." And he said: *Electra*. And I found:

Οὐ ταῦτα πρὸς κακοῖσι δειλίαν ἔχει;

Shall we to all our ills add cowardice?

But by now we had all had enough of Greek tragedy. Even Boris, who had handled himself and everybody else with tact

[306]

and flexibility. Soon after his arrival Babbo had exclaimed: What a relief: finally a real couple: Felix nupsit,/an end.

But we were approaching a different end. Love, gone as lightning, and If love be not in the house there is nothing.

We thought it would be good for Babbo's spirits to have a change, and be in the company of men instead of women. So he went to Rome with an old friend of Boris, a brave man, but whose head was still too full of the *Eia Eia Allalà* spirit. It worked for a while; they traveled, went to concerts and parties. But for Babbo the social life was too strenuous and he fell ill, this time seriously. I went to Rome and was frightened. I wrote to Mamile to come. Babbo wanted to see her. And she came and helped me drive him back home — to Martinsbrunn. A long illness. But he recovered. And by the time the magnolia I had first seen in bloom when my son was born was in full bloom once more, he came out and walked in the garden. It was decided that as soon as he was strong enough to travel I would take him back to Sant' Ambrogio for a visit. And ever since, he and Mamile have been taking care of each other.

Citations

Quotations from *The Cantos* printed in boldface type in the text are taken from *The Cantos of Ezra Pound* (London: Faber and Faber, 1964), to which the page and line references following the Canto number refer, unless otherwise specified. Sources of other quotations are given in conventional form.